GOOD FOOD

GOOD COMPANY

EXTRAORDINARY RECIPES & IDEAS FOR EASY TO ELEGANT ENTERTAINING

JUNIOR SERVICE LEAGUE
OF THOMASVILLE, GEORGIA

ON THE COVER
Melissa's Spinach Salad Quiche (page 159) and Bran Muffins (page 111).

EDITORIAL CONSULTANT
Mary A. Krier

NUTRITIONAL CONSULTANT
Barbra A. Crumpacker, R.D.
JOHN D. ARCHBOLD
MEMORIAL HOSPITAL

TECHNICAL ASSISTANT
Raye Strickland

For information, contact:
JUNIOR SERVICE LEAGUE
OF THOMASVILLE
P.O. BOX 279
THOMASVILLE, GA 31799

Printed by
Rose Printing Company
Tallahassee, FL

Library of Congress Catalog Card Number
93-060311

Good Food,
Good Company

ISBN 0-9636402-0-8

Our DEEPEST GRATITUDE

The Junior Service League of Thomasville appreciates the contributions of the following professionals who gave unselfishly of their time and talents in the making of GOOD FOOD, GOOD COMPANY. Their involvement was extremely important to the successful publishing of this cookbook.

PHOTOGRAPHY
Jerry M. Turner
Canopy Road Gallery

FLORAL DESIGN
Jimmy Singletary
Singletary's Flowers & Gifts

DESIGN CONSULTANT
Al Cuneo
Cuneo Creative Group

About JUNIOR SERVICE LEAGUE

Junior Service League of Thomasville is a 65-member women's organization dedicated to meeting the economic, cultural, and medical needs of children in the community. All proceeds from the group's activities support children's programs in Thomasville and Thomas County. Among the charitable contributions are the staffing and funding of children's orthopedic, seizure, hearing, and vision clinics; the funding of eyeglasses and dental services for children who otherwise would not receive those services; and numerous other opportunities to assist area children.

*S*outherners know that the essential elements of a successful party are good food and good company. That holds true for small family gatherings, casual outdoor events, and even the most elegant formal dinner parties.

Here in the South, hospitality is a way of life. We relish even the smallest opportunity to entertain our friends and family. Bringing people together to enjoy each others' company and to share great food is pure enjoyment for us!

Thomasville's gracious style of entertaining dates back to the late 1800's when the city was one of the South's first resort towns. Wealthy northerners flocked here to enjoy our famous hotels, mild winter climate, and most importantly, our easy style of living. Today, Thomasville continues that tradition of hospitality, gracious living, and elegant entertaining.

In GOOD FOOD, GOOD COMPANY, Thomasville Junior Service League shares the secrets of southern entertaining. You'll find ideas for preparing invitations, creating the perfect atmosphere, developing exciting menus, and of course, almost 500 delectable, triple-tested recipes--all the ingredients you'll need to serve good food to the good company at your next party!

SPECIAL THANKS

Junior Service League of Thomasville owes a huge debt of gratitude to the many people who have contributed to GOOD FOOD, GOOD COMPANY *in countless ways. They have given of their time, talents, and knowledge, and have even opened up their homes and businesses to us. We cannot express how much we appreciate the part they have played in the publication of this book.*

Leesa Arce
Pam Barnett
Mary Beverly
Paul and Lisa Bryan
Marie Chambers
Melanie Chavaux
Lee Chubb
Barbra Crumpacker
Janice Faircloth
Robin Fink
Jane Guy
Andrea Hancock
Tommy and Brona Harrison
Joe and Donna Harvard
Harriet Hawkins
Emily Hjort
Janet Hutchings
Marilyn Jefferson
Mary A. Krier

Ralph Krier
Jane Lewis
Libba McKinney
Amos and Jackie McMullian
Elizabeth Krier Matlin
Betty Claire Neill
Anna NeSmith
Sara Shipp
Raye Strickland
Maurice and Peggy Tanner
Jerry Turner
Carolyn Wight
Bernice Woodward

———————

Ann's Accents
Barnes Printing Co.
Books-Gifts & Co.
Brantley's Seafood Resturant

The Bridal Boutique
Canopy Road Gallery
Cargo Unlimited
Chrysalis Fabrics
Cuneo Creative Group
Dogwood Gifts & Baskets
Dunn's Discount Furniture
Flowers Industries, Inc.
Lewis Produce Co.
Melissa's
Neel's, Inc.
Nick's Package Store
Paxton House Bed & Breakfast
Singletary's Flowers & Gifts
Snapdragon Ltd.
Stafford's
The Gift Shop
Travel Time
Turner's Fine Furniture

SPECIAL FRIENDS

Financial backing is a key element in any undertaking, especially one of this scope. The publication of GOOD FOOD, GOOD COMPANY *would not have been possible without the support of the very generous patrons listed below. Junior Service League of Thomasville thanks its many special friends.*

Canada Dry of South Georgia
Coca-Cola Bottling Company
    of Thomasville
Conradi Pest Control, Inc.
Dekle-Allen Funeral Chapel
First Thomasville Realty, Ltd.
Flowers Baking Company of Thomasville
Flowers Properties, Inc. as developers of:
        The Fairways at Glen Arven
        The Woodlands at Glen Arven
        and Pine Summit Subdivisions
Hardee's
Hicks Clothing Company
J.C. Penney Company
Kirkland Croy Hughes Home for Funerals
Loftiss, Van Heiningen & Ward, Attorneys
MBI Metal Buildings Inc.

Modern Cleaners & Laundry, Inc.
Muller, Reynolds & Reed, MD's, PA
Southern Asphalt & Construction, Inc.
Stanley F. Smith, Architect, AIA, ASID
The Bookshelf, Inc.
The Grand Victoria Inn Bed & Breakfast
The Open Door Adoption Agency
Thomas Drug Stores
Travel Time
Winn-Dixie Stores, Inc.

———————

David and Sandra Daniel
Frances H. Eubanks
Janice P. Faircloth
  - In memory of Blanford Bass McKenzie

A Friend
Mark and Diane Glaccum
Chip and Andrea Hancock
Harry and Lella Jones
Harry T. and Jamie Jones
Powell and Caren Jones
Monty and Jane Lewis
Gaston and Kathy Loomis
Nancy McCollum
Donald J. McKenzie
George and Connie Mathes
Dick and Charlotte Miller
Jim Pettigrew
Joan R. Thomas
Jerry and Marta Turner
Mildred Vann
Pete and Mary Wolek

Commercial Bank
Flowers Industries, Inc.
John D. Archbold Memorial Hospital
Marguerite Neel Williams Charitable Lead Annuity Trust

Lanigan & Associates, PC

Thomasville Times-Enterprise

Thomas County Federal Savings & Loan Association

A.G. Edwards & Sons, Inc.
First Merchants Bank
Jones Tractor & Rental Company
NationsBank
Plantation Propane, Inc.

Shields & Company
Thomasville Community Bank
Thomasville Orthopedic Center, PC
Trust Company Bank
W. J. Powell Company, Inc.

 Each rose represents a donation of $1,000.

Junior Service League of Thomasville extends very special appreciation to our corporate sponsors who provided much of the funding for GOOD FOOD, GOOD COMPANY. Without these sponsors, our task of publishing this cookbook would have been impossible. Through their generous support, Junior Service League of Thomasville will be able to increase contributions to the many projects we support. The League realizes that our ability to meet the needs of the children of Thomasville and Thomas County is enhanced by the generosity of the community. We especially appreciate the corporate sponsors who have always given financial support to our projects, including the publication of GOOD FOOD, GOOD COMPANY.

5

COOKBOOK COMMITTEE

CO-CHAIRMEN

Marta Jones Turner

Caren McKenzie Jones

EDITOR
Diane Glaccum

RECIPE CHAIRMEN

Susan Harvard
Appetizers

Denise Watt
Side Dishes

Rebecca Sanford
Game and Grilling

Jamie Jones
Soups and Salads

Shannon Balfour
Meats

Beverly Cox
Seafood

Mary Wolek
Pastas and Breads

Dale Gurley
Game and Grilling

Diana Cone
Desserts

Sharon C. Johnson
Preliminary Recipe Editor

PHOTO STYLIST
Natalie Braswell

FOOD STYLISTS
Cindy Lawson and Diana Cone

PHOTO TEAM LEADERS
Sara Martha Vann   Julia Taylor   Penny Woodward

SIDEBAR RESEARCH
Boo Ivey

BUSINESS MANAGER
Sherri Burks

TABLE OF CONTENTS

A GUIDE TO THE COOKBOOK 8

ENTERTAINING IDEAS 9

APPETIZERS AND BEVERAGES 35

SOUPS AND SALADS 71

PASTAS AND BREADS 97

SIDE DISHES 127

ENTRÉES 157

DESSERTS 239

ACKNOWLEDGMENTS 300

INDEX 304

EVENT PLANNER 323

YOUR GUIDE TO THE COOKBOOK

There are interesting and stylish alternatives to the usual tablecloth. Quilts, shawls, lace, fabric remnants, sheets, and rugs are wonderfully creative ways to top a table. Look around your home--the possibilities are endless!

Throughout GOOD FOOD, GOOD COMPANY, the wine bottle symbol introduces you to dozens of wonderful entertaining ideas. Included are suggestions for decorations, invitations, flowers, table settings, and linens as well as organizational pointers that make entertaining a breeze. Don't miss the Event Planner on page 323--it is certain to become an invaluable part of all your future parties.

The caffeine in coffee has been studied in relation to a number of health problems. The word today for most Americans is that caffeine used in moderation does not pose a health hazard. That advice can be applied in all areas of nutrition and life-- everything in moderation!

The heart symbol in GOOD FOOD, GOOD COMPANY identifies nutritional tips offered by Barbra Crumpacker, Registered Dietitian at Thomasville's Archbold Memorial Hospital. Ms. Crumpacker suggests variations of recipes that lead to important reductions in fat, cholesterol, and calories.

LAMB CHOPS MADE SIMPLE

- *2 loin lamb chops*
- *black pepper*
- *Dijon mustard*
- *bread crumbs*
- *1 teaspoon rosemary*

Sprinkle lamb chops with pepper. Coat both sides
(continued on page 192)

Recipes appearing in the shaded areas and marked with this decorative symbol are wonderfully easy, yet crowd-pleasing additions to any menu. Although these recipes are often simple, you will find them simply <u>delicious</u>!

GOOD FOOD
GOOD COMPANY

ENTERTAINING IDEAS

New Year's Day Buffet

It's time to ring in the New Year
with old friends and new,
Cornbread, ham, and black-eyed peas, too.
Mark your calendar for three o'clock
New Year's Day
And start the New Year in a timely way!

Menu

BOURBON & PRALINE HAM *page 191*

BLACK-EYED PEAS & SAUSAGE *page 184*

MARINATED ZUCCHINI *page 43*

FRESH COLLARD GREENS *page 137*

SOUR CREAM CORN BREAD *page 122*

SPICED PEARS *page 275*

❏ Update traditional menus with new twists on classic recipes. Here, black-eyed peas are combined with tomatoes, sausage, and rice to create a new "old" favorite. Ham is given a fresh look with a pecan glaze, and familiar cornbread gets a flavor boost with sour cream. Excellent appetizer choices for this menu include Jo's Cheese Ball and Hot Onion Canapés (page 47).

❏ Contrasts are important in a menu--contrasts in tastes, colors, and textures. When selecting recipes, pair foods that are soft and crunchy, sweet and sour, spicy and delicate.

❏ Everyday materials from around your home can decorate your buffet in a special way. Pages torn from a large calendar can be used as table runners. Enhance the time theme by using watches--old and new--as napkin rings. Be inventive with serving pieces. Here, a brass cricket box serves cornbread sticks with special southern flair.

Darling,
Apecial plans
for tonight! Meet
me fireside, 8:00 P.M.
Love, J.

MENU

NUTTY BRIE APPETIZER *page 64*

VEAL CHOPS À LA PALMER *page 236*

SAUTÉED FRESH SPINACH *page 148*

ANGEL HAIR PASTA WITH
TOMATO-BASIL SAUCE *page 99*

LUSCIOUS CHOCOLATE MOUSSE *page 264*

❏ Make ordinary tablesettings extraordinary by moving them off the table! By placing settings on a large ottoman an intimate mood is created.

❏ Even simple garnishes add sophistication to food--try quartered cherry tomatoes, toasted slivered almonds, or fresh parsley. With a little effort, you can create chocolate leaves to add a gourmet touch to a pie, mousse, or cheesecake (see page 264).

❏ Don't forget that lighting and music can extend the mood. Soft candlelight, a warm fire, and relaxing music add romance to a setting. With prior planning, the host will enjoy the evening more by having the meal components at hand on a nearby tea cart or buffet. Bring in everything you'll need before your guest arrives.

❏ Often, less is more. A table set for two calls for a single rose rather than an elaborate floral arrangement. If the occasion calls for a gift, choose wrapping that complements the setting.

PICNIC IN THE PARK

Our
Basket
is Brimming!
Join us at Paradise Park
Easter Sunday
Twelve Noon

MENU

PENNE PASTA &
GRILLED CHICKEN
page 108

COOL VEGETABLE TRAY
WITH FRESH DILL DIP
page 44

PARMESAN
BREAD STICKS
page 121

RAINBOW TART
page 270

❑ When planning a picnic, keep it simple. Choose foods that are easily transported. Prepared salads or quiche can be transported in their serving containers to the backyard or park with ease.

❑ Take advantage of nature's seasonal offerings for spring events including your picnic in the park. Dress up your baskets and serving dishes with backyard vines or small limbs from flowering shrubs.

❑ A red-checked cloth is not your only option for a picnic table covering. An antique quilt or a pretty rag rug will work well in an outdoor setting. Or, take your invitation to a local fabric store and choose a coordinating print for a special look.

❑ Colorful Easter eggs are great for children's games, but keep eggs chilled if you plan to let the children eat them.

ROSE SHOW BRUNCH

Rose Show Brunch
on the Terrace

Eleven O'clock   April Twenty-eighth

please respond

MENU

FRESH FRUIT WITH HONEY DRESSING *page 96*

MOLDED CHICKEN SALAD *page 90*   RASPBERRY CREAM *page 265*

ZUCCHINI MUFFINS *page 111*   CIDER SPRITZER *page 69*

❏ At an event clearly centered around roses, it is only fitting that the reigning queen of the garden should be the focal point of the table. By keeping the table covering solid rather than floral, the rose topiary has no competition. Scattering fresh rose petals among the place settings adds interest to the table top. Carry out the rose theme by offering each guest a rose as they arrive.

❏ Color contrasts can be dramatic and appealing. A dark-bordered plate frames light-colored chicken salad, accented with flowering kale. Dark breads and muffins offset the plate's light center. Ribbons in complementary colors make excellent napkin rings. Add more color and flavor to your table with sprigs of mint in drinks and on desserts.

❏ Topiaries make excellent centerpieces and can be ordered from the florist or created at home with your own garden's blooms or purchased flowers.

And she has her reward; not fame
Or baubles tonight in any mart;
But motherhood's brave crown, the love
And homage of her own child's heart.

Clare Aiken Speer

Luncheon   Noon   Mother's Day

Menu

Chicken Breasts in Triple Mustard Sauce *page 161*

Seasoned Rice *page 147*

Marinated Asparagus *page 129*

Peaches & Mincemeat *page 133*

Butter Dips *page 120*

Coconut Sour Cream Cake *page 241*

❏ Often it's the little touches that count. Tucking fresh flowers into napkins is a great way to add a festive feeling to a table setting. Complete the look by using the same flowers in floral arrangements or as a cake ornament.

❏ Set the mood for any celebratory meal by placing the gifts and cards associated with the occasion on the table. Use brightly colored wrapping paper and ribbons on packages and add a special touch with flowers.

❏ Garnishes can make the difference between an ordinary lunch and an extraordinary event. Slices of fresh mushrooms adorn wild rice, while bright maraschino cherries add contrast to a mincemeat topping. Try tying asparagus bundles neatly together with spring onion tops or very thin strips of celery. For a final colorful touch, add both lemon and lime slices to the rims of your water or tea glasses.

BRIDAL TEA

MENU

CUCUMBER LITES
page 38

OUR CHEESE STRAWS
page 41

SHRIMP STUFFED CHERRY TOMATOES
page 52

SUMMER FRUIT TRAY
page 45

PINEAPPLE CHEESE BALL
page 48

SUPER SANDWICH FILLING
ON PARTY BREADS
page 39

ORANGE BLOSSOMS
page 250

PARK AVENUE SQUARES
page 291

FRUITED TEA PUNCH
page 67

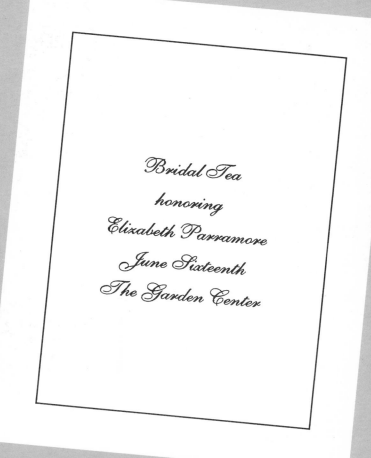

Bridal Tea
honoring
Elizabeth Parramore
June Sixteenth
The Garden Center

❏ Silver and white are perfect tones for a formal occasion such as a bridal tea. An heirloom lace tablecloth and white floral centerpiece highlight the bridal theme. Use the bride's favorite colors for accent. Since there is no seating at the table, a taller, more formal floral arrangement can be used. Use a variety of sizes and shapes of hollowware and china to carry out the silver and white theme.

❏ When planning the menu, remember to serve both sweet and savory finger foods along with fruits and vegetables. A small amount of chicken or shrimp adds a nice touch to a tea buffet, but it is best to avoid heavy meats and breads.

❏ Dress up simple foods for a party by presenting them in uncommon ways. Use heart-shaped cookie cutters for finger sandwiches and fruit slices. Drape a watermelon bowl with a soft tangle of ivy. Ordinary red and green grapes become decorative pearls when dipped in honey and granulated sugar.

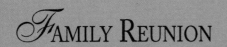

FAMILY REUNION

PLEASE COME

FOR: Our 5th Family Reunion

TIME: 4pm

DATE: July 24th

PLACE: The Farm

MENU

SOUTHERN POPCORN *page 42*

BARBECUED CHICKEN & RIBS *page 238*

MARINATED COLE SLAW *page 88*

FAMOUS POTATO SALAD *page 87*

DELICIOUS BAKED BEANS *page 131*

GRANNY'S ROLLS *page 119*

SUMMER DESSERT *page 268*

BROWN SUGAR CHOCOLATE CAKE *page 242*

❏ A family reunion doesn't have to be predictable. Serve the family favorites, but add a twist by trying a new recipe. Be sure to offer a variety of foods to satisfy everyone's tastes.

❏ Informality is the key to a relaxed event. Enhance this mood with a madras tablecloth, spectacular sunflowers, and simple ferns.

❏ Special garnishing touches add interest to traditional dishes. Onions turn floral atop baked beans, while carrot curls and celery brushes dress up a platter of barbecued chicken and ribs. Even the family's favorite Brown Sugar Chocolate Cake (page 242) takes on a new look adorned with fresh flowers.

❏ Casual tableware is perfect for this type of occasion. Simplify the buffet line by wrapping the silverware in napkins tied with coordinating ribbons.

Alfresco Seafood Dinner
4125 Parkway Drive
August 19   7:30pm
RSVP

MENU

SMOKED SALMON *page 228*

KEY WEST SHRIMP *page 232*

GRILLED VEGETABLES *page 236*

IRISH POTATO CASSEROLE *page 144*

MARINATED ONION & TOMATO SLICES *page 141*

KEY LIME PIE *page 277*

❑ The calm blues and greens of the sea set the tone for this event. Whimsical fish and seashell serving pieces carry out the theme.

❑ Scatter small seashells on the table and serving cart for an interesting accent. Large scalloped-shaped shells can be used as bowls for lemon wedges or cocktail sauce.

❑ Set simple votive candles on galax leaves from your yard for a tropical accent. Don't forget to put a tablespoon of water in the candle holder before lighting to make cleaning up melted wax easier. Tiki torches are a wonderful way to light alfresco parties.

❑ When planning an outdoor event, have an alternate plan in case of inclement weather. Be ready to move the party indoors and to change your menu accordingly.

❑ Of course, bug spray and cirtronella candles are a must! If your party is scheduled outdoors during daylight hours, have sunscreen available for your guests' comfort.

Tailgate Party

Push em back, Push 'em back way back!

Back up to our tailgate lunch
Meet us at 10:00 Saturday
to drive to the game!

Menu

MARINATED MUSHROOMS *page 43*

SOUTHERN FRIED CHICKEN *page 169*

MARINATED GREEN BEAN SALAD *page 88*

CRUNCHY PICNIC COOKIES *page 282*

DIVINE CHOCOLATE MINT SQUARES *page 290*

VERY BLOODY MARYS *page 66*

❑ With a football theme, creating a memorable tailgate party is easy. A football helmet filled with potted mums serves as a centerpiece and a stadium blanket makes an ideal tablecloth. Line your serving baskets with cloth napkins and finish your "table" with cheerleader pompoms.

❑ Transport your party food in sealed plastic bags or bowls and clean up is a snap. Baskets, Lucite bowls, and earthen crockery are perfect for serving lunch at the stadium.

❑ Don't skip the garnishes just because you're on the road. Prepare parsley, whole cherry tomatoes, and onion slices ahead of time and transport them in a plastic bag.

❑ With any tailgate party, alcohol should be limited to those not driving! The Very Bloody Mary recipe can be prepared without vodka. Those not driving can add it if desired.

Join Us Lakeside for a Traditional Harvest Dinner October 28 6:30 p.m. Wood's Mill

MENU

SWISS ONION SPREAD *page 47*

CURRIED PUMPKIN SOUP *page 74*

GRILLED PORK TENDERLOIN *page 235*

HERBED GREEN BEANS *page 130*

PRALINE SWEET POTATOES &
ORANGE SAUCE *page 146*

QUICK MAYONNAISE ROLLS *page 120*

APPLE CRANBERRY CASSEROLE *page 274*

❏ Simple decorations are perfect for a harvest dinner. Gourds and dried leaves accent the table, while berry-laden hawthorn and pyracantha branches complement the outdoor theme. Raffia-tied leaves encircle votive candles that add a warm touch and a hurricane lamp enhances the overall look of the harvest table.

❏ There's no better way to serve Curried Pumpkin Soup than in a hollowed-out pumpkin. Use this creative idea for other food presentations, such as vegetable dip in a cabbage "bowl" or cut fruit in a scooped out pineapple half.

❏ For your guests' comfort, be sure the invitation includes information on the level of formality, whether the party is inside or out, and a brief description of the setting. The style of the invitation can convey the appropriate dress. A description of the setting can help your guests more easily make their wardrobe selections.

ℋUNT BUFFET

The Huntboard is groaning!
Ride over for Supper.

Saturday, November 15
7:00 p.m.

Menu

Always-A-Hit Spinach Dip *page 50*

Stuffed Quail *page 227*

Merrily Plantation Deep Dish Dove Pie *page 226*

Charcoaled Marinated Duck Breasts *page 224*

Garlic Cheese Grits *page 230*

Creamy Peas with Bacon and Mushrooms *page 143*

Bread Pudding with Whiskey Sauce *page 267*

❑ For a hunt supper, consider a less formal setting. Serve the meal buffet-style off a hunt board. Although space is more limited, placing foods close together gives a hearty, bountiful look. There's no need for a large centerpiece--a small arrangement placed at one end of the buffet is perfect.

❑ The obvious menu choices for a hunt supper include game and fowl. Garnish these entrées with autumn-colored fall fruits such as persimmons, apples, and cranberries.

❑ Keep room decorations simple and natural. Magnolia leaves, nandina berries, and pine cones can be combined in countless creative ways throughout the house. Place them in decorative bowls on your coffee table, in large floor containers, and beside your front door in an oversized basket or urn.

❑ When planning any buffet, think about traffic flow and food placement. You'll want your guests to find it simple to fill their plates and enjoy the bounty of your table.

Holiday Dinner
8 p.m.
December 15
Black Tie
RSVP

MENU

GRILLED BEEF TENDERLOIN WITH BÉARNAISE SAUCE *page 232*

CHEESY CHIVE POTATOES *page 144*

BEAN BUNDLES *page 130*

CRANBERRY SALAD RING *page 81*

HIGH RISE ROLLS *page 119*

ROBIN'S CARAMEL FLAN *page 260*

MOCHA ALMOND TORTE *page 254*

❑ Candelabras, crystal, silver, holiday china, and place cards make this a very formal event. Add linen napkins tied with gold and fabulous charger plates, and the room is nothing short of elegant--perfect for a large dinner party for very special guests.

❑ The table is adorned with an exquisite arrangement of gilded fruit, shimmering gold bows, and votive candles. The centerpiece is kept low to allow easy conversation flow.

❑ Organization is the key to planning any party, but especially a large formal gathering. Plan the menu well ahead of time and check the availability of all special ingredients. It's also a good idea to wash, count, and set out your tableware several days before the party. Preparing ahead allows you more time to spend with your guests.

NOTES

GOOD FOOD

GOOD COMPANY

APPETIZERS
and
BEVERAGES

Never Fail Cocktail Meatballs

1 pound lean ground beef
⅓ cup minced onion
1 egg
1 teaspoon salt
1 teaspoon Worcestershire sauce
1 tablespoon parsley flakes
1 teaspoon garlic powder
½ cup vegetable oil
Party Meatball Sauce (see below)

Mix all ingredients. Shape into 1" balls. Brown in oil in a large skillet.

Makes 30 meatballs

Party Meatball Sauce

1 cup brown sugar
½ cup melted butter
½ cup apple jelly
1 cup ketchup
½ teaspoon cloves
1 teaspoon allspice
1 teaspoon black pepper
1 teaspoon sugar
Juice of 1 lemon

Mix ingredients in a saucepan and simmer over low heat for 45 minutes to 1 hour. Pour sauce over meatballs.

Makes 2½–3 cups

♡ *Quickly transform this tempting recipe into one that promotes heart health with a few simple changes, such as choosing extra-lean ground beef, using 2 egg whites in place of 1 whole egg, and eliminating butter from the sauce. These alterations result in less than 1 gram of fat per meatball, 0 grams of fat in the sauce, and no sacrifice at all in taste!*

Barbra Crumpacker, Registered Dietitian

This recipe is a "hit" at parties. It also is good served over cooked noodles as a main dish.

For a delicious sandwich spread, gradually cream 1 can evaporated milk into 1 pound butter. Add a little salt and chill. Spread on party breads and top with thinly sliced meats or vegetables.

Cucumber Lites

15 slices of bread
6   ounces cream cheese, softened
2   tablespoons mayonnaise
2   tablespoons sour cream
2   tablespoons minced onion
Dash Worcestershire sauce
Dash garlic powder
Salt
Pepper
2   cucumbers, thinly sliced
Fresh parsley

Cut out small rounds of bread with cookie or biscuit cutter. Mix together all remaining ingredients, except cucumbers and parsley. Spread mixture on bread. Top with cucumber slices and sprigs of parsley.

Makes 2½ dozen

To keep parsley fresh longer, wash in cold water, then place stems in warm water for several hours. Dry parsley, wrap in a paper towel, and then put in a plastic bag. Refrigerate.

Open-Faced Ham Sandwiches

1   (8 ounce) package cream cheese, softened
¼   cup butter, softened
½   cup grated Parmesan cheese
½   teaspoon dried whole oregano
½   teaspoon paprika
½   teaspoon garlic powder
4   English muffins, split
8   slices cooked ham
8   slices tomato

Combine cream cheese and butter. Stir until smooth. Add Parmesan cheese, oregano, paprika, and garlic powder; stir. Spread ⅔ of mixture evenly over English muffins. Top each muffin half with 1 slice of ham and tomato. Spoon remaining cheese mixture onto center of each tomato slice. Place on baking sheet and broil until golden brown.

Makes 8

When making sandwiches ahead of time for a party, spread the mixture on the bread and then refrigerate. Cut when firm with a serrated knife.

Super Sandwich Filling

1   (8 ounce) package cream cheese, softened
¼   cup chopped green pepper
3   tablespoons chopped pimientos
¾   teaspoon salt
3   hard boiled eggs, finely chopped
¾   cup chopped pecans
¼   cup chopped onion
1   tablespoon ketchup
¼   teaspoon lemon pepper

Combine all ingredients.

Makes 2⅓ cups

Sandwiches can be made the day before a party. To keep them fresh, place a paper towel in the bottom of a plastic container. Put wax paper between sandwich layers and on top. Cover with a damp paper towel, place lid on container, and refrigerate until the party.

Blue Cheese Biscuits

1   cup blue cheese, softened
½   cup butter, softened
1   cup flour
½   cup coarsely chopped nuts
½   cup finely chopped nuts

Cream cheese and butter. Mix in flour and coarsely chopped nuts. Take teaspoons of mixture and form into balls. Roll balls in finely chopped nuts and bake at 350° for 15 to 17 minutes. Serve cold.

Makes 3 dozen

To keep nuts from sticking together in a food processor, lightly flour the knife blade before chopping nuts.

When planning appetizers, make sure that each item is small enough to be eaten with fingers or a fork. Using a knife while standing is awkward and diverts attention from conversation.

Parmesan Pastry Twists

½ cup grated Parmesan cheese
¾ teaspoon pepper
¾ teaspoon parsley flakes
¼ teaspoon garlic powder
1 package frozen puff pastry sheets, thawed
1 egg, slightly beaten

Combine first 4 ingredients in a small mixing bowl. Brush 1 pastry sheet with egg. Sprinkle with ¼ of dry mixture. Press into pastry with palm of hand. Repeat this process on the other side of pastry sheet. Cut pastry sheet in half; cut each half into 1" strips (about 9 strips per half). Twist each strip into a spiral shape. Repeat entire process with remaining pastry sheets. Place twists on a lightly greased baking sheet. Bake at 350° for 15 minutes or until golden.

Makes 3 dozen

Curried Cheese Toast

1 cup chopped black seedless olives
½ cup thinly sliced green onions
1½ cups grated sharp Cheddar cheese
½ cup mayonnaise
½ teaspoon salt
½ teaspoon curry powder
6 English muffins, split and toasted

Mix first 6 ingredients together. Spread mixture on toasted English muffin halves. Place on baking sheet under broiler and broil until mixture melts. Cut English muffin halves into quarters before serving. Serve warm.

Serves 12

Spicy Greek Toast

1   tablespoon drained and minced pepperoncini
1½ tablespoons minced kalamata olives
3   slices of Genoa salami, minced
1   tablespoon minced fresh parsley
8   ½" thick slices of Italian bread, lightly toasted
2   teaspoons Dijon mustard
3   tablespoons freshly grated Parmesan cheese

In a bowl, combine the pepperoncini, olives, salami, and parsley. Spread 1 side of the toasted bread with the mustard. Divide the pepperoncini mixture among the slices and spread evenly. Sprinkle toasted bread with Parmesan cheese. On a baking sheet, broil the toast under preheated broiler about 3 inches from heat for 1 minute or until cheese is golden.

Serves 4

Our Cheese Straws

4   cups grated extra sharp Cheddar cheese
1   pound butter
4   cups flour
1   teaspoon salt
¾   teaspoon cayenne pepper

Place cheese and butter in a bowl. Let mixture reach room temperature. Cream together with an electric mixer until soft and well-blended. While mixing, gradually add flour, salt, and cayenne pepper. Using a cookie press with a star plate, pipe cheese mixture out in short bite-sized cheese straws. Bake at 350° for 10 to 15 minutes.

Makes 12 dozen

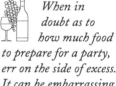

Southern Popcorn

2 pounds fresh okra
1 tablespoon buttermilk
4 eggs, well beaten
1½ cups cornmeal
1½ cups flour
Salt and pepper to taste
Vegetable oil

Wash okra, remove tops, and slice. Add buttermilk to eggs. Dip okra in egg mixture and roll in mixture of cornmeal and flour. Fry in oil over medium heat until brown. Drain on paper towels and season with salt and pepper. Serve immediately.

Serves 8–10

Carter's Mushroom Caps

1 (8 ounce) package cream cheese, softened
1 medium onion, grated
12 bacon slices, fried and crumbled
2 pounds large mushrooms

Remove and discard mushroom stems. Blend first 3 ingredients. Fill mushroom caps with cream cheese mixture. Place on baking sheet and bake at 350° for 10 minutes or until thoroughly heated.

Serves 12

Down-Home Boiled Peanuts

• *4–5 pounds green peanuts in shell*
• *1 tablespoon salt to each quart of water*
• *water to cover*

Wash peanuts. Place in large pot; add water and salt. Bring to boil; reduce heat to brisk simmer. Cook for 2 ½ to 3 hours. Add water as needed. To increase saltiness, allow peanuts to stand in salted water after cooking.

MARINATED MUSHROOMS

1   pound fresh mushrooms, whole
1   tablespoon salt
Pinch red pepper
⅛   teaspoon black pepper
⅛   teaspoon white pepper
⅛   teaspoon crushed oregano leaves
1   tablespoon sugar
1   teaspoon minced onion
Pinch fresh ground garlic
1   cup red wine vinegar
1   cup vegetable oil

Wash mushrooms. Place in container with tight-fitting lid. Add remaining ingredients. Refrigerate 24 hours. Shake occasionally.

Serves 8-10

MARINATED ZUCCHINI

1   pound zucchini, thinly sliced
1   tablespoon olive oil
Juice of 1 large lemon
2   cloves garlic, minced
¼   teaspoon salt
½   teaspoon freshly ground black pepper
2   tablespoons chopped fresh parsley or basil or 1 teaspoon dried
     parsley or basil

In a bowl, toss sliced zucchini in olive oil, lemon juice, garlic, salt, and pepper. Cover and refrigerate for 4 to 8 hours, stirring occasionally. Toss with parsley or basil just before serving. (If dried herbs are used, add with other ingredients from the start.)

Serves 12

Fruits make nice bases in which to place toothpicks. Try apples, oranges, pineapples-- they add nice color and interest to your table, too!

Cool Vegetable Tray with Fresh Dill Dip

1   cup sour cream
1   cup mayonnaise
1   tablespoon fresh lemon juice
⅛   teaspoon salt
⅛   teaspoon freshly ground pepper
½   cup finely minced fresh dill
1   fresh red or green cabbage, hollowed out
Assorted fresh vegetables, such as sliced yellow squash, whole snow
      peas, whole baby carrots, broccoli and cauliflower flowerets, or
      whole asparagus.

Mix first 6 ingredients in a bowl. Refrigerate until ready to serve.
Carefully spoon dip into hollowed-out cabbage "bowl." Serve with
fresh vegetables.

Serves 30

Kiwi and Prosciutto

½   pound prosciutto, sliced paper thin
12   kiwi, quartered lengthwise.

Wrap kiwi quarters with slices of prosciutto. Refrigerate until
serving time.

Makes 4 dozen

Herb Dip

• 1 cup yogurt
*• ¼ cup finely
chopped and
seeded cucumber*
*• ½ teaspoon
snipped fresh dill*
• ¼ teaspoon salt
*• 1 clove garlic,
pressed*

*Combine all
ingredients well.
Refrigerate.
Serve as dip for
raw vegetables.*

Summer Fruit Tray

1 (8 ounce) package cream cheese, softened
1 (8 ounce) container marshmallow cream
Assorted fresh melons and fruit cubes or balls

In a bowl, combine the cream cheese and marshmallow cream. Serve dip in a hollowed-out melon or pineapple placed in the center of a large serving platter. (Save the inside of the fruit for dipping.) Surround the dip with honeydew, cantaloupe, and pineapple cubes or balls.

Serves 20–25

Chili Cheese

1 pound sharp Cheddar cheese
1 (4 ounce) jar pimientos
1 (4 ounce) can chili peppers
1 small onion
1 cup mayonnaise

Grate cheese and place in large bowl. Add mayonnaise. Cut the onion in 4 pieces. Put onion, pimientos, and chili peppers in blender or food processor and purée. Add purée to cheese mixture and blend until very smooth. For best flavor, refrigerate 1 day before serving. Serve with large corn chips.

Serves 15–20

Potatoes Nouveau

- *1 dozen small new potatoes*
- *1 (8 ounce) container sour cream*
- *1 (6 ounce) can caviar*

Boil potatoes for 15 minutes. Slice thinly. Put a dollop of sour cream on each potato slice and top with a small amount of caviar.

Makes 15–20

Shrimp Mousse

1 (10¾ ounce) can tomato soup
1 package unflavored gelatin
¼ cup cold water
1 (8 ounce) package cream cheese, softened
1 cup mayonnaise
2 (4¼ ounce) cans small shrimp
½ cup chopped onion
½ cup chopped celery
½ cup chopped green pepper

Heat soup to boiling. Dissolve gelatin in cold water and add to soup. In a bowl, mix cream cheese with mayonnaise. Add soup and beat with an electric beater. Add shrimp and chopped vegetables. Pour into mold and chill. Serve with crackers.

Serves 20

Charleston Cheese

½ cup mayonnaise
1 (8 ounce) package cream cheese, softened
1 cup grated sharp Cheddar cheese
2 green onions, chopped
6 round, buttery crackers, crushed
8 slices bacon, fried and crumbled

In a bowl, mix mayonnaise, cream cheese, Cheddar cheese, and onions. Put mixture into a greased quiche dish. Top with crushed crackers. Bake at 350˚ for 15 minutes. Remove from oven and top with crumbled bacon. Serve with crackers.

Serves 15–20

Florida Lobster Butter Log

- *½ pound cooked Florida lobster meat, fresh or frozen*
- *6 tablespoons butter, softened*
- *1 teaspoon minced onion*
- *½ teaspoon seasoned salt*
- *¼ teaspoon paprika*
- *½ cup chopped fresh parsley*

Thaw lobster meat if frozen. Pat dry with paper towel, and finely chop. Combine all ingredients, except parsley, in a medium bowl. Roll mixture in plastic wrap and shape into a log. Refrigerate for about 4 hours or until firm. Before serving, remove plastic wrap and roll log in parsley. Serve with crackers or melba toast.

Makes 1¾ cups spread

Hot Onion Canapé

½ cup minced onion
½ cup mayonnaise
4 drops hot pepper sauce
1 teaspoon paprika
Salt and pepper to taste
32 saltine crackers

Combine onion, mayonnaise, pepper sauce, paprika, salt, and pepper. Spread on crackers. Brown on top rack at 400° until bubbly.

Makes 32

Jo's Cheese Ball

2 (8 ounce) packages cream cheese, softened
¼ pound blue cheese
1 onion, grated
½ teaspoon garlic powder
½ cup chopped nuts
2 tablespoons paprika
2 tablespoons parsley

Combine softened cream cheese and blue cheese. Add onion and garlic powder to taste. Divide mixture in half and shape into 2 balls. Combine nuts, paprika, and parsley in a shallow dish. Roll balls in nut mixture to coat completely.

Serves 25–30

Swiss Onion Spread

• *1 cup chopped onion*
• *1 cup grated Swiss cheese*
• *1 cup mayonnaise*
• *fresh celery stalks*

Mix onion, cheese, and mayonnaise together. Bake at 350° for 18 to 20 minutes. Stuff in fresh celery stalks.

Serves 12

The recipe above also makes an excellent side dish or cracker spread. It is the onion lover's dream!

PINEAPPLE CHEESE BALL

1   (8 ounce) can crushed pineapple, drained
2   (8 ounce) packages cream cheese
½   cup chopped bell pepper
2   teaspoons chopped onion
3   tablespoons seasoned salt
½   cup chopped pecans

Combine all ingredients, except pecans. Form into 2 balls or rings and roll in chopped pecans.

Serves 20–25

TUNA CREAM BALL

1   (8 ounce) package cream cheese, softened
¼   teaspoon hot pepper sauce
3   tablespoons mayonnaise
1   (6 ½-7 ounce) can tuna
1   tablespoon lemon juice
⅓   cup finely chopped onion
½   cup chopped pecans

In a bowl, combine cream cheese with pepper sauce, mayonnaise, tuna, lemon juice, and onion. Shape into 2 balls and roll in chopped nuts. Refrigerate before serving.

Serves 10–15

Tomato Salsa

½ teaspoon dried basil or 1 tablespoon fresh basil
3 ripe tomatoes, peeled, diced, with juice reserved
1 clove garlic, minced
3 tablespoons finely chopped onion
2 tablespoons finely chopped green bell pepper
1 tablespoon finely chopped jalapeño peppers
Salt and sugar to taste
2 tablespoons white wine or apple cider vinegar
1 tablespoon reserved jalapeño juice (optional)

The day before serving, combine all ingredients and stir together.
Refrigerate. Serve with tortilla chips.

Makes 1½ –2 cups

For a colorful addition to your table, hollow out acorn squash, small pumpkins, and large red or green bell peppers. Fill with dips or spreads, and enjoy!

Mexi-Dip

2 (8 ounce) cans bean dip
1 (8 ounce) container sour cream
⅔ cup mayonnaise
1 package taco seasoning
1 cup grated Cheddar cheese
2 medium chopped tomatoes
¼ cup sliced black olives
½ cup chopped green onion
¼ cup chopped green chilies

Cover the bottom of a 12" quiche dish with bean dip. In a small dish, mix sour cream, mayonnaise, and taco seasoning; spread mixture over bean dip. Layer any or all of the other toppings. Serve with tortilla chips.

Serves 10–12

Shape up this Mexican dish with the reduced-fat and fat-free products on the market today. Choosing fat-free sour cream and mayonnaise will reduce the fat content substantially. Also, try low-fat cheese and save half the fat. By using non-fat sour cream, low-fat mayonnaise, and low-fat cheese, you can save 134 grams of fat and 1,206 calories per recipe. Your hips will thank you!

Barbra Crumpacker, Registered Dietitian

Use large sea-shells or miniature flower pots lined with plastic wrap to hold dips and spreads for pool parties.

Always-A-Hit Spinach Dip

2 cups mayonnaise
1 (10 ounce) package frozen chopped spinach, cooked and drained
½ cup chopped bell pepper
½ cup chopped fresh parsley
½ cup chopped green onion
Salt and pepper to taste
2 loaves round French or Hawaiian bread

Mix all ingredients, except bread, and refrigerate. Cut out the center of one bread loaf and place dip inside. Cube remaining bread and use it for dipping.

Serves 15–20

Spinach Beef Dip

1 (10 ounce) package frozen chopped spinach, thawed and drained
1 (8 ounce) package cream cheese, softened
1 cup mayonnaise
½ cup chopped green onions
1 tablespoon dillweed
1 (2 ½ ounce) jar dried beef, chopped
Dash salt
Dash pepper

Combine spinach, cream cheese, mayonnaise, and onions together and put in electric blender or food processor. Blend 1 minute. Add dillweed and blend 1 minute longer. Fold in dried beef, salt, and pepper. Chill. Serve with corn chips.

Makes 3 cups

Alligator Eyes Dip

4   (2¼ ounce) cans black olives, chopped
2   fresh tomatoes, chopped
20 fresh green onions, chopped
3   (4 ounce) cans Mexican chilies, chopped
¾   cup salad oil
⅓   cup vinegar
2   tablespoons garlic salt or to taste

Mix all ingredients. Refrigerate overnight. Serve with cheese-flavored chips.

Serves 20

Newlywed Crab Dip

1   pound crabmeat
1   cup sour cream
½   cup mayonnaise
1   package Italian dressing mix

Combine all ingredients. Chill 1 hour before serving with crackers.

Serves 10-15

Fernandina Shrimp Dip

1   (8 ounce) package cream cheese, softened
⅓   cup sour cream
2   teaspoons lemon juice
½   teaspoon grated onion
¼   teaspoon Worcestershire sauce
⅛   teaspoon paprika
1   cup shrimp, boiled, cleaned, and chopped

Combine cream cheese, sour cream, and seasonings. Mix thoroughly. Add shrimp and mix well. Serve with round buttery crackers.

Serves 4-6

Shrimp In Suds

• 1 pound shrimp, cleaned and peeled
• 2 cans beer
• 1 beer can of water

Boil shrimp in water and beer for approximately 5 minutes or until shrimp turns pink.

Serves 2

♡ While small
recipe modifi-
cations may not turn a
dish into a perfect low-
fat alternative, they can
definitely improve the
nutritional profile. Do
not hesitate to substitute
the light version of
regular products, such as
cream cheese and
mayonnaise, in recipes.
Applying that rule in
the recipe at right for
Shrimp Stuffed Cherry
Tomatoes would save
about 50 grams of fat.

Barbra Crumpacker,
Registered Dietitian

Pawley's Island Pickled Shrimp

2   pounds cooked shrimp, cleaned and peeled
1   cup chopped onions
1   cup chopped bell pepper
2   cloves garlic, minced
2   tablespoons capers
2   tablespoons whole cloves
1¼ cups olive oil
¾   cup white vinegar
2   tablespoons salt
Pepper sauce to taste

Layer first 6 ingredients in a glass bowl. In a jar with a tight-fitting lid, mix together the remaining 4 ingredients and shake. Pour oil and vinegar mixture over layered shrimp. Refrigerate at least a day. Keeps well several days.

Serves 6

Shrimp-Stuffed Cherry Tomatoes

2   pints cherry tomatoes
1   (8 ounce) package cream cheese, softened
1   teaspoon Worcestershire sauce
1   small onion, chopped
½   teaspoon salt
2   teaspoons mayonnaise
Dash of garlic powder
½   pound small shrimp, cooked and peeled

Hollow out cherry tomatoes and place in ice water to chill. Combine cream cheese, Worcestershire sauce, onion, salt, mayonnaise, and garlic powder. Chop shrimp very fine, add to mixture. Stuff tomatoes and refrigerate.

Serves 10–12

Shrimp in Fresh Dill Marinade

1   quart water
1   tablespoon salt
1   teaspoon dillweed
1   lemon, sliced
2½ pounds shrimp, unpeeled
½   cup olive oil
½   cup dry white wine
4   teaspoons chopped fresh dill
1   teaspoon freshly ground pepper
Dash garlic powder
2   drops hot red pepper sauce
½   cup lemon juice
Salt to taste
1   tablespoon snipped chives

Bring salted water, dillweed, and lemon to a boil. Add shrimp and
simmer until shrimp are pink, about 3 to 4 minutes. Drain and
chill shrimp. Peel and devein shrimp and place in a bowl. In
another bowl, mix together olive oil, white wine, and remaining
ingredients. Pour over shrimp. Cover and store in refrigerator for
24 hours.

Serves 8-10

Steve's Shrimp Spread

1   (8 ounce) package cream cheese
2   pounds medium shrimp, boiled and peeled
¾   cup cocktail sauce with horseradish
Assorted crackers
2   fresh lemons, cut in wedges lengthwise

Remove cream cheese from wrapper and place in center of large
platter. Surround block with shrimp. Pour cocktail sauce over the
cream cheese. Surround shrimp with crackers. Using a portion of 1
lemon, squeeze juice on shrimp. Garnish with remaining lemon
wedges.

Serves 4-6

*Buy fresh herbs when
they're most abundant,
and freeze them for
year-round use. Wash,
dry, and pick off sprigs
from stems. Place
sprigs in freezer storage
bags, seal, label, and
freeze. Use herbs
directly from the
freezer.*

♡ *The link
between
cholesterol and heart
disease has been clearly
acknowledged and
Americans are
searching for ways to
decrease the cholesterol
in their diets. While
ingesting an excess of
cholesterol does increase
blood cholesterol levels,
saturated fat actually
has a stronger impact
on your blood choles-
terol level than actual
cholesterol from food.
For example, 15
shrimp supply 155 mg
of cholesterol, but less
than 1 gram of total
fat and .2 grams of
saturated fat. Four
ounces of lean ground
beef, however, provides
only 82 mg. of
cholesterol, but in
comparison has 16
grams of total fat and
6.3 grams of saturated
fat. Clearly, shrimp--
and all shellfish--are
still a healthier choice.*

*Barbra Crumpacker,
Registered Dietitian*

All Seasons Seafood Marinade

1   (6 ounce) package Italian dressing mix
¾   cup olive oil
¼   cup vinegar
1   teaspoon oregano
1   tablespoon lemon juice
⅛   teaspoon minced garlic
¼   cup parsley flakes
¼   teaspoon salt
½   teaspoon pepper
¼   cup grated Parmesan cheese
1   tablespoon white wine
1   tablespoon Worcestershire sauce
1   pound boiled shrimp or steamed crab claws

Combine all ingredients except for seafood in a glass bowl. Add shrimp or crab. Cover bowl and marinate for 5 to 6 hours in refrigerator before serving.

Serves 2–4

Happy Hour Ham Biscuits

5   pounds uncooked smoked ham
2   cups butter, melted
2   (8 ounce) cartons sour cream
4   cups self-rising flour
6   ounces honey mustard
6   ounces mayonnaise

Bake ham 8 to 10 hours at 225°. While ham is cooking, mix together butter and sour cream in large bowl. Add flour and mix well. Drop mixture by teaspoonfuls into greased mini-muffin pan. Bake at 450° for 15 minutes. Remove biscuits from pan and let cool. When ham is cooked, let cool and slice thinly. Slice biscuits in half. Put small slices of ham between biscuit slices. Serve with honey mustard and mayonnaise.

Makes 4 dozen

Savory Tenderloin with Horseradish Sauce

1   (8 pound) beef tenderloin
1   (15 ounce) bottle Worcestershire sauce
2   (8 ounce) cartons sour cream
4   tablespoons prepared horseradish
Salt and pepper to taste
½   cup butter, softened
1½ teaspoons salt
1   tablespoon black pepper
1½ teaspoons garlic powder

Remove excess fat and skin from tenderloin. Place in a bowl and pour half the bottle of Worcestershire sauce over the meat. Cover and refrigerate for 5 to 7 hours.

While meat is marinating, prepare horseradish sauce. In a bowl, combine sour cream, horseradish, salt, and pepper. Chill until ready to serve.

Before cooking meat, remove it from marinade. Coat both sides of meat with butter and seasonings. Place on broiling pan and broil 6 inches from heating element for 15 minutes. Turn over and broil another 15 minutes. Remove meat from oven. Place on platter and let cool at room temperature. When cooled, place meat in a hot oven-proof skillet. Sear meat on both sides. Pour remaining Worcestershire sauce over meat. Place skillet in preheated oven and bake at 350° to desired doneness. Refrigerate and slice thinly. Serve with assorted party breads.

Makes 50 sandwiches

Start your menu planning with appetizers that feature meat. They're often the most popular, but also the most expensive and time-consuming to prepare. So, choosing your meat appetizers first helps you to fit the rest of the menu into your schedule and budget.

Fabulous Franks

3 packages regular-size beef franks
2 cups ketchup
4 tablespoons Worcestershire sauce
¾ cup bourbon
½ cup lightly packed light brown sugar
2 tablespoons dry mustard

Cut franks diagonally into bite-sized pieces (about 6 per hotdog). Mix remaining ingredients in large saucepan. Heat until bubbly. Add frank pieces. Cook over low heat until franks are hot. Pour into a chafing dish to serve.

Serves 30–40

Stuffed Artichoke Hearts

1 bunch green onions, chopped
3 teaspoons minced garlic
2 tablespoons olive oil
¾ cup regular breadcrumbs
1 cup Italian breadcrumbs
½ cup Romano cheese
1 (8 ½ ounce) can artichoke hearts, drained

Sauté green onions and garlic in 2 tablespoons of olive oil. In a bowl, combine bread crumbs and Romano cheese. Add enough water to mix to make it stick together. Cut each artichoke heart into 4 pieces. Make round balls with the stuffing mix and place on top of the artichoke pieces. Press the stuffing down. Place on an ungreased baking sheet and bake at 350° until brown. Serve hot.

Serves 4–6

The artichoke dish at right freezes well, so it can be prepared ahead of time.

Freckled Cheese Sticks

1 loaf thin-sliced bread
1 pound margarine
1 cup grated Parmesan cheese
2 tablespoons poppy seeds
1 teaspoon celery salt
1 teaspoon paprika

Trim crust from bread and cut bread into thirds. Grease cookie sheet. Melt margarine. In shallow dish, mix cheese, poppy seeds, celery salt, and paprika. Brush bread strips with melted butter. Roll in cheese mixture. Bake at 325° for 15 to 20 minutes or until crisp and brown.

Serves 15-20

Tortilla Roll-Ups

6 ounces cream cheese, softened
1 (4 ounce) jar chopped pimientos
1 (4¼ ounce) can chopped black olives
1 (4 ounce) can chopped chili peppers
12-16 flour tortillas
Salsa (see recipe on page 49)

Mix first 4 ingredients. Spread mixture on 1 side of each tortilla. Roll tortillas up jelly-roll style. Wrap each tortilla individually in plastic wrap or place in a covered container. Refrigerate 2 hours or more. To serve, cut tortilla rolls into bite-sized slices. Serve on toothpicks with a bowl of salsa.

Serves 10-12

Whirligigs

• 1 (12 ounce) package sliced sandwich ham
• 1 (8 ounce) package cream cheese, softened
• 1 bunch fresh green onions

Spread cream cheese on each slice of ham. Roll 1 onion in each slice of ham. Slice the roll into bite-sized servings. Serve with toothpicks.

Variation: Use a dill pickle instead of green onion. Perfect for picnics.

Serves 5

Pizza Popcorn

• ⅓ cup butter, melted
• ¼ cup grated Romano cheese
• ¾ teaspoon Italian seasoning
• 2 teaspoons garlic salt
• 10 cups hot popcorn

Mix well.

Serves 5

Bacon-Wrapped Surprise

1 (1 pound) package sliced bacon
Regular and/or frilled toothpicks

Cut bacon slices equally into 3 pieces. Wrap a "surprise" in each bacon piece and secure with a toothpick. "Surprise" recipes follow.

Surprise 1

1 box dates, pitted
Walnut, pecan, or almond halves
1 (8 ounce) container plain yogurt

Stuff dates with walnut, pecan, or almond halves. Wrap each date in a bacon piece. Bake on cookie sheet at 350° for 10 minutes. Turn on broiler and continue cooking until bacon is crisp, about 1 to 2 minutes. Place yogurt in small serving dish and use as a dip.

Surprise 2

1 can water chestnuts, drained
Worcestershire sauce
Soy sauce

Wrap each water chestnut with a bacon piece. Put a dash of each sauce on each wrapped chestnut. Bake on cookie sheet at 350° for 10 minutes. Turn on broiler and continue cooking until bacon is crisp, about 1-2 minutes.

Surprise 3

3 dozen fresh oysters
Lemon juice
Worcestershire sauce
Salt and pepper to taste

Season each oyster with a dash of lemon juice, Worcestershire sauce, salt, and pepper. Wrap in bacon pieces. Bake at 350° for 10 minutes. Turn on broiler and continue cooking until bacon is crisp, about 1-2 minutes.

SURPRISE 4

3   ripe bananas, sliced thickly
Black pepper

Wrap banana slices in bacon pieces. Sprinkle bacon with a generous dash of black pepper. Broil for 5 minutes or until bacon is crisp, turning twice.

SURPRISE 5

3   dozen party wieners
Brown sugar

Wrap wieners with bacon pieces. Sprinkle with brown sugar. Bake in a glass baking dish at 350° for 30 to 45 minutes.

MAGNIFICENT MINI-REUBENS

2   packages crescent rolls
Spicy mustard
1   (16 ounce) can sauerkraut, rinsed and drained
½   pound cooked corned beef, sliced thinly
1   egg yolk, beaten lightly
Caraway seeds

Separate dough into triangles. Spread with mustard. Top with thin layer sauerkraut and corned beef. Roll to close. Brush with egg yolk and dip into caraway seeds. Place on greased cookie sheet and bake at 375° for 10 to 12 minutes or until golden. Serve hot.

Serves 10–12

VERSATILE COCKTAIL PUFFS

¼ cup butter
½ cup boiling water
½ cup flour
2 eggs

Add butter to boiling water and stir until butter melts. Add flour all at once and stir vigorously until ball forms in center of pan. Remove from heat and add eggs 1 at a time, beating after each addition. Spoon out 18 tiny puffs. Shape on buttered cookie sheet. Bake 15 minutes at 450°, then lower heat to 375° and bake 20 minutes longer. Remove from pan and let cool. Cut puffs in half horizontally. Fill halves with chicken, shrimp, crab, or ham salad.

Makes 3 dozen

CRAB MOLD

1 cup mayonnaise
Juice of 2 lemons and the peel, grated
1 small carton low-fat cottage cheese
1 (8 ounce) can crabmeat, drained
¼ teaspoon salt
½ cup chopped green bell pepper
1 medium onion, chopped
4 stalks celery, chopped
⅛ teaspoon white pepper
1 (4 ounce) jar pimientos, chopped
1 tablespoon unflavored gelatin soaked in 2 tablespoons water

In a small bowl, combine mayonnaise, lemon juice, and peel. Set aside. In a separate bowl, mix together the cottage cheese, crab, and remaining ingredients. Add just enough of lemon-mayonnaise mixture to crab mixture to blend. Spoon crab mixture into a ring mold and refrigerate overnight. Refrigerate remaining lemon-mayonnaise mixture. To serve, invert mold onto serving tray. Place remaining lemon-mayonnaise mixture in a small bowl that fits in the center of the ring.

Serves 8–10

HEARTS OF PALM SPREAD

• 1 (14 ounce) can hearts of palm, drained and chopped
• 1 cup shredded mozzarella cheese
• ¾ cup mayonnaise
• ½ cup grated Parmesan cheese
• ¼ cup sour cream
• 2 tablespoons minced green onions

Combine all ingredients. Spoon into a lightly greased 9" quiche pan. Bake at 350° for 20 minutes or until brown and bubbly. Serve with stone-ground crackers or toasted pita chips.

Serves 6–8

Lona's Hot Mushroom Turnovers

3 (3 ounce) packages cream cheese, softened
½ cup butter or margarine, softened
1½ cups flour, sifted
½ pound mushrooms
1 medium onion, minced
3 tablespoons butter or margarine
2 teaspoons salt, divided
¼ teaspoon thyme
2 tablespoons flour
¼ cup sour cream

In a bowl, mix together the cream cheese, ½ cup butter or margarine, and flour. Cover and refrigerate for 1 hour. In a skillet over medium-high heat, sauté mushrooms, onion, 3 tablespoons butter or margarine, and 1 teaspoon salt for about 5 minutes. Stir in remaining salt, thyme, and flour, then add sour cream. Remove from heat. Roll out dough to ¼" thickness. Cut with a 2¾" round cutter. Place a spoonful of mushroom-onion mixture on half of the dough circle. Brush edges of circle with beaten egg. Fold dough over and press edges together. Prick top of turnover with a fork. Place turnovers on an ungreased cookie sheet; brush with egg. Bake at 350° for 12 to 15 minutes or until golden.

Makes 4 dozen

Aim for variety in the texture, color, and flavor of recipes you choose for appetizers. It's most appealing for 1 or 2 of the selections to be hot.

When planning your menu, choose appetizers that are prepared in a variety of ways. In doing so, you'll avoid the common mistake of preparing too many dips and spreads.

Sweet Vidalia Spread

1   cup sugar
2   cups water
¼   cup vinegar
½   teaspoon celery seed
2   medium Vidalia onions, finely chopped
3   tablespoons mayonnaise

In a saucepan, bring sugar, water, vinegar, and celery seed to a boil. Add chopped onion, cover, and remove from heat. Let stand covered 15 to 20 minutes. Drain. Mix with mayonnaise to desired consistency. Serve with crackers.

Serves 6-8

Before you grate (or shred) cheese, brush a little oil on your grater so that the cheese will wash off easily. Use a pastry brush or paper towel dampened with oil and coat the grater, starting at the bottom. Simply brush the shredding side of the grater from the bottom to the top (this prevents bristles from getting caught in the holes). Make sure the cheese is very cold--it will be easier to grate.

Margaret's Pimiento Spread with Bagel Chips

1¼ cups grated sharp Cheddar cheese
1¼ cups grated Swiss cheese
12 ounces pimientos, chopped
8   ounces jalapeño slices, chopped
1   cup mayonnaise
6   bagels, sliced thin
1   teaspoon garlic salt

In a bowl, mix together cheeses, pimientos, jalapeños, and mayonnaise. Cover and chill overnight. To make bagel chips, place bagel slices on baking sheet and sprinkle with garlic salt. Bake at 300° for 20 minutes or until light brown and crisp. Cool on wire rack and store in air tight container. Serve cooled chips with pimiento spread.

Serves 6

Barbecued Spareribs

5 pounds spareribs
Curry powder
Salt and pepper
Barbecue sauce (recipe follows)

Remove excess fat from ribs and cut into as many pieces as desired. Place spareribs, flesh side up, on a rack in a shallow roasting pan. Sprinkle with salt, pepper, and lightly with curry powder. Bake at 400° for 1 hour, basting with warm sauce every 10 minutes. When ribs are done, brush with the remaining sauce and serve.

Serves 4–6

Barbecue Sauce

1	cup finely chopped onion
1	clove garlic, minced
¼	cup butter, melted
1	cup ketchup
½	cup dry sherry
1	tablespoon light brown sugar
1	teaspoon dry mustard
1	tablespoon lemon juice
½	cup white vinegar
2	teaspoons Worcestershire sauce
⅓	cup water

In a deep saucepan, sauté the onion and garlic in melted butter for 3 to 4 minutes. Add remaining ingredients. Bring to a boil. Lower heat and simmer, uncovered, for 1 hour, stirring frequently to prevent scorching. Strain through a fine sieve.

Makes 2½ cups

Brie Wrapped In Pastry

• *1 (14 ounce) round mini Brie*
• *1 package refrigerated crescent rolls*
• *3–5 fresh apples or pears*

Remove rind from round Brie. Spread out 1 package of uncooked crescent rolls. Wrap Brie in crescent rolls, pressing firmly to make uniform, even crust. Bake at 350° until pastry begins to brown slightly. Serve with apple or pear slices.

Serves 3–5

QUICK AND EASY QUESADILLAS

1 pound ground beef
Taco seasoning packet
8 ounces Monterey Jack cheese, shredded
8 ounces Cheddar cheese, shredded
8 (8") flour tortillas
1 (4 ounce) can chopped green chilies
¾ cup sliced green onions
Guacamole
Sour cream
Picante sauce

Brown ground beef in a skillet. Drain off fat. Add taco seasoning packet and cook according to directions. Set aside. Combine the 2 cheeses and set aside. Lightly spray two 8" cake pans with non-stick vegetable oil. Place a tortilla in bottom of each pan. Sprinkle ⅓ of cheese mixture, ⅓ of chilies and onions, and ⅓ of meat mixture between the two pans. Continue to alternate layers, ending with tortillas. Brush with melted butter. Bake at 400° for 20 minutes or until cheese melts and tops are lightly browned. Cool 5 minutes and invert onto serving platters. Cut into wedges. Serve with guacamole, sour cream, and picante sauce.

Serves 4-6

CRABMEAT CRISPS

½ cup butter, softened
1 (5 ounce) jar sharp pasteurized processed cheese spread
1½ teaspoons mayonnaise
½ teaspoon garlic powder
¾ teaspoon Cajun salt or seasoned salt
1 (7 ounce) can crabmeat, drained, or fresh lump crabmeat
6 English muffins, split

Mix first 6 ingredients together and spread on English muffin halves. Cut halves into 4 wedges. Place on cookie sheet and bake at 400° until bubbly.

Serves 6-8

NUTTY BRIE APPETIZER

• ¾ cup finely chopped toasted pecans
• ¼ cup coffee liqueur
• 3 tablespoons brown sugar
• 1 (14 ounce) mini Brie

Stir together pecans, liqueur, and brown sugar. Mix well. Remove rind from top of Brie. Place Brie on a micro-wave-safe serving dish. Spoon pecan mixture over top of Brie. Microwave uncovered on high 1½ to 2 minutes or until Brie softens, giving dish a half-turn after 1 minute. Serve with crackers.

Serves 6-8

Fuzzie Peach

1   (6 ounce) can pink lemonade concentrate, thawed
6   ounces vodka
6   ounces water
3   large fresh peaches, peeled, pitted, and sliced
1   dozen ice cubes

Empty the lemonade concentrate into blender. Add the vodka and water. (Use the empty lemonade can to measure the vodka and water.) Blend. While blending add peaches, then ice. Blend until smooth.

Serves 4

When planning food for an afternoon party, allow 3 to 4 cups of punch, 2 to 3 cups of tea or coffee, and 10 "bites" per person.

Coffee Punch

2   quarts strong coffee
2   cups cold milk
2   teaspoons vanilla extract
½   cup sugar
½   gallon vanilla ice cream
½   pint whipping cream, whipped (optional)
Dash ground nutmeg

Mix first 4 ingredients. Chill. Just before serving, break ice cream into chunks and place in punch bowl. Pour chilled coffee mixture over ice cream. If desired, spoon mounds of whipped cream on top of punch in individual cups. Sprinkle with nutmeg.

Serves 12

For subtle flavor and a wonderful aroma, add a cinnamon stick or vanilla bean to the coffee maker basket. Delicious!

To make children's punch, save the juices from canned fruits. Combine several kinds and add orange juice and/or ginger ale.

Georgia Peach Punch

3 (12 ounce) cans frozen orange juice concentrate
3 (12 ounce) cans frozen lemonade concentrate
6¾ quarts water
6 (12 ounce) cans apricot nectar
3 (46 ounce) cans pineapple juice

Mix concentrates with water. Combine with apricot nectar and pineapple juice. Chill and serve.

Makes 4 gallons

"Frost" beer or champagne glasses by placing in freezer for 1 hour. Frosted glasses look pretty and keep

Very Bloody Mary

1 (64 ounce) jar beef and tomato cocktail juice
1 (12 ounce) can cocktail vegetable juice
1 can beef bouillon
½ teaspoon bitters
½ teaspoon hot pepper sauce
¼ cup steak sauce
¼ cup Worcestershire sauce
2 cups vodka
½ teaspoon salt
½ teaspoon celery salt
½ teaspoon coarse black pepper

Mix together all ingredients in large pitcher. Refrigerate. Serve cold.

Makes 3 quarts

For delicious crisp celery, let stand in a quart of cold water to which 1 teaspoon sugar has been added.

Warm Winter Coffee

2   cups non-dairy coffee creamer
1½ cups hot cocoa mix
1½ cups instant coffee granules
1½ cups sugar
1   teaspoon ground cinnamon
½   teaspoon ground nutmeg

Combine all ingredients and store in airtight container. To serve, put 2 tablespoons of mix in a coffee mug and add boiling water.

Makes mix for 40 cups

Fruited Tea Punch

1   gallon water
8   tea bags
2½ cups sugar
2   cups water
2   tablespoons whole cloves
1   (46 ounce) can pineapple juice
1   (46 ounce) can orange juice

Bring 1 gallon water to a boil. Add tea bags. Remove from heat and steep tea for 3 minutes. In saucepan, boil sugar and 2 cups water. Add cloves. Boil 10 minutes, stirring often until syrupy. Strain to remove cloves. Add syrup to steeped tea. Mix in juices. Refrigerate overnight. Serve cold or hot.

Makes 2 gallons

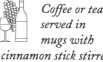

Coffee or tea served in mugs with cinnamon stick stirrers adds a festive, fun flair to any gathering!

$\mathscr{P}$OPPA TOM'S EGGNOG

12 eggs, separated
12 ounces bourbon
12 tablespoons sugar, divided
1 pint whipping cream
1 tablespoon confectioners' sugar

Separate eggs by placing all the yolks in 1 mixing bowl and the whites in another. Beat yolks until thick. Slowly add bourbon, while beating constantly. Add eight tablespoons sugar one at a time. Beat until mixture is smooth. Beat whites, adding 4 tablespoons sugar a small amount at a time. Beat until stiff but not dry. In a third mixing bowl, whip the cream while slowly adding the confectioners' sugar. Whip until soft peaks form. Put egg white mixture in chilled punch bowl. Pour whipped cream on top and then egg yolk mixture. Fold all 3 together.

Serves 12–15

$\mathscr{C}$OZY COCOA MIX

1 (8 quart) box instant dry milk
1 (16 ounce) box white confectioners' sugar
1 (16 ounce) box instant chocolate mix
1 (8 ounce) jar non-dairy creamer

Combine all ingredients and store in air-tight container. To serve, put 3 heaping tablespoons in a coffee mug and add hot water.

Makes mix for 50 cups

PINK BABY SHOWER PUNCH

• *1 (12 ounce) can frozen pink lemonade concentrate*
• *1 (24 ounce) bottle white grape juice*
• *½ cup sugar*
• *2 drops red food coloring*

Mix lemonade as directed on can. Add grape juice, sugar, and food coloring and mix. Refrigerate 1 day before serving. Serve cold.

Makes 2 quarts

Wassail Supreme

12 sticks cinnamon, broken into pieces
2 teaspoons whole allspice
1 medium can whole cloves
6 medium oranges
12 cups apple cider
4 cups cranberry juice cocktail
½ cup sugar

On a piece of cheesecloth, place broken cinnamon sticks, allspice, and 16 cloves. Secure the ends of the cloth with a piece of cooking string to form a small bag. Stud oranges generously with cloves. In large saucepan, combine juices, sugar, oranges, and spice bag. Cover and simmer over low heat for 10 minutes. Remove spice bag and oranges. Pour into a warmed serving bowl. Float studded oranges in bowl. Serve hot.

Makes 1 gallon

Ciderific

1 coffee mug apple cider
1 dash cinnamon
1 teaspoon butter or margarine
Rum to taste

Combine all ingredients in mug and warm in microwave.

Serves 1

Cider-Spritzer

• *4 cups dry white wine*
• *1 quart apple cider*
• *1 quart ginger ale*
• *1 (12 ounce) can frozen orange juice concentrate*
• *1 orange, sliced very thin*

Combine first 4 ingredients and stir well. Garnish with orange rounds. Serve over ice.

Serves 15–20

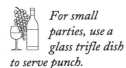

For small parties, use a glass trifle dish to serve punch.

Christmas Punch

1   cup sugar
1   cup water
4   cups cranberry juice
1½ cups lemon juice
2   cups orange juice
2   cups unsweetened pineapple juice
2   (28 ounce) bottles ginger ale
2   ice rings

Combine sugar and water in a small saucepan. Bring to boil, stirring until sugar dissolves. Cover and continue boiling over medium heat, without stirring, for about 5 minutes. Add all fruit juices. Chill thoroughly. Just before serving, put ice ring in punch bowl; save second ice ring to place in bowl when first ring melts. Ladle juice over ice ring. Add ginger ale.

Makes 24–30 servings

GOOD FOOD

GOOD COMPANY

SOUPS
and
SALADS

Sweet and Sour Cabbage Soup

1½ pounds ground chuck, browned
1 medium cabbage, shredded
2 (16 ounce) cans stewed tomatoes
2 (16 ounce) cans water
1 package onion soup mix
1 tablespoon brown sugar
1 tablespoon white sugar
Juice of 1 lemon
Salt and pepper to taste

Mix all ingredients in large pot. Cover and simmer 2 hours.

Serves 8–10

For soup that's too salty, add a sliced raw potato and cook a few minutes, then remove the potato. Abracadabra! The soup is just right!

Wild Rice Soup

1 pound ground venison, browned or 1 pound round steak, cut into thin strips and browned
2 cups cooked wild rice
1 (10¾ ounce) can cream of mushroom soup
1 (10¾ ounce) can cream of asparagus soup
2 soup cans milk
1 cup (4 ounces) shredded Cheddar cheese
Garlic salt or pepper to taste
1 scant tablespoon dried parsley

In large pot, combine soups, milk, and cheese. Blend. Add wild rice and meat, and simmer until cheese has melted. Add garlic salt and parsley.

Serves 8

♡ *Building bone density early is important in preventing osteoporosis later in life. Skim milk, buttermilk, low-fat yogurt, and cottage cheese are excellent sources of calcium, which is a major component of bones and teeth. To get the recommended daily allowance for calcium, eat calcium-rich foods 3-4 times each day. Young adults and pregnant or breast-feeding women need at least 1200 mg. Adult women need at least 800 mg. One cup of skim milk has 302 mg. of calcium. Remember Mom's advice, "Drink your milk, it's good for you!". Why is it that Mom is always right?*

Barbra Crumpacker, Registered Dietitian

Billy's Brunswick Stew

3   pounds ground pork
3   pounds ground beef
3   pounds chicken breasts, ground
3   medium onions, diced
3   (16½ ounce) cans cream-style corn
3   (16 ounce) cans chopped tomatoes
1   pound butter
Salt and black pepper to taste

Cover all meats with water and boil until tender. Remove from stock. Skim fat and reserve stock. Combine meats and remaining ingredients in large pot. Simmer for 3 to 4 hours, gradually adding the remaining stock.

Serves 25

Simmer bones for soup (never boil) to extract the best flavor and gelatin from bone marrow. Adjust salt after cooking.

Curried Pumpkin Soup

1   medium pumpkin
1   stick butter
1½ (14½ ounce) cans chicken broth
2   tablespoons maple syrup
Salt and black pepper
1   tablespoon curry powder

Pierce pumpkin in several places. Bake in 400° oven for 1 hour or until soft when pierced. Cut cooked pumpkin in half; scoop out seeds. Separate pumpkin flesh from outer skin and set aside. Melt butter in stock pot. Add pumpkin flesh and cook over medium heat, mashing pumpkin until completely soft and blended. Add chicken broth, maple syrup, and all seasonings. Simmer for about 10 minutes. Remove from heat. When soup is cool, purée in a blender or food processor until smooth. Soup can be stored in the freezer or refrigerator. Reheat before serving. Thin soup with cream or chicken broth if necessary.

Serves 4-6

Freeze any leftover chicken broth in ice cube trays or mini-muffin tins. Remove from trays or tins and store in labeled freezer bags. Add to fresh or canned vegetables when cooking or add to basic white sauce to enhance flavor.

CREAM OF BROCCOLI SOUP

2   tablespoons butter
2   tablespoons all-purpose flour
1   cup milk
Salt and pepper to taste
1   (10 ounce) package frozen chopped broccoli
1   cup strong chicken broth
¼   cup dry white wine
Nutmeg or mace to taste
Small fresh broccoli flowerets

Prepare white sauce by melting butter in a heavy saucepan over low heat; add flour, stirring until smooth. Cook 1 minute, stirring constantly. Gradually add milk; cook over medium heat, stirring constantly until mixture is thickened and bubbly. Stir in salt and pepper. Cook frozen broccoli according to package directions. Purée cooked broccoli and white sauce together in blender. In a medium saucepan, blend purée, chicken broth, and wine. Heat to serving temperature. Garnish with nutmeg or mace and broccoli flowerets.

Makes 4 (1-cup) servings

WHITE BEAN SOUP

2   tablespoons olive oil
3   cups thinly sliced celery
1   cup diced onion
1   cup thinly sliced carrots
2   (16 ounce) cans white kidney beans or great Northern beans
2   (14½ ounce) cans chicken broth
¼   teaspoon crushed rosemary leaves

In a 3-quart or larger saucepan, heat olive oil until hot. Add celery, onion, and carrots; cook about 5 minutes until vegetables are tender-crisp. Stir in beans, broth, and rosemary leaves. Bring to a boil. Reduce heat and simmer about 10 minutes until flavors are blended.

Makes 8 (1-cup) servings

SAVANNAH OPEN-FACED TOMATO SANDWICH

• *1 pkg. mini–French bread loaves*
• *garlic butter spread*
• *ripe tomatoes*
• *Parmesan cheese*
• *mozzarella cheese slices*

Cut mini loaves in half length-wise. Spread garlic butter to cover top of cut side of bread. Add sliced tomato; sprinkle generously with Parmesan cheese and top with a slice of mozzarella cheese. Place in a 350° oven until cheese melts. Wonderful with soup or pasta salad. Ham could be added to make a meal in itself. Easy and delicious.

Makes 20

Onion Soup Les Halles

Soup

4 tablespoons unsalted butter
2 tablespoons olive oil
6 cups sliced yellow onions
4 cloves garlic, minced
1 teaspoon sugar
⅓ cup cognac
1 tablespoon Dijon mustard
½ teaspoon dried thyme
3 tablespoons unbleached all-purpose flour
3 quarts beef stock
1½ cups dry white wine
Salt and pepper to taste

Heat butter and oil in a large stock pot. Add the onions and cook for 15 minutes over high heat, stirring occasionally. Add the garlic and sugar. Reduce heat to medium and cook until onions are golden brown, stirring occasionally, about 40 minutes. Pour in the cognac, warm and flame with a match. When the flame subsides, add the mustard and thyme. Stir in the flour and cook for 3 minutes, stirring frequently. Gradually stir in the stock and wine. Season to taste with salt and pepper. Simmer uncovered over medium heat for 1 hour.

Cheese Gratiné

8 ounces shredded Gruyère cheese
8 ounces shredded smoked mozzarella cheese
4 ounces grated Parmesan cheese

Combine the 3 cheeses. Preheat broiler for soup. Ladle the hot soup into 8 oven-proof bowls and fill ¾ full. Float a crouton (see recipe at left) in the center of each bowl. Top each bowl lavishly with the mixed cheeses. Broil 6" away from heat, until the cheese is melted and bubbling, about 4 minutes. Serve immediately.

Serves 8

Croutons

• 8 thick slices French bread
• 4 tablespoons butter
• 4 tablespoons olive oil
• 3 cloves garlic, minced

Spread 1 side of each bread slice with 1½ teaspoons butter and 1½ teaspoons olive oil. Sprinkle with garlic. Toast the prepared side only at 350° on a baking sheet until crusty and golden, about 10 to 12 minutes.

POTATO SOUP

4   cups cubed and peeled potatoes
1   medium onion, chopped
¼   stick butter
1   teaspoon salt
½   teaspoon pepper
1   (10¾ ounce) can cream of chicken soup
¾   pound processed cheese, cubed
2   cups milk

In a Dutch oven or large saucepan, sauté onion in melted butter. Add cubed and peeled potatoes. Barely cover with water; season with salt and pepper and cook over medium heat until well done. Mash. Add cream of chicken soup and cheese; stir until cheese is melted. Add milk and heat thoroughly.

Serves 5

Summer heat got you down? This soup is delicious served cold!

CREAM OF CHEESE SOUP

½   cup coarsely chopped carrots
½   cup chopped celery
1   cup water
2   tablespoons finely chopped onion
¼   cup butter or margarine
6   tablespoons all-purpose flour
2   cups milk
2   cups chicken broth
½   pound processed cheese, diced
Fresh parsley, chopped

Cook carrots and celery in boiling water until tender. Transfer vegetables and liquid to a blender or food processor and process until finely chopped. Sauté onion in butter until tender, but not brown. Stir in flour. Add milk and chicken broth; cook over low heat until thickened, stirring constantly. Add cheese; stir to blend. Stir in vegetables. Garnish with chopped parsley.

Makes 6 cups

Wonderful in a thermos for a chilly tailgate party!

Have a soup party! In summer, use cold soups; in winter, hot soups. Prepare all soups in advance; have plenty of breads, butters, some cheeses. Serve buffet-style using oversized ladles and old-fashioned enameled pots as containers.

Zucchini Soup

1   quart chopped zucchini squash
3   ounces cream cheese, softened
1   cup water
1½ teaspoons curry powder
4   teaspoons chicken bouillon granules
Pepper to taste

Cut zucchini into 1" pieces. Boil in water until soft. Add cream cheese. Place in blender and mix. Add all other ingredients in blender and mix again. Serve hot or cold.

Serves 5

Smoked Turkey, Bean, and Barley Soup

1   tablespoon oil
1   medium onion, chopped
2   ribs celery, chopped
1   (1 pound) package smoked turkey sausage, cut into ½" slices
5   cups chicken broth or water
1   (14½ ounce) can stewed tomatoes
½   cup pearl barley
2   medium carrots, sliced
1   (15½ ounce) can black or Northern beans
½   teaspoon dried basil leaves
2   teaspoons Worcestershire sauce
¼   teaspoon garlic powder
Salt and pepper to taste

In a 4-quart pot, sauté onion and celery in oil until tender. Stir in all other ingredients and bring to a boil over medium heat. Cover and simmer until all vegetables are tender, about 1 hour.

Serves 10

Greek Salad

• *2 heads lettuce, chopped*
• *8 celery stalks, chopped*
• *2 purple onions, sliced in rings*
• *1 green pepper, sliced in strips*
• *1 can pitted black olives*
• *2 baskets cherry tomatoes, halved*
• *2 blocks feta cheese, crumbled*
• *1 cup olive oil*
• *Greek seasoning*

Mix all ingredients together except seasonings and olive oil. About 10 minutes before serving, drizzle olive oil over salad. Season to taste with Greek seasoning.

Serves 10-12

Tomato Zucchini Soup

1   stick butter
1   large sweet onion, diced
8   large tomatoes, diced
1   medium zucchini, diced
1   (14½ ounce) can chicken broth
Fresh thyme
Salt and pepper to taste
Half and half cream

Sauté onion in melted butter over medium heat until soft. Add tomatoes and zucchini and continue to cook until mushy. Season to taste and add several fresh thyme leaves. Pour in ¼ of chicken broth. Purée in batches in a food processor or blender. Thin to taste with more chicken broth. Store in refrigerator overnight so that flavors can blend. Reheat with a small amount of half and half cream if desired.

Serves 4–6

Pimiento Cheese

• 8 ounces grated medium Cheddar cheese
• ⅓ cup mayonnaise
• 1 teaspoon Dijon mustard
• garlic salt
• 1 teaspoon minced onion
• 1 (4 ounce) jar pimiento, drained

Mix all ingredients. Add additional mayonnaise if a softer texture is desired.

Serves 4

It takes less sugar to sweeten fruits if added at the end of cooking. A little soda added to cooked sour fruits (such as apricots) lessens the amount of sugar required for sweetening.

Layered Cranberry Salad

1 (3 ounce) package vanilla pudding mix
1 (3 ounce) package lemon flavored gelatin
2 cups water
2 tablespoons lemon juice
1 (3 ounce) package raspberry flavored gelatin
1 cup boiling water
1 (16 ounce) can whole cranberry sauce
½ cup chopped celery
¼ cup chopped pecans
1 (1.4 ounce) package whipped topping mix
½ teaspoon nutmeg

Combine first 3 ingredients in a 2-quart saucepan. Cook, stirring constantly, until gelatin dissolves. Stir in lemon juice. Chill until mixture has the consistency of unbeaten egg whites. In a bowl, dissolve the raspberry gelatin in 1 cup boiling water. Stir in cranberry sauce and blend well. Stir in celery and pecans. Chill until partially set. In another bowl, prepare whipped topping mix according to package directions and add nutmeg. Fold this mixture into lemon gelatin mixture. Spoon 1½ cups of mixture into a lightly oiled 7-cup mold. Chill until set. Spoon raspberry gelatin mixture over lemon mixture; chill until set. Spoon remaining lemon mixture over raspberry layer. Chill until firm.

Serves 8

Bing Cherry Salad

Grease gelatin mold with mayonnaise before pouring in gelatin.

1 (16 ounce) can dark pitted sweet cherries
1 (20 ounce) can crushed pineapple in heavy syrup
1 (3 ounce) package cream cheese, crumbled
1 (3 ounce) package strawberry gelatin
1 (3 ounce) package cherry gelatin
1 cup chopped pecans
2 (10 ounce) bottles cola, chilled

Drain cherries and pineapple; reserve juices. Use mixture of cherry and pineapple juices to dissolve gelatin. Add crumbled cream cheese to gelatin, then the fruit and nuts. Add chilled cola and mix well. Put in greased 13" x 9" pan. Refrigerate.

Serves 12

CRANBERRY SALAD RING

4　(3 ounce) packages raspberry gelatin
2　cups boiling water
½　cup cold water
2　cups chopped fresh cranberries
2　unpeeled oranges, seeded and ground
2　unpeeled apples, cored and ground
1　(15¼ ounce) can crushed pineapple, undrained
2　cups sugar
1　cup chopped pecans
Lettuce
Mayonnaise

In a bowl, dissolve gelatin in boiling water. Add cold water. Chill until consistency of unbeaten egg whites. In another bowl, combine the next 6 ingredients. Mix well. Fold fruit mixture into gelatin. Pour into lightly oiled 10-cup ring mold. Chill until set. Unmold onto lettuce. Fill center with mayonnaise.

Serves 8–10

Decorate outside as well as inside your home. Encourage the party to flow outdoors by outlining your wooden deck with votive candles. Outlining the pool with luminaries is another beautiful and inviting touch.

CONGEALED SPICED PEACH SALAD

1　(16 ounce) can of sliced peaches in heavy syrup, drained, with 1 cup liquid, reserved
¼　cup vinegar
½　cup sugar
12　whole cloves
⅛　teaspoon cinnamon
1　(3 ounce) package orange gelatin
¾　cup cold water

Chop peaches coarsely. In a saucepan, bring syrup, vinegar, sugar, and spices to a boil and simmer uncovered for 10 minutes. Strain syrup and discard cloves. Dissolve gelatin in hot syrup and add cold water and peaches. Chill until slightly thickened. Pour into a mold or 9" x 9" dish.

Serves 4

Citrus fruits "juice" best at room temperature. To increase amount of juice from citrus fruit -- dip fruit in hot water before squeezing. Then roll the fruit between the palm of your hand and the kitchen counter, applying gentle pressure.

Frozen Fruit Salad

1 (8 ounce) package of cream cheese, softened
1 (20 ounce) can crushed pineapple
¾ cup sugar
1 cup finely chopped pecans
3 bananas, mashed
2 (10 ounce) packages frozen sliced strawberries, thawed
1 (9 ounce) carton nondairy whipped topping

Mix cream cheese and pineapple together. Add sugar, pecans, bananas, strawberries, and whipped topping. Put ingredients in a 13" x 9" dish and freeze. Cut into 2" x 2" squares.

Serves 8-10

Tangy Spinach Salad

1 (6 ounce) package lemon gelatin
2 cups hot water
1 cup cold water
3 tablespoons vinegar
1 cup mayonnaise
½ teaspoon salt
Dash of pepper
2 cups chopped fresh spinach
2 cups cottage cheese
⅔ cup diced celery
1 tablespoon chopped onion

Dissolve gelatin in 2 cups hot water. Add 1 cup cold water plus vinegar, mayonnaise, and seasonings. Chill in freezer for 20 minutes or until firm 1" from edge of bowl. Remove from freezer and whip until fluffy. Fold in spinach, cottage cheese, celery, and onion. Pour into a 9" x 13" pan and refrigerate until firm.

Serves 12

Golden Glow Salad

1   (6 ounce) package lemon gelatin
1   cup boiling water
1   cup canned pineapple juice
1   tablespoon vinegar
½   teaspoon salt
1   cup canned pineapple chunks
1   cup grated carrot

Dissolve gelatin in boiling water; add all but last 2 ingredients.
Chill mixture until it is the consistency of unbeaten egg whites.
Add pineapple and carrots. Spoon into mold. Chill until firm.

Serves 4-6

Molded Broccoli Salad

2½ envelopes plain gelatin
1   (13 ounce) can consommé
1   cup mayonnaise
1   teaspoon hot pepper sauce
1   teaspoon black pepper
3   tablespoons Worcestershire sauce
1½ teaspoons salt
3   tablespoons lemon juice
3   (10 ounce) packages frozen chopped broccoli, cooked, drained, and mashed
4   hard boiled eggs, mashed

In a saucepan, soften gelatin in undiluted consommé. Heat, stir-ring to dissolve. Add remaining ingredients, except broccoli and eggs, to consommé and gelatin. In a separate bowl, mix eggs and broccoli together and fold into consommé mixture. Blend well. Grease an 8-cup mold with a small amount of mayonnaise. Pour mixture into mold and chill well. Serve with crackers or toast points.

Serves 10

Tomato Aspic

1 (3 ounce) package lemon gelatin
1 envelope plain gelatin
1 (14½ ounce) can stewed tomatoes
1 tablespoon Worcestershire sauce
1 cup cocktail vegetable juice
1 cup boiling water
¼ cup vinegar
2 tablespoons chopped parsley
2 tablespoons horseradish
5 drops hot pepper sauce

Soften plain gelatin in 2 tablespoons of juice. Dissolve lemon gelatin in boiling water in large bowl. Add softened gelatin. Purée the tomatoes in a food processor or blender. Mix all ingredients together. Pour into a mold and refrigerate.

Serves 8

Congealed Asparagus Salad

¾ cup sugar
½ cup vinegar
½ teaspoon salt
2 envelopes plain gelatin
½ cup cold water
½ cup chopped pecans
½ cup chopped celery
1 (16 ounce) can cut asparagus, drained, reserve juice
1 (2 ounce) jar diced pimientos, drained
1 (15 ounce) can English peas, drained, reserve juice
½ lemon, juiced
1 small onion, grated
1 (2.5 ounce) jar mushrooms

In a saucepan, boil sugar, vinegar, 1 cup reserved vegetable juices, and salt until sugar is dissolved. Set aside. In a bowl, dissolve gelatin in water then add to boiled ingredients. Let cool. Add remaining ingredients to gelatin mixture. Pour into oiled pan or mold and chill until set. Serve on bed of lettuce.

Serves 6-8

Quick Basic Mayonnaise

• 1 large egg
• 5 teaspoons lemon juice
• 1 teaspoon Dijon mustard
• ¼ teaspoon salt
• ¼ teaspoon white pepper
• 1 cup olive or vegetable oil

Have all ingredients at room temperature. Blend first 5 ingredients at high speed. Add oil in a thin steady stream until well blended. Store in a tightly covered container and refrigerate. Will last 5 days.

Molded Tomato Salad

1   envelope plain gelatin
1   cup cold water
½   cup boiling water
1   (8 ounce) package cream cheese, softened
1   cup mayonnaise
7   medium tomatoes, cubed and drained
2   small cucumbers, chopped
1   medium onion, chopped
Salt and pepper to taste

Dissolve gelatin in cold water. Add ½ cup boiling water. In a separate bowl, mix cream cheese and mayonnaise. Add cream cheese mixture to gelatin. Add vegetables and mix. Salt and pepper to taste. Pour into 13" x 9" x 2" dish and chill until set.

Serves 10–12

Garden Vegetable Rice Salad

1   (6 ounce) box long-grain wild rice
1   (12 ounce) can corn
1½ cups chopped and seeded cucumber
2   medium carrots, chopped
2   green onions, chopped
⅓   cup chopped parsley
½   cup olive oil
¼   cup lemon juice
2   cloves garlic, minced
½   teaspoon dill
¼   teaspoon dry mustard
¼   teaspoon pepper

Cook rice according to directions on package. In a bowl, mix cooked rice with the next 5 ingredients. In another bowl, mix together olive oil and remaining ingredients. Pour olive oil dressing over salad and stir gently. Chill before serving.

Serves 6–8

To unmold a gelatin salad, loosen the edge and around the center of the ring mold with a metal spatula. For just a few seconds, dip the mold up to its rim in warm water. Tilt the mold slightly, easing the gelatin salad away from one side to let in air. Tilt and rotate the mold so that air can loosen the gelatin salad all the way around. Place a serving plate upside down over the mold. Hold the plate and mold together, then invert. Lift off the mold.

Alice's Rice Salad

1 (5 ounce) package chicken-flavored rice
½ cup finely chopped green pepper
5 green onions, chopped
8 stuffed olives, chopped
1 (6½ ounce) jar marinated artichoke hearts, drained, liquid reserved
½ teaspoon mayonnaise
¼ teaspoon curry powder

Cook rice according to package directions, omitting butter. Cool. In a bowl, combine cooled rice, green pepper, onions, olives, and artichoke hearts. In a separate bowl, mix reserved artichoke liquid with mayonnaise and curry powder. Add to rice mixture and refrigerate for several hours.

Serves 8

Greek Potato Salad

1½ pounds red potatoes, boiled and cut into ¾" cubes
¼ cup fresh lemon juice
¼ teaspoon salt
1 sweet red pepper, cut into julienne strips
½ cup pitted ripe olives
3 green onions, minced
4 ounces feta cheese, crumbled
¾ teaspoon dried whole oregano
½ cup olive oil
Salt and pepper to taste

Pour 2 tablespoons lemon juice and salt over cubed potatoes. Toss gently. Boil red pepper strips in small amount of water for 1 to 2 minutes. Drain. Combine potatoes, red pepper, olives, green onion, and feta cheese. Toss gently. Combine remaining 2 tablespoons lemon juice and oregano in small bowl. Add oil in thin, steady stream, beating well with wire whisk. Pour dressing over salad. Salt and pepper to taste.

Serves 4-6

Famous Potato Salad

25 medium potatoes
¼ cup bottled Italian dressing
1 small onion, chopped
1 (6 ounce) can pitted and sliced olives
1 teaspoon celery seed
¾ cup mayonnaise
1 tablespoon Dijon mustard
1 teaspoon salt
1 teaspoon garlic salt
1 teaspoon pepper

Boil potatoes until tender. Cool completely, then cube. In a separate bowl, mix all other ingredients together. Pour over cooled potatoes and toss gently.

Serves 12

 When planning a party in someone else's honor, be certain to let the guest of honor assist with the guest list.

Ham Salad in Cantaloupe Rings

¾ pound cooked ham, diced
½ large green pepper, diced
4 stalks celery, diced
½ cup chopped walnuts
¼ cup sour cream
¼ cup mayonnaise
½ teaspoon curry powder
½ teaspoon fresh lemon juice
½ teaspoon soy sauce
2 ripe cantaloupes
Lettuce leaves
Parsley or watercress sprigs

Mix ham, pepper, celery, and walnuts together in mixing bowl. In a separate bowl, combine sour cream, mayonnaise, curry powder, lemon juice, and soy sauce. Stir well. Add to ham mixture, blending well. Peel and seed each cantaloupe. Slice each cantaloupe into 4 rings. Line individual salad plates with lettuce leaves, place 1 cantaloupe ring on each plate. Fill center with ham mixture. Garnish with parsley or watercress.

Serves 8

Marinated Cole Slaw

1   large head cabbage, shredded
1   large onion, thinly sliced or shredded
1   large green pepper, thinly sliced
¾-1 cup sugar
¾   cup salad oil
1   cup vinegar
1   teaspoon dry mustard
1   teaspoon celery seed
1   tablespoon salt

Place cabbage in a large bowl. Top with onion and green pepper. Sprinkle with sugar until green peppers are completely covered. Do not stir. In a saucepan, boil salad oil, vinegar, and dry seasonings. Immediately pour over cabbage, onions, and green peppers. Do not stir. Refrigerate at least 4 hours or overnight.

Serves 10-12

Marinated Green Bean Salad

1   (16 ounce) can cut green beans, drained
1   (15 ounce) can English peas, drained
2   medium onions, sliced into rings
1   green bell pepper, chopped
1   (2 ounce) jar diced pimientos
5   celery stalks, chopped
1   teaspoon salt
¾   cup sugar
½   cup salad oil
1   teaspoon water
1   cup white vinegar

Mix green beans, peas, onions, green pepper, pimientos, and celery in a bowl. In another bowl, mix remaining ingredients. Pour oil dressing over vegetable mixture. Marinate overnight, stirring several times. May be kept 3 days in the refrigerator.

Serves 6-8

Tangy Green Bean Salad

4 (16 ounce) cans whole green beans
1 purple onion, sliced
¼ cup oil
¼ cup vinegar
1 tablespoon pepper
1 teaspoon salt
1 cup sour cream
½ cup mayonnaise
¼ teaspoon dry mustard
1 tablespoon prepared horseradish

Drain green beans and mix with onions. In another bowl, mix together oil, vinegar, salt, and pepper. Blend oil mixture into green beans and onions. Let stand 4 hours. In another bowl, mix together sour cream and remaining ingredients. Pour dressing over salad, refrigerate, and marinate for another 4 hours.

Serves 16

Broccoli Mushroom Salad

½ cup sugar
1 teaspoon salt
1 tablespoon onion powder
¼ cup wine vinegar
1 cup oil
1 teaspoon paprika
1 teaspoon celery seed
2 bunches fresh broccoli
1 pound fresh mushrooms
¼ cup finely chopped green onions

Mix together first 7 ingredients and let sit for 1 hour. Wash broccoli and cut into bite-sized pieces. Wash mushrooms and thinly slice. In a large bowl, combine broccoli, mushrooms, and green onions. Pour dressing over vegetables and marinate overnight.

Serves 6–8

If you plan on hiring help for the party, interview potential candidates beforehand. Ask about previous experience and be sure to check references. You will want your staff to be pleasant, trustworthy, and neat in appearance.

• 6–8 slices stale bread, cut in ¾" cubes
• ¼ cup butter
• 1 teaspoon minced garlic
• 1 teaspoon Greek seasoning

Melt butter in small saucepan. Add garlic and Greek seasoning. Pour over bread cubes and toss to coat. Bake on oiled cookie sheet at 350° until toasted. Can be stored in an airtight container for up to 2 weeks.

MOLDED CHICKEN SALAD

6   cups cooked chicken, diced
3   envelopes gelatin
¾   cup cold water
3   (10¾ ounce) cans cream of chicken soup
2   cups chopped celery
1   medium onion, chopped
½   cup lemon juice
6   hard boiled eggs, chopped
1   (6 ounce) can sliced black olives
1½ cups mayonnaise
3   tablespoons Worcestershire sauce
4   tablespoons salad pickles

Soften gelatin in cold water. Heat 1 can of soup and add gelatin. Stir until dissolved. Add the remaining 2 cans of soup and all other ingredients. Pour into 9" x 11" glass dish and refrigerate overnight. Garnish with parsley.

Serves 10–12

EXOTIC CHICKEN SALAD

3   whole chicken breasts, cooked, boned, cut into bite-sized pieces
2   cups grapes
6   green onions, chopped
1   cup lightly steamed (1 minute) snow peas
½   cup raisins
½   package spinach leaves, torn
1   large bunch celery with leaves, chopped
1   kiwi, sliced
7   ounces cooked cheese-stuffed ravioli
1   (6 ounce) jar marinated artichokes, drained
⅔   cup mayonnaise
½   cup freshly grated Parmesan cheese
½   cup fresh lemon juice
Salt and pepper to taste

In large bowl, mix together first 10 ingredients. In a separate bowl, blend together mayonnaise, cheese, lemon juice, salt, and pepper. Toss mayonnaise dressing with chicken mixture; mix well.

Serves 6–8

JAPANESE CHICKEN SALAD

6   chicken breast halves
Salt and pepper
1   small head iceberg lettuce, broken into pieces or chopped
3   stalks celery, chopped
3   tablespoons sugar
1½ teaspoons salt
¾   cup salad oil
1½ tablespoons sesame oil
5   teaspoons vinegar
Chow mein noodles
⅓   cup chopped cashew nuts, toasted
3   tablespoons sesame seeds, toasted

Season chicken with salt and pepper, wrap in foil, and bake at 350°
for 45 minutes. Let cool; bone chicken and shred. Set aside. Combine lettuce, celery, and chicken in large bowl. Refrigerate for
several hours. Mix sugar, salt, salad oil, sesame oil, and vinegar;
store in refrigerator until serving time. When ready to serve, toss
lettuce mixture with cashew nuts, sesame seeds, and dressing. Top
salad with chow mein noodles and serve immediately.

Serves 8

*Use a vinegar-based
dressing with meats
and vegetables and a
lemon-based dressing
with fruits.*

CRISS CROSS SALAD

1   bunch broccoli
½   cup chopped red onion
2   tomatoes, diced
1   (8 ounce) can red kidney beans, drained
1   cup shredded medium Cheddar cheese
⅔   cup bottled Italian or Catalina dressing

Wash broccoli and break into bite-sized flowerets. Toss with all
remaining ingredients and marinate in the refrigerator for 8 hours
or overnight before serving.

Serves 4-6

*Prepare as
much as possible
of the meal in
advance; this includes
trimming vegetables,
washing salad greens,
and making salad
dressing.*

Avocado Crab Salad

1   pound imitation crabmeat
½   cup chopped green onions
1   cup finely chopped celery
Seafood seasoning to taste
1¼ cups mayonnaise
2   avocados

Cut crabmeat into 1" pieces. Mix all ingredients together. Chill thoroughly. Serve on avocado halves.

Serves 4

Mandarin Orange Salad

¼   cup sliced almonds
3   tablespoons sugar, divided
¼   head lettuce, chopped or broken into bite-sized pieces
2   celery stalks, chopped
2   green onions, chopped
1   (11 ounce) can mandarin oranges, drained
¼   cup vegetable oil
2   tablespoons red wine vinegar
1   tablespoon parsley
1   teaspoon salt
1   teaspoon black pepper

In a nonstick saucepan, cook almonds and 1 tablespoon sugar over low heat, stirring constantly until sugar melts. Cool in pan, then break apart. Place lettuce, celery, and onions in a large plastic food storage bag. In a saucepan, heat remaining ingredients, except oranges and almonds, stirring until sugar melts. Let cool. Add oranges, almonds, and dressing to ingredients in bag. Seal bag and shake to mix. Serve immediately.

Serves 4

Blue Cheese Dressing

1   cup extra virgin olive oil
¼   cup red wine vinegar
2   cloves garlic
7   ounces blue cheese
Salt and pepper to taste

In blender or food processor, mix first 3 ingredients until well blended. Add cheese, salt, and pepper. Blend until creamy. Use immediately or store in airtight container. Shake before using.

Serves 4

Allow 1 cup tossed salad (about ¾ salad greens and ¼ other salad ingredients) per person. When serving a crowd, buy salad greens by weight. A pound of greens yields about 5 cups of torn leaves (enough for 6 servings). Because most people like 1–2 tablespoons of salad dressing on a salad, plan on 16–32 servings from a 16-ounce bottle.

Fresh Ginger Salad Dressing

3½ teaspoons peeled and grated fresh ginger
3   limes
¾   teaspoon sugar
¾   teaspoon salt
1½ teaspoons basil
6   tablespoons olive oil
1½ teaspoons soy sauce
1½ teaspoons red wine vinegar
¾   teaspoons garlic salt

Grate ginger into bowl, add the sugar, the juice of 3 limes and zest of 1 lime. Mix with a fork. Add rest of ingredients, stirring quickly with fork until well blended. Serve over green salad.

Makes 1 cup

The colorful blossoms and peppery-flavored leaves of nasturtium will add zip to any salad.

To receive rave reviews for your salads, make your own salad dressings. It cuts the cost, too!

Julie's Fresh Italian Dressing

¾   cup extra virgin olive oil
3   tablespoons red wine vinegar
¾   teaspoon salt
1   clove garlic, minced
1   tablespoon minced onion
½   teaspoon freshly ground pepper
½   teaspoon Italian seasoning

Combine ingredients in a shaker or jar with tight lid. Shake well to mix. Refrigerate overnight. Shake before using.

Makes 1 cup

Delicious on a fruit salad!

Golden Dressing

2   eggs
¼   cup pineapple juice
¼   cup lemon juice
½   cup sugar

Beat eggs sufficiently to blend, but not until foamy. Add remaining ingredients and cook in double boiler, stirring constantly until thickened. Cool or refrigerate before serving.

Makes 1 cup

Wilted cucumbers? Pare and slice thinly using a vegetable peeler. Place in layers in a bowl, salting each layer. Place a weighted plate over cucumbers. Cover and refrigerate 3-6 hours. Drain and toss with sour cream or yogurt and garnish with chopped dill, parsley, basil.

Green Goddess Salad Dressing & Dip

1   cup mayonnaise
½   cup cream
2   tablespoons vinegar
2   rounded teaspoons anchovy paste (½ tube)
¼   cup finely sliced green onions
½   cup finely chopped parsley
Dash garlic powder
1   teaspoon curry powder

In medium bowl, mix together the first 3 ingredients. Add the rest and mix thoroughly. Refrigerate.

Makes 2 cups

Poppy Seed Dressing

2   small onions
1½ cups sugar
2   teaspoons dry mustard
2   teaspoons salt
⅔   cup apple cider vinegar
2   cups salad oil
3   tablespoons poppy seeds

In a food processor, mince onions on high. Add next 4 ingredients, mixing until blended. With food processor on, slowly add all oil until mixture is thickened. Add poppy seeds and mix. Store in refrigerator.

Makes 3 cups

To prevent lettuce from wilting, add salad oil first, then add your spices and vinegar.

Spinach Salad Dressing

2   tablespoons sesame seeds
⅓   cup oil
¼   cup lemon juice
2   tablespoons soy sauce
⅛   teaspoon hot sauce

Heat sesame seeds in large saucepan over medium heat until toasted. Remove from heat. Add remaining ingredients. Stir and chill.

Makes ⅔ cup

The best gauge of freshness when choosing greens is how they look and smell. Choose greens that are sparkling fresh with a good color and no wilted, dry, or yellowing leaves. Greens are almost all water -- if they feel light, they're drying out.

In preparing salads, balance the textures -- crunchy with soft, cooked with raw, succulent with crisp.

Strawberry Dressing

2   tablespoons confectioners' sugar
2   tablespoons lemon juice
1   cup crushed fresh strawberries
1   cup sour cream
1   cup mayonnaise

Combine first 3 ingredients. Add sour cream and mayonnaise. Chill and serve over fruit.

Makes 3 cups

As a general rule, it is best to store greens and fresh vegetables unwashed and packed loosely in plastic bags in the refrigerator crisper drawer until needed.

Honey Dressing for Fresh Fruit

⅔   cup sugar
1   teaspoon dry mustard
1   teaspoon paprika
1   teaspoon celery seed
¼   teaspoon salt
⅓   cup strained honey
5   tablespoons vinegar
1   tablespoon lemon juice
1   teaspoon grated onion
1   cup salad oil

 If you are planning an outdoor party, don't forget to spray beforehand for insects. It also is a good idea to set out citronella candles during the party.

Mix together dry ingredients. Add honey, vinegar, lemon juice, and onion. Slowly pour in oil while mixing with electric mixer at low speed. Keeps in refrigerator indefinitely.

Makes 1¼ cups

GOOD FOOD

GOOD COMPANY

PASTAS
and
BREADS

Angel Hair Pasta with Tomato-Basil Sauce

1-2 tablespoons olive oil
2   cloves garlic, minced
5   large basil leaves or ½-1 teaspoon dried basil
2   large tomatoes, peeled and chopped
Salt and pepper to taste
Fresh Parmesan cheese, grated
1   pound fresh angel hair pasta, cooked and cooled

Sauté garlic in olive oil. Add tomatoes, basil, and seasonings.
Simmer 20 to 30 minutes. Toss with cooled angel hair pasta.
Sprinkle with fresh grated Parmesan cheese.

Serves 8

Apricot Linguine

¾   cup olive oil
15   cloves garlic, 6 minced and 9 cut into thin slices
1   cup dry white wine
1   tablespoon fresh rosemary or 1½ teaspoons dried rosemary
¾   cup dried apricots, cut into slivers
Salt and pepper to taste
1   pound linguine
½   cup chopped fresh parsley

Heat olive oil in skillet over medium heat. Add minced and sliced
garlic and sauté just until browned. Stir in white wine; reduce heat
and simmer uncovered for 5 minutes. Add the rosemary and apricots. Season with salt and pepper. Simmer 5 to 10 minutes longer.
Meanwhile, cook pasta in boiling salted water until tender, but still
firm; drain. Place the pasta, sauce, and parsley in serving bowl and
toss to coat. Serve immediately.

Serves 4-6

Many recipes call for much more margarine or oil than necessary. Enjoy the flavor of the garlic in this recipe without the 162 grams of extra fat by reducing the amount of olive oil to ¼ cup -- that will provide plenty of flavor while saving 18 grams of fat per serving. With this simple change, the apricot linguine takes on a whole new nutritional look with only 9 grams of fat per serving and only 19% of the calories from fat. This falls well within the guideline set by the American Heart Association that encourages a total fat intake of less than 30% of calories.

Barbra Crumpacker,
Registered Dietitian

CARTWHEEL PASTA SALAD

2   cups cartwheel pasta or mixed trio, cooked
1   cup sliced fresh green beans, cooked
½   cup olive oil
3   tablespoons red wine vinegar
2   cloves garlic, crushed
1   teaspoon dried sweet basil
Black pepper to taste
½   cup grated Parmesan cheese
2   cups diced ham
1   (7 ounce) jar chopped pimiento
½   cup pitted, sliced black olives
⅓   cup chopped green onions
½   cup whole almonds, toasted

Combine all ingredients together in a large bowl. Refrigerate before serving.

Serves 4-6

CHICKEN PASTA SALAD

3   whole chicken breasts
1   (8 ounce) box sea shell pasta
1   cucumber, peeled and sliced
2   (6-ounce) cans sliced, pitted black olives
1   (8-ounce) bottle olive oil Italian dressing
½   cup mayonnaise

Boil chicken breasts. Cool, remove bones from meat, and chop into large chunks. Cook pasta until almost done, but firm, about 2 minutes less than cooking time on package. Drain pasta, cool, and place in a large bowl with chopped chicken. In another bowl, mix mayonnaise and Italian dressing. Place cucumbers and olives on top of pasta and chicken; add mayonnaise-dressing mixture and combine well. Salad flavor improves if it is refrigerated 2 to 3 hours or overnight before serving. Serve on lettuce.

Serves 4-6

CURLY PASTA WITH BREADCRUMBS

1 cup olive oil
4 cloves garlic, minced
1½ cups fine breadcrumbs
1 cup chopped fresh parsley
Salt and pepper to taste
1 pound curly pasta

Heat 1 tablespoon oil in medium skillet. Add garlic and sauté until lightly golden. Remove garlic from pan and set aside. Add remaining oil to skillet. Add breadcrumbs and stir to coat evenly with the oil. Toast the crumbs over medium heat, watching closely so they do not burn. Stir frequently until the crumbs are a deep golden brown. Remove skillet from heat. Stir in garlic and parsley. Season with salt and pepper. Cook pasta in boiling salted water until tender but still firm. Drain and toss immediately with breadcrumb mixture.

Serves 4–5

FETTUCCINE ALFREDO

16 ounces fresh fettuccine
½ cup butter
⅔ cup grated Gruyère cheese
⅔ cup grated Parmesan cheese
1 cup heavy cream
1 teaspoon salt
Freshly ground black pepper
2 tablespoons cooking sherry

Cook fettuccine until tender; drain. Return pasta to pan over medium heat. Add remaining ingredients and toss lightly with two forks to blend. Serve immediately in warm serving bowl.

Serves 8

Rinsing pasta is a good way to keep cooked pasta from sticking together. Use cold water when preparing a cold pasta dish and hot water when making a hot pasta dish.

♡ *Modifying recipes can be scary when serving guests, so always experiment with your family and eliminate that unnecessary stress. The 90 grams of fat and 832 calories in the cup of cream called for in the recipe at left can be greatly reduced by substituting evaporated skim milk in its place. The evaporated skim milk can be used just as cream, yet it supplies less than 1 gram of fat and 200 calories per cup. Wary of changing the recipe? Use half cream and half evaporated skim milk the first time you try this. The next time, you'll find it easy to substitute the whole cup because you will never know what you're missing.*

*Barbra Crumpacker,
Registered Dietitian*

GARLIC ITALIAN BREAD

• 1 loaf Italian bread
• 1 stick butter, melted
• 1 teaspoon garlic powder
• 2 teaspoons dill
• 4 tablespoons grated Parmesan cheese

Slice bread in half, horizontally. Combine butter and garlic. Spread on each half with pastry brush. Sprinkle with dill and Parmesan cheese. Bake at 425° for 8-10 minutes or until golden brown. Cut in 1" slices and serve hot.

Serves 8-10

FANCY FETTUCCINE

½ cup margarine
1 bunch green onions, chopped
1 celery stalk, chopped
½ pound fresh mushrooms, sliced
1 small clove fresh garlic, minced
6 tablespoons flour
1 (10¾ ounce) can chicken broth
1 (8 ounce) carton cream
2 chicken breasts, cooked, cooled, and diced
½ pound fresh shrimp, cooked, cooled, and diced
1 (8 ounce) box fettuccine noodles
Salt and pepper to taste
Fresh parsley

Melt margarine in a skillet. Add onions, celery, mushrooms, and garlic. Cook until tender. Stir in flour until thickened like a gravy mixture. Add chicken broth and cream. Transfer mixture to a double boiler and simmer until thick. Stir in chicken and shrimp. Simmer a few minutes longer. Pour over fettucine noodles and sprinkle with parsley.

Serves 4-6

GREEN PASTA SALAD

10 ounces green noodles, cooked and drained
½ cup pitted black olives
¼ cup diced pimiento
½ cup sliced water chestnuts
¼ cup grated Parmesan cheese
½ cup chopped scallions
4 ounces mozzarella cheese, diced
4 ounces fresh mushrooms, sliced
1 tablespoon Dijon mustard
1 (8-ounce) bottle Italian dressing

Mix all ingredients together. Chill before serving.

Serves 4-6

Greek Shrimp and Pasta Salad

¼ cup lemon juice
1 tablespoon red wine vinegar
½ cup olive oil
2 teaspoons oregano leaves
⅛ teaspoon garlic powder
¼ teaspoon salt
8 ounces rainbow rotini, cooked and drained
1 pound cooked shrimp, shells and tails removed
½ cucumber, unpeeled
1 cup cherry tomatoes, cut into halves
1 (4 ounce) package feta cheese, crumbled
½ cup sliced salad peppers
¼ cup finely chopped red onion
¼ cup sliced, pitted black olives
Pepper to taste

Combine lemon juice and red wine vinegar. Gradually whisk in olive oil. Whisk in oregano leaves, garlic powder, and salt. Set aside. Rinse cooked rotini with cold water and drain. Place rotini and shrimp in a large bowl. Add dressing and mix well. Cut cucumber half into 2 lengthwise pieces; remove seeds and cut into ¼" thick slices. Combine all ingredients and mix well. Refrigerate several hours to blend flavors.

Serves 8

Orzo with Onions and Parsley

3 quarts water
1½ teaspoons salt
2 cups orzo
6 tablespoons butter
2 medium onions, chopped
2 tablespoons parsley

In a large pot, bring salted water to a boil. Add orzo and cook for 12 minutes or just until tender. Drain. In a skillet, melt butter and sauté onions over medium heat for 5 minutes. Add orzo and parsley to the onions. Stir well and serve immediately.

Serves 8

Marinara Sauce

• 3 tablespoons olive oil
• 1 teaspoon butter
• 2 cups chopped onion
• 1½ cups thinly sliced carrots (optional)
• 1 teaspoon minced fresh garlic
• 1 (28 ounce) can whole tomatoes, undrained and crushed
• 2 tablespoons chopped fresh basil or 1 tablespoon dried basil
• ¼ teaspoon salt
• ¼ teaspoon pepper

Heat oil and butter in large saucepan; sauté onions, carrots, and garlic over medium heat until tender. Stir in remaining ingredients. Simmer, covered, over low heat for 20 minutes. Blend or purée to a creamy consistency. Return sauce to pan and simmer 10 more minutes.

Makes 4 cups

DINNER PARTY SALAD

• *2 heads red leaf lettuce*
• *1 head Bibb lettuce*
• *2-3 bunches green onions*
• *1 (8-ounce) carton mushrooms*
• *1 head iceberg lettuce*
• *1 box Caesar salad croutons*
• *1 bottle olive oil Caesar dressing or olive oil red wine vinaigrette*

Wash all lettuce and dry by spinning. Tear iceberg, red leaf, and Bibb lettuce into bite-sized pieces. Put in large bowl. Slice green onions thinly, up to ⅓ of the dark green. Sprinkle over lettuce. Slice mushrooms and sprinkle over lettuce. Just before serving add croutons. Cover with dressing and mix well.

Serves 10-12

LEAGUE LASAGNA

1   pound ricotta cheese
1   teaspoon parsley
2   eggs
1   tablespoon salad oil
2   cloves garlic, minced
2   pounds ground beef
1   (16 ounce) can tomato sauce
1   (16 ounce) can tomatoes
1½ teaspoons salt
¼   teaspoon pepper
½   teaspoon basil
½   teaspoon oregano
½   pound lasagna noodles
12   ounces shredded mozzarella cheese
¾   cup grated Parmesan cheese

Beat together eggs, ricotta cheese, and parsley; set aside. Sauté ground beef and garlic in oil, then add next 6 ingredients and simmer for 20 minutes. Cook noodles in boiling salted water for about 15 minutes. Drain. Cover the bottom of a 3-quart buttered casserole dish with a thin layer of meat sauce. Layer noodles, meat sauce, mozzarella cheese, ricotta mixture and then sprinkle with Parmesan cheese. Repeat process, ending with a layer of meat sauce and Parmesan cheese. Bake uncovered at 350° for about 40 minutes or until bubbly. Let stand 10 minutes before cutting.

Serves 10

Spinach Lasagna

8   ounces lasagna noodles, cooked
3   (10 ounce) packages frozen chopped spinach, cooked and well drained
2   pounds cottage cheese
2   eggs
1   tablespoon parsley
½   cup butter, softened
Salt, pepper, garlic powder to taste
1   pound grated Monterey Jack cheese
1   cup grated Parmesan cheese

Mix together cottage cheese, seasonings, eggs, and butter. Grease a 9" x 13" pan. Place a layer of noodles in pan, followed by a layer of cottage cheese mixture, Monterey Jack cheese, spinach, and Parmesan cheese. Repeat layer. Bake uncovered for 30 minutes at 350°. Let stand 10 minutes before cutting.

Serves 10

Reheat pasta by running it under hot tap water in a strainer while shaking vigorously.

Macaroni Supreme

1   (8 ounce) box macaroni
¼   cup diced pimiento
1   (3 ounce) can mushrooms
¼   cup chopped onions
¼   cup chopped bell pepper
1   pound Cheddar cheese, grated
1   (10¾ ounce) can cream of celery or cream of chicken soup
1   cup mayonnaise

Cook macaroni until tender. Drain. Mix all ingredients together. Place in greased 9" x 13" casserole. Bake at 350° until bubbly, about 15 to 20 minutes.

Serves 4-6

If pasta is to be used in a dish that requires other cooking, reduce pasta cooking time by ⅓.

SeaShell Salad

1   (8 ounce) package shell macaroni, cooked and drained
1   cup bottled coleslaw dressing
½   cup mayonnaise
1   teaspoon celery seed
¼   cup chopped onion
½   cup chopped bell pepper
Paprika

In a bowl, mix together coleslaw dressing and mayonnaise. In a separate bowl, mix together celery seed, onion, and bell pepper. Add to dressing mixture, stirring well. Pour over cooked macaroni and stir to mix well. Refrigerate overnight. Before serving, add another ¼ cup of coleslaw dressing if necessary. Sprinkle top with paprika and serve.

Serves 4-6

Patsy's Pasta Salad

1   (8 ounce) box sea shell macaroni
1   package hard salami, diced
1   stick pepperoni, sliced
1   cup cubed mozzarella or provolone cheese
½   cup chopped celery
½   cup sliced green olives
1   (6 ounce) can sliced, pitted black olives
1   onion, chopped
1   (8 ounce) bottle Italian dressing
Fresh tomatoes, cut in wedges

Cook macaroni until tender and drain. Mix macaroni with next 7 ingredients. Sprinkle with Italian dressing until just moist. Toss and refrigerate for several hours. Before serving, garnish with tomatoes.

Serves 8

Pasta Primavera

2 cups fresh broccoli flowerets
1 medium onion, chopped
1 large clove garlic, chopped
1 tablespoon olive oil
1 large carrot, sliced
1 medium red bell pepper, chopped
1 cup fresh corn
1 cup whipping cream
½ cup chicken broth
3 green onions, chopped
2 tablespoons fresh basil or 2 teaspoons dried whole basil
½ teaspoon salt
8 ounces uncooked linguine
½ pound fresh mushrooms, sliced
1 cup freshly grated Parmesan cheese
¼ teaspoon pepper

Place broccoli in a vegetable steamer. Cover and steam 6 to 8 minutes or until crisp-tender. Remove from heat; set aside. Sauté onion and garlic in oil in a large skillet until tender. Add carrot, peppers, and corn to onion mixture; sauté until crisp-tender. Remove from heat; drain. Combine whipping cream, broth, green onions, basil, and salt in a medium skillet. Cook over medium-high heat for 5 minutes, stirring occasionally. Cook linguine according to package directions, breaking uncooked linguine in half before boiling. Drain; place in a large serving bowl. Add vegetables, whipping cream mixture and sliced mushrooms; toss gently. Sprinkle with Parmesan cheese and pepper; toss. Serve immediately.

Serves 8

Pasta Salad

- *12 to 14 ounces vermicelli*
- *1 cup grated Cheddar cheese*
- *1 cup chopped celery*
- *1 cup chopped bell pepper*
- *1 cup chopped green onions*
- *1 cup diced cucumber*
- *1 (6-ounce) can chopped olives*
- *1 cup chopped ham or steak*
- *1 (8-ounce) bottle zesty Italian dressing*
- *1 (2.6 ounce) package salad seasoning*

Boil vermicelli. Drain. Mix in all other ingredients. Chill.

Serves 8

Variation: Add 1 cup of your favorite vegetables to this salad, such as carrots, radishes, and broccoli.

Easy Spaghetti Meat Sauce

• *1 pound ground beef*
• *1 (8-ounce) can tomato sauce*
• *1 cup water*
• *2 tablespoons dried onion flakes*
• *2 teaspoons Worcestershire sauce*
• *½ teaspoon garlic powder*
• *¼ teaspoon pepper*
• *1 (14-ounce) jar spaghetti sauce*

Brown ground beef in a small Dutch oven, stirring until it crumbles; drain well. Stir in tomato sauce, water, dried onion flakes, Worcestershire sauce, garlic powder, and pepper. Bring to a boil over medium heat. Cover, reduce heat, and simmer 20 minutes, stirring occasionally. Add spaghetti sauce, and simmer, uncovered, 20 minutes, stirring occasionally. Serve over cooked spaghetti. Sprinkle with Parmesan cheese.

4 servings

Spaghetti and Minced Clams

½ pound spaghetti, cooked
4 tablespoons olive oil
4 tablespoons butter
1 clove garlic, chopped
3 tablespoons chopped shallots
1 cup clam juice
1 cup minced clams
½ cup chopped fresh parsley

Heat butter and olive oil and sauté lightly. Combine garlic and shallots and add to oil mixture; sauté lightly. Add clam juice and simmer for 5 minutes. Stir in minced clams and parsley. Bring to a boil; blend sauce with cooked spaghetti. Serve hot.

Serves 4

Penne Pasta and Grilled Chicken

2 whole chicken breasts, halved (about 1½ pounds)
2 tablespoons lemon juice
1 pound penne pasta
2 large red bell peppers, diced in ½" pieces
2½ cups thinly sliced celery
1 red onion, chopped
1¼ cups thinly sliced black olives
¼ cup minced fresh dill
3 tablespoons mayonnaise
2 tablespoons Dijon mustard
Salt and pepper to taste
⅔ cup olive oil

Grill chicken and sprinkle with lemon juice; allow to cool. Cook pasta in salted boiling water; drain and rinse. Toss pasta with peppers, celery, onion, olives, and dill in a large bowl. Slice chicken thin and add mayonnaise, mustard, salt, and pepper. Add oil in a slow, steady stream. Add chicken mixture to pasta salad and toss.

Serves 8-10

Swordfish, Pasta, and Pecan Salad

1½ pounds swordfish steaks, ¾-1" thick
4   tablespoons fresh lemon juice, divided
¼   cup mayonnaise
1   pound thick spaghetti, cooked al dente and drained
¼   cup olive oil
1   cup black olives, pitted and sliced
1½ cups pecan halves, toasted in 350° oven for 10 minutes
Béarnaise mayonnaise (recipe at right)
Fresh dill and tarragon sprigs (optional)

Sprinkle fish on both sides with 1 tablespoon lemon juice. Spread
1 side of fish with half of the regular mayonnaise. Broil steaks,
regular mayonnaise side up, 6 inches from heat for 5 minutes. Turn
steaks over, spread with remaining regular mayonnaise and broil
until done, another 3 to 4 minutes. Let fish cool and then cut into
½" cubes. Toss pasta with oil and remaining 3 tablespoons lemon
juice. Add olives, pecans, and swordfish and toss together. Make
Béarnaise mayonnaise. Top pasta mixture with Béarnaise mayonnaise and toss lightly. Garnish with fresh dill and tarragon. Refrigerate several hours to allow flavors to blend. Serve cold or allow to
reach room temperature.

Serves 6

Béarnaise Mayonnaise

- *2 shallots, minced*
- *½ cup dry white wine*
- *¼ cup white wine vinegar*
- *2 tablespoons dried tarragon*
- *2 tablespoons dried dill*
- *2 egg yolks*
- *2 tablespoons fresh lemon juice*
- *2 tablespoons tarragon mustard*
- *1 cup vegetable oil*
- *½ cup olive oil*
- *salt and pepper to taste*

Heat shallots, wine, vinegar, tarragon, and dill to boiling in small saucepan. Cook until almost all of liquid has evapo-rated. Remove from heat. Process egg yolks, lemon juice, and mustard in food processor fitted with steel blade for 10 seconds. With machine running, add the oils in a thin, steady stream through the feed tube to make a thick mayonnaise. Turn off processor and add the reduced shallot mixture. Process just until blended. Season with salt and pepper.

Makes 2 cups

Use an ice cream scoop (the kind with a lever and spring) to drop cupcake and muffin batter into baking tins.

Pat's Applesauce Muffins

2 cups flour
2½ teaspoons baking powder
¾ teaspoon salt
¼ cup sugar
1 teaspoon cinnamon
½ cup applesauce
¼ cup milk
1 egg, slightly beaten
2 tablespoons oil
2 tablespoons butter or margarine, melted
2 teaspoons cinnamon
¼ cup sugar

Combine first nine ingredients together and beat for 30 seconds with an electric mixer. (Take care not to over mix). Bake in greased muffin tins for 12 minutes at 400°. Remove muffins from pan. Dip tops of warm muffins in melted margarine or butter; roll in cinnamon and sugar mixture for topping.

Makes 2 dozen

Banana Oatmeal Muffins

The following can be substituted for the bananas and cinnamon:
• 1 cup applesauce and ½ teaspoon cinnamon;
• 1 cup mashed pumpkin, ½ teaspoon allspice, and ½ teaspoon cinnamon;
• 1 cup blueberries and ½ teaspoon nutmeg.

1½ cups rolled oats
1¼ cups all-purpose flour
2 teaspoons baking powder
1 egg
½ cup brown sugar
1 tablespoon vegetable oil
½ cup milk
½ cup water
1 cup mashed bananas
½ teaspoon cinnamon

Mix ingredients together. Line 12-cup muffin pan with paper liners. Fill muffin cups ⅔ full. Bake at 350° for 20 minutes.

Makes 1 dozen

Bran Muffins

2 cups boiling water
2 cups bran buds
5 cups all-purpose flour
5 teaspoons baking soda
1 teaspoon salt
4 cups all bran cereal
1 cup vegetable shortening
3 cups sugar
4 eggs
1 quart buttermilk

Combine boiling water with bran buds and set aside. Combine flour, soda, and salt; sift together and then add all bran cereal. In another bowl, cream together shortening and sugar, then add eggs 1 at a time. Add this to flour mixture. Add soaked bran buds and buttermilk to flour mixture. Store in large covered container in refrigerator. Will keep up to 7 weeks. Bake in lightly greased muffin tins at 375° for 15 minutes. Raisins or nuts may be added.

Makes 8 dozen

For a great gift, place bran muffin batter in a decorative jar with baking instructions attached.

Zucchini Muffins from Red Rocker Inn, Black Mountain, NC

3 eggs, beaten
1 cup granulated sugar
1 cup firmly packed brown sugar
1 cup vegetable oil
4 tablespoons vanilla
3 cups flour
3 teaspoons cinnamon
1 teaspoon baking soda
¼ teaspoon baking powder
¼ teaspoon salt
2 cups unpeeled and shredded zucchini
½ cup chopped nuts

In a bowl, gradually add sugars to beaten eggs. Stir in oil and vanilla. Mix dry ingredients and fold into eggs, adding zucchini and nuts. Bake in greased muffin tins at 325° for about 25 minutes.

Makes 2 dozen

For fluffy, tender muffins, mix batter gently and minimally. Beating or over-handling batter will result in tough muffins.

CARAMEL COFFEECAKE

1   loaf frozen bread, broken into 12 or 18 pieces
2   teaspoons water
¼   cup butter
½   cup brown sugar
1   (3 ounce) box butterscotch pudding (not instant)
2   teaspoons vanilla
½   cup chopped nuts

Place frozen bread pieces in well greased tube pan. Mix water, butter, brown sugar, and pudding together until melted. Add vanilla and nuts to melted mixture. Pour this melted mixture over bread pieces. Let rise at room temperature overnight. Bake next morning at 350° for 35 minutes. Turn out (upside down) immediately.

Serves 6–8

Sometimes cranberries may be difficult to find. Buy cranberries when they're in season and freeze them in a plastic bag. They will last up to one year.

CRANBERRY COFFEECAKE

1   cup butter or margarine, softened
1   cup sugar
2   eggs
2   cups self-rising flour
1   (8 ounce) carton sour cream
1   teaspoon vanilla, divided
1   can whole berry cranberry sauce
½   cup chopped pecans or walnuts
1   cup sifted confectioners' sugar
2   tablespoons milk

Cream butter and sugar; add eggs 1 at a time, beating after each. Add flour alternately with sour cream, beginning and ending with flour. Stir in ½ teaspoon vanilla. Pour batter into a greased 13" x 9" pan or 2 round cake pans. Spread cranberry sauce evenly over batter; sprinkle with nuts. Bake at 350° for 35 to 45 minutes until wooden pick comes out clean. To make glaze, combine confectioners' sugar, milk, and remaining vanilla. Stir until smooth. Drizzle over coffeecake.

Serves 16

Holiday Coffee Wreath

4⅓ cups flour
⅓ cup plus 2 tablespoons sugar
1 teaspoon salt
1 teaspoon cardamom (or mace, optional)
1 teaspoon cinnamon
2 packages yeast
½ cup butter
½ cup water
½ cup milk
½ cup raisins
2 eggs, slightly beaten
2 tablespoons chopped nuts

Mix 1 cup flour, ⅓ cup sugar, salt, cardamom, cinnamon, and yeast. Set aside. In a saucepan, melt butter, add liquids and raisins. Cool slightly before adding to flour mixture. Remove 2 tablespoons of beaten eggs; set aside to use later as glaze. Add remaining egg and 1 cup flour. Stir in enough flour for soft dough. Let rise 1 hour. Knead and braid and let rise for 45 minutes. Brush with reserved beaten egg and sprinkle with sugar and nuts. Bake at 375° for 25-30 minutes.

Makes 2 wreaths

Floral arrangements in the dining area should have little or no perfume. You won't want a heavy floral fragrance to interfere with the taste and aroma of the food.

Favorite Pancakes

1 egg
1 cup buttermilk
2 tablespoons vegetable shortening, melted
1 cup all-purpose flour
1 tablespoon sugar
1 teaspoon baking powder
½ teaspoon baking soda
½ teaspoon salt

Beat egg; add remaining ingredients in order listed and beat with rotary egg beater or electric mixer until smooth. Grease heated griddle. Test griddle. Pour batter from tip of large spoon or from pitcher onto hot griddle. Turn pancakes as soon as they are puffed and full of bubbles, but before bubbles break. Cook other side until golden brown.

Makes 10 four-inch pancakes

Turn ordinary pancakes into fruity roll-ups kids love! Spoon fresh berries on large pancakes, roll tightly, sprinkle with confectioners' sugar. Serve immediately on warmed plates.

JACK'S FAVORITE COFFEECAKE

2   eggs
½   cup butter or margarine, softened
2   cups sugar
1   cup sour cream
1   teaspoon vanilla
2   cups flour
¼   teaspoon salt
1   teaspoon baking powder
⅛   teaspoon baking soda
1   cup chopped nuts
2   teaspoons cinnamon
8   tablespoons brown sugar

Mix together the eggs, butter or margarine, and sugar. Add sour cream and vanilla. Mix. Add flour, salt, baking powder, and soda. In a separate bowl, mix the nuts, cinnamon, and brown sugar. Grease and flour a tube pan. Pour half of batter mixture in bottom of pan, cover with half of the nut mixture. Top with remaining batter and then the rest of nut mixture. Bake at 325° for 1 hour or until done.

Serves 10

OVERNIGHT CINNAMON ROLLS

A wonderful addition to a Christmas breakfast--all the work is done the day before.

1   cup milk
1   cup water
½   cup butter or margarine
6-6½ cups all purpose flour, divided
½   cup sugar
3   packages dry yeast
2   teaspoons salt
1   egg, beaten
2   tablespoons butter or margarine, melted
⅓   cup firmly packed brown sugar
1½   teaspoons ground cinnamon
1   cup confectioners' sugar, sifted
2   tablespoons milk
½   teaspoon vanilla extract

Combine first 3 ingredients in a small saucepan; heat until very warm, about 120°. Combine 2 cups flour, sugar, yeast, and salt in large bowl; stir well. Gradually add milk mixture to flour mixture, stirring well; add egg. Beat at medium speed with an electric mixer until smooth. Gradually stir in enough remaining flour to make slightly stiff dough. Turn out dough onto a well-floured surface and knead until smooth and elastic, about 10 minutes. Place in a greased bowl, turning to grease top. Cover and let rise in a warm place (85°), free from drafts, for 1 hour or until doubled in bulk. Punch down dough, cover, and let rest 15 minutes. Set half of dough aside. Turn remaining half of dough out onto lightly floured surface; roll to a 20" x 12" rectangle. Brush 2 tablespoons butter over dough, leaving a half-inch border. Combine brown sugar and cinnamon; sprinkle over rectangle. Beginning at long side, roll up jelly roll fashion, press edges and ends together securely. Cut into 1" slices; place cut side down in a greased 13" x 9" x 2" pan. Cover pan with greased plastic wrap; refrigerate 8 hours or overnight. Repeat with remaining dough. Before baking, cover and let rise in a warm place, free from drafts for 1 hour or until doubled in bulk. Bake at 375° for 20 minutes. Make glaze by combining confectioners' sugar, milk, and vanilla; drizzle over warm rolls.

Makes 3½ dozen

Mama's Gingerbread has been a holiday tradition since 1920.

MAMA'S GINGERBREAD

1   cup molasses
1   cup brown sugar
1   cup butter
3   eggs
3½ cups flour
1   teaspoon cinnamon
1   teaspoon nutmeg
1   teaspoon ginger
½   teaspoon salt
1   teaspoon baking soda
1   cup sour milk, buttermilk, or water

Place molasses, brown sugar, and butter in a bowl and let stand in warm place until butter has softened. Beat the mixture to a cream. Beat in eggs and add flour (sifted with spices, salt, and baking soda) alternately with milk. Bake in greased loaf pans in a 300°-325° oven until done.

Makes 2 loaves

Hydrogenated vegetable oil is found in many processed foods as it extends the shelf life of products. Hydrogenation is a process that changes a liquid vegetable oil to a more solid form. Hydrogenation changes the oil into a more saturated fat that is similar to other saturated fats in its cholesterol-raising ability. When looking at ingredient labels, use products with hydrogenated fats in moderation.

Barbra Crumpacker,
Registered Dietitian

CRANBERRY BREAD

2   cups all-purpose flour
1   cup sugar
1½ teaspoons baking powder
½   teaspoon baking soda
1   teaspoon salt
¼   cup shortening
¾   cup orange rind
1   egg, well beaten
½   cup chopped nuts
2   cups fresh cranberries, chopped
½   cup raisins (optional)

Sift together first 5 ingredients. Add remaining ingredients and mix together. Spoon batter into a greased 9" x 5" loaf pan. Bake at 350° for approximately 1 hour.

Makes 1 loaf

Poppy Seed Bread

1 package yellow cake mix
½ cup oil
1 cup hot water
4 eggs
1 (3 ounce) package instant coconut pudding mix
½ cup poppy seeds

Mix together all ingredients for 4 minutes. Pour into a greased loaf pan. Bake at 400° for 30 to 40 minutes.

Makes 1 loaf

Strawberry Bread

½ cup butter or margarine
1 cup sugar
½ teaspoon almond extract
2 eggs, separated
2 cups flour
1 teaspoon baking powder
1 teaspoon baking soda
1 teaspoon salt
1 cup fresh strawberries or 1 (10 ounce) package frozen strawberries, crushed or chopped

Cream together butter, sugar, and almond extract. Beat in egg yolks, 1 at a time. Sift together flour, baking powder, soda, and salt. Add dry ingredients alternately with strawberries to creamed mixture. Beat egg whites until stiff. Fold into strawberry mixture. Line 9" x 5" loaf pan with wax paper; grease. Turn batter into pan. Bake at 350° for 50 to 60 minutes or until a toothpick placed in the center of the bread comes out clean. Cool 15 minutes on rack. Remove from pan and continue to cool on rack.

Makes 1 loaf

Add some of your favorite preserves or jelly to softened butter, whip until blended. Serve with English muffins or bagels for a neighborhood coffee.

For a tasty plain muffin, omit dill.

Remove muffins and bread from pans as soon as they come out of the oven; standing in hot pans will cause them to become soggy.

DILL MUFFINS

¼   cup butter, softened
1   cup unsifted self-rising flour
½   cup sour cream
1   teaspoon dill
½   cup milk

Mix all ingredients well. Fill greased muffin tins ½ full. Bake at 350° for 20 minutes.

Makes 1 dozen

For Parkerhouse rolls, roll dough into circles, brush with melted butter, and fold in half in pan. Dough freezes well or may be kept in refrigerator for a few days before you roll out and bake.

DIXIE ROLLS

2   packages yeast, dissolved in ¼ cup lukewarm water
⅓   cup sugar
1   cup milk (lukewarm)
1   cup water
5   cups self-rising flour
½   cup vegetable shortening

In a bowl, add sugar to dissolved yeast. Let stand 5 to 10 minutes until sugar dissolves. Pour yeast mixture into a bowl containing the milk and water. Set aside. Cut shortening into flour with pastry blender. Add all liquid to flour mixture; stir. Dough will be sticky. Turn onto floured board and knead until smooth. Place in a greased bowl. Cover. Let rise for 30 minutes in a warm place. Punch down. Cover and refrigerate. Roll into desired shape. Let rise in greased muffin tin for 1 hour (covered in a warm place). Bake 10 to 15 minutes at 400°.

Makes 4–5 dozen

Granny's Rolls

1   package dry yeast
2   cups lukewarm water
4   cups self-rising flour
½   cup sugar
¾   cup oil or melted vegetable shortening
1   egg (optional)

Mix yeast, water, and flour together in bowl. Add sugar, shortening, and egg. Put in greased muffin pans. Bake at 350° for 12 to 15 minutes until golden brown. Dough will last for a week or so in the refrigerator.

Makes 2 dozen

High Rise Rolls

1   package yeast, dissolved in ¼ cup warm water
¾   cup evaporated milk
¾   cup hot water
3   tablespoons butter, melted
3   tablespoons sugar
1   teaspoon salt
½   teaspoon baking soda
Flour enough for stiff dough (about 4 cups)

Dissolve yeast; add milk and hot water, then butter, sugar, and salt. Add flour and soda. Mix. Turn out on floured board and knead. Place in greased bowl and let rise 2 to 3 hours. Punch down. Form into rolls and place in greased muffin pan. Let rise until doubled. Brush with melted butter. Bake at 400° until golden brown, about 10 minutes.

Makes 2 dozen

Not sure how many people can sit comfortably at your table? Allow 24" per person.

Test freshness of yeast by adding a pinch of sugar when dissolving it in water. If mixture doesn't foam within 10 minutes the yeast is dead.

Butter Dips

1¼ cups self-rising flour
2 teaspoons sugar
⅔ cup milk
¼ cup margarine, melted

Measure flour and sugar into bowl. Add milk, stir until dough forms, about 30 strokes. Knead dough approximately 10 times on a heavily floured sheet of wax paper. (The dough mixture will be soupy at first.) Pat down dough in a greased pie pan, pour ¼ cup melted margarine over dough. Cut into desired number of pie-shaped wedges. Bake at 450° for 15 to 20 minutes.

Serves 4–6

Sesame Parmesan Rolls

1 can biscuits
Melted butter
Grated Parmesan cheese
Sesame seeds

Grease a shallow baking pan very generously. Cut biscuits into quarters and place them in pan. Brush generously with melted butter. Sprinkle with Parmesan cheese and then with sesame seeds. Bake at 350° approximately 10 minutes. Put pan on next to bottom rack for 5 minutes, then move to top rack until brown. Watch carefully for they burn easily.

Serves 10–15

Quick Mayonnaise Rolls

• 1 cup self-rising flour
• 3 tablespoons mayonnaise (do not use salad dressing)
• ½ cup milk

Mix together flour and mayonnaise; add milk and stir well. Fill greased muffin tins half full. Bake at 400° for 15 to 20 minutes.

Makes 6 rolls

Hushpuppies

1   cup cornmeal
1   egg
1   teaspoon baking powder
3   teaspoons sugar
1   small onion, diced
⅔   cup buttermilk
Vegetable oil

Mix together all ingredients. Heat 2-4 inches of oil in a fryer or large, heavy pan. Make sure there is enough oil in pan for hushpuppies to float up. Scoop small amount of batter with a teaspoon. Place spoon into hot oil. Batter will slide off spoon into oil. When hushpuppies begin to float, they are ready to turn. Approximate cooking time per side is 2 to 4 minutes.

Makes 1½ dozen

Lacy Cornbread

1   egg, well beaten
¾   cup buttermilk
1   cup cornmeal
2   tablespoons all purpose flour
2   teaspoons baking powder
¼   teaspoon salt
1   tablespoon melted shortening or cooking oil

Combine egg and buttermilk; mix well. In a separate bowl, combine dry ingredients and stir into egg mixture. Lightly grease skillet or griddle with shortening. Drop batter by tablespoon onto hot skillet or griddle. (Stir batter frequently to prevent cornmeal from settling.) Turn patties when tops are covered with bubbles and edges are browned. It may be necessary to regrease your griddle or add oil to skillet while frying the bread.

Makes 1 dozen

Parmesan Bread Sticks

• *1 loaf white bread*
• *2 sticks butter*
• *2 cups grated Parmesan cheese*
• *1 tablespoon garlic powder*

Remove crusts from bread and cut each slice into 4 pieces. Melt butter in shallow dish. Mix cheese and garlic powder in another shallow dish. Dip each piece of bread lightly in butter and then roll in cheese mixture. Place on baking sheet. Bake at 400° for 10 minutes or until golden. Serve warm or at room temperature.

Makes 5–6 dozen

Mexican Cornbread

1¾ cups yellow cornmeal
3 teaspoons baking powder
⅓ teaspoon baking soda
1 teaspoon salt
2 eggs
1 cup buttermilk
⅓ cup cooking oil
1 (8 ounce) can cream-style corn
1 cup grated Cheddar cheese
4 jalapeño peppers, chopped (about ¼ to ⅓ cup)
1 small onion, chopped (optional)

Mix dry ingredients. Add other ingredients. Mix well. Grease 9" iron skillet. Bake for 30 to 35 minutes at 400°.

Serves 4-6

Sour Cream Cornbread

¾ cup yellow cornmeal
¾ cup all-purpose flour
1 teaspoon salt
3 teaspoons baking powder
1 cup sour cream
2 eggs
½ cup vegetable oil
Butter, softened

Combine all dry ingredients. Add sour cream, eggs, and oil; stir and mix well. Pour into a 9" x 9" greased pan and bake at 400° for 25 to 30 minutes. Spread top with softened butter while warm.

Serves 4

Southern Spoon Bread

1 cup cornmeal
2 cups milk
1 teaspoon salt
1 teaspoon baking powder
2 tablespoons vegetable shortening, melted
1 cup milk
3 egg yolks, well beaten
3 egg whites, stiffly beaten

Cook cornmeal and milk over medium heat until consistency of mush. Remove from heat; add salt, baking powder, vegetable shortening, and milk. Add egg yolks and fold in egg whites. Bake in greased 2-quart baking dish at 325° for 1 hour. Spoon into warm dishes and serve with butter.

Serves 6

One Hundred Percent Whole Wheat Bread

1 package yeast
¼ cup warm water
6 cups whole wheat flour
2½ cups hot water
1 tablespoon salt
⅓ cup oil
⅓ cup honey
1 cup wheat germ

Sprinkle yeast in ¼ cup warm water. Do not stir. Mix 3 cups flour and hot water; add salt, oil, honey, and wheat germ. Add yeast-water mixture and then the rest of flour. Knead 10 minutes or so, until dough is firm and is handled easily. Form into loaves. Place in greased loaf pans and cover with damp cloth in warm place. Let rise about 35 minutes. Bake at 350° for 40 minutes.

Makes 2 loaves

To bake hole-free bread follow this guide: Knead the dough at least 10 to 12 minutes the first time. Knead it a second time, but just enough to break the dough down. It should have the consistency of elastic. Let the dough rise at least twice before it is shaped into loaves.

Pandora's Box

All-Purpose Mix

5   pound bag flour
5   cups instant dry milk
½   cup sugar
¾   cup baking powder
3   tablespoons salt
2   tablespoons cream of tartar
2   pounds vegetable shortening

Pour flour into a large pan. Add dry milk, sugar, baking powder, salt, and cream of tartar. Sift all together once. Cut in shortening until mixture looks like cornmeal. Store in gallon jars or large plastic containers with tight lids. This recipe will fill a 1½ gallon jar. Store at room temperature until used. Mix can be used in the following recipes.

Pandora's Biscuits

3   cups mix
⅔   cup water

Combine mix and water. Drop spoonfuls of batter onto ungreased baking sheet. Bake at 450° for 10 minutes.

Makes 12 large or 18 medium biscuits

Pandora's Pancakes

3   cups mix
1   egg
1½ cups water

Combine ingredients until smooth. Drop by spoonfuls onto heated griddle and cook until desired doneness.

Makes 10 pancakes

PANDORA'S COFFEECAKE

3 cups mix
½ cup sugar
1 egg
⅔ cup water
1 cup brown sugar
⅓ cup butter, softened
1 teaspoon cinnamon

Beat egg and add to water. Stir sugar into mix. Add liquid all at once and stir to blend. Pour into greased 8" x 9" pan. In a separate bowl, mix together brown sugar, butter, and cinnamon. Sprinkle mixture evenly over batter. Bake at 400° for 25 minutes.

Makes 1 coffeecake

PANDORA'S MUFFINS

3 cups mix
2 tablespoons sugar
1 egg
1 cup water

Combine all ingredients. Spoon into a muffin tin. Bake at 425° for 20 minutes.

Makes 1½ dozen

FLAKY BISCUITS

• 2 cups all–purpose flour
• 1 tablespoon baking powder
• 1 teaspoon salt
• ⅔ cup milk
• ¼ cup oil

Mix together first 3 ingredients. Combine milk and oil; add to dry ingredients. Roll out to ½" thickness. Cut with 2" biscuit cutter. Bake on ungreased sheet at 450° for 8 to 10 minutes.

Makes 1 dozen

Sourdough Bread

Sourdough Starter
1   package dry yeast
2½ cups lukewarm water (110°), divided
2   tablespoons sugar
2½ tablespoons all-purpose flour
¾   cup sugar
3   tablespoons instant potatoes
1   cup warm water

Mix yeast with ½ cup lukewarm water. In another bowl, mix two tablespoons sugar with 2 cups warm water and flour. Add yeast mixture to flour mixture. Put in glass jar or bowl. Cover with a clean cloth and allow to set for 5 days at room temperature. Place in the refrigerator for 3 to 5 days; pour out all but 1 cup; and feed. Feed starter every 3 to 5 days or at least once a week with the ¾ cup sugar, instant potatoes, and 1 cup warm water.

Sourdough Bread
1   cup starter
1   tablespoon salt
1½ cups warm water
½   cup oil
6   cups bread flour

Mix ingredients together. Place in a well-greased bowl; turn to grease top of dough as well. Cover with a towel and let rise at room temperature overnight. In the morning, punch dough down and knead 8 to 10 times. Divide into 2 equal parts and knead again 8 to 10 times. Place in greased 9" x 5" loaf pans; brush tops with butter. Let rise 4 to 6 hours and bake at 350° for 30 to 45 minutes.

Makes 2 loaves

GOOD FOOD

GOOD COMPANY

SIDE DISHES

Artichoke and Spinach Casserole

2   (6 ounce) jars marinated artichokes
3   (10 ounce) packages frozen chopped spinach
3   (3 ounce) packages cream cheese, softened
⅓   cup grated Parmesan cheese
4   teaspoons butter
6   teaspoons milk
Salt and pepper to taste

Cook spinach according to package directions. Drain. Season with butter, salt, and a little of the artichoke marinade. Spread artichokes and remaining marinade on the bottom of a 1½-quart glass baking dish. Top with spinach. Beat cream cheese, butter, and milk together. Spread over spinach. Dust with pepper. Cover with Parmesan cheese. Refrigerate for 24 hours. Bake at 375° for 40 minutes.

Serves 8

Need more table space? Top card tables with 48" rounds cut from particle board and drape with pretty cloth.

Marinated Asparagus

2   pounds fresh asparagus, trimmed
¼   cup white wine vinegar
¼   cup chopped green onion
½   teaspoon sugar
¼   teaspoon salt
½   cup vegetable oil
¼   cup lemon juice
2   tablespoons chopped parsley
½   teaspoon dry mustard
⅛   teaspoon freshly ground pepper

Lightly steam asparagus until crisp-tender, about 5 to 8 minutes. In a bowl, combine remaining ingredients. Place asparagus and marinade in a 13" x 9" x 2" glass dish or a 1-gallon plastic bag. Refrigerate several hours or overnight before serving.

Serves 6

To revive limp, uncooked asparagus, stand them upright in a small amount of ice water in a deep pot and cover with a plastic bag. Let stand in the refrigerator 30 minutes before serving.

Asparagus and Pea Casserole

1 (16 ounce) can small green peas
1 (10½ ounce) can asparagus
1 (4 ounce) can mushrooms
1 (10¾ ounce) can cream of celery soup
½ cup grated Cheddar cheese

Drain peas, asparagus, and mushrooms. Mix together in 12" x 6" casserole dish. Pour undiluted soup over vegetables. Place in 350° oven until bubbly. Remove and sprinkle with grated cheese before serving.

Serves 8

Herbed Green Beans

1 pound fresh green beans
2 tablespoons vegetable oil
¼ cup chopped fresh parsley
½ teaspoon dried basil
½ teaspoon dried oregano
⅛ teaspoon crushed red pepper
2 medium tomatoes, cut into 1" pieces
2 cloves garlic, finely chopped
1 tablespoon grated Parmesan cheese

Wash beans and remove ends. Leave whole or cut crosswise into 1" pieces. Place beans in 1" salted water (½ teaspoon salt to 1 cup water). Heat to boiling; reduce heat and boil uncovered 5 minutes. Cover and boil until tender, about 5 to 10 minutes longer. Drain. Heat oil in skillet until hot. Add remaining ingredients, except cheese. Cook until tomatoes are soft, stirring frequently. Stir in beans. Cook, stirring occasionally, just until beans are hot, about 1 to 2 minutes. Sprinkle with cheese.

Serves 6

Bean Bundles

• 1 (16 ounce) can whole green beans or 3 cups fresh green beans, cooked
• 1 (8 ounce) bottle Catalina dressing
• 5 pieces bacon, halved, partially cooked, and drained

Drain beans and divide into bundles of 5–7 beans. Wrap each bundle with ½ piece of bacon. Place in a glass dish. Pour dressing over beans and marinate for several hours. Bake 20 minutes at 350°.

Serves 4–6

Bourbon Beans

2   (16 ounce) cans pork and beans
1   tablespoon molasses
½   cup chili sauce
1   tablespoon dry mustard
½   cup strong coffee
1   cup bourbon
½   cup crushed pineapple, drained
¼   cup brown sugar, packed

In a bowl, combine all ingredients except brown sugar and pineapple. Place mixture in a 2-quart casserole dish. Cover and let stand at room temperature for 4 hours. Bake in covered casserole at 350° for 45 minutes. Uncover and top with pineapple and then brown sugar. Return to oven and bake for an additional 35 minutes.

Serves 8–10

Delicious Baked Beans

1   pound ground chuck
1   tablespoon butter
1   medium onion, chopped
1   green pepper, chopped
¾   cup light brown sugar
2   (15 ounce) cans pork and beans
6   tablespoons ketchup
1   tablespoon chili powder
4   tablespoons barbecue sauce
5   tablespoons Worcestershire sauce
1   teaspoon prepared mustard

Brown meat in skillet. Remove meat from skillet, drain, and set aside. In same skillet, melt butter. Sauté onions and green peppers. Add remaining ingredients and return meat to mixture. Pour into 9" x 13" baking dish and bake at 350° for 1 hour.

Serves 8–10

Baked beans are a favorite at picnics, cookouts, and family reunions. Beans are an excellent source of fiber with more than 6½ grams per cup. That's a hefty dose towards the recommended daily intake of 20 to 30 grams. Baked beans also are a good low-fat source of protein. This recipe for Bourbon Beans includes only fat-free additions, so just remove the pork and serve a hearty dish that is sure to be a hit!

Barbra Crumpacker, Registered Dietitian

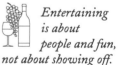

Entertaining is about people and fun, not about showing off.

Baked Lima Beans

1   (1 pound) package large dried lima beans
1½ teaspoons salt
½   pound sliced bacon
1   cup chopped onion
2   (8 ounce) cans tomato sauce
¼   cup light brown sugar, firmly packed
2   teaspoons dry mustard
2   teaspoons Worcestershire sauce
¼   teaspoon dried oregano leaves
½   cup water

Soak beans overnight in enough water to allow for swelling. Drain and rinse. Place beans in a large saucepan and cover with water. Add 1 teaspoon salt and bring to a boil; reduce heat, and simmer 40 minutes or until beans are tender. Drain. Cut all but 6 slices of bacon into ½" pieces. In a skillet, sauté bacon pieces and onion until onion is tender and bacon is brown. In a large bowl, combine beans, onion, bacon, tomato sauce, brown sugar, dry mustard, Worcestershire sauce, ½ teaspoon salt, oregano, and ½ cup water. Blend well. Place beans and sauce in a 2½-quart baking dish. Bake at 350°, covered, 30 minutes. Remove cover and bake 15 minutes longer. Meanwhile, fry remaining bacon until crisp. Drain. Arrange bacon slices over beans before serving.

Serves 6

Mildred's Beets

2   (1 pound) cans whole or sliced beets
½   cup sugar
3   tablespoons cornstarch
½   teaspoon salt
⅔   cup water
¼   cup cider vinegar
2   tablespoons butter or margarine
1   cup sweet pickle relish

Drain beets. In a saucepan, mix sugar, cornstarch, and salt. Add water and vinegar. Cook, stirring constantly, until thick. Add butter and relish. Pour over beets. Serve hot.

Serves 6

Broccoli Balls

2   (10-ounce) packages frozen chopped broccoli
6   eggs, beaten
2   cups herb-seasoned stuffing mix
½   cup grated Parmesan cheese
½   teaspoon salt
3   tablespoons chopped green onion
¾   cup margarine, melted
1   teaspoon celery seed
2   fresh tomatoes, sliced

Cook broccoli according to package directions. Drain well. Place broccoli in a bowl. Add all other ingredients and mix well. Place tomato slices on a cookie sheet. Using an ice cream scoop, top each tomato slice with a broccoli ball. Bake at 350° for 30 minutes.

Serves 6–8

Broccoli Surprise

1   (16 ounce) package broccoli pieces, thawed
1   (24 ounce) package broccoli spears, thawed
2   (10¾ ounce) cans condensed New England clam chowder
1   cup cottage cheese
1   cup sour cream
1   cup grated Cheddar cheese

Place broccoli cuts in bottom of buttered 3-quart casserole. Arrange spears on top with flowerets facing casserole rim. In a bowl, mix chowder, cottage cheese, and sour cream. Pour over center of dish, leaving the flowerets exposed. Sprinkle with cheese and bake at 325° for 1 hour.

Serves 8

PEACHES AND MINCEMEAT

• *1 (16 ounce) can peach halves, drained*
• *1 (12 ounce) can mincemeat*
• *1 stick butter*

Place desired number of peach halves in baking dish with seed cavity up. Fill each cavity with 1 tablespoon of mincemeat. Dot the top of mincemeat with butter and heat in oven at 300° for 10 minutes.

Serves 10

Choose a menu that is within your time, space, and budget limitations. Serve dishes you feel comfortable and confident with--don't experiment with daring new recipes when time and energy are limited.

Broccoli Ring with Parmesan Cheese Sauce

2	tablespoons butter
3	(10 ounce) packages chopped broccoli, thawed, squeezed and drained
½	cup chopped onion
4	eggs
⅓	cup light cream
1	teaspoon salt
⅛	teaspoon pepper
¼	teaspoon ground nutmeg
3	tablespoons butter
3	tablespoons flour
½	teaspoon salt
¼	teaspoon white pepper
2	cups light cream or milk
¾	cup grated Parmesan cheese

Butter a 6-cup ring mold. Purée broccoli and onions in blender or food processor. In a large bowl, beat eggs until light; add puréed broccoli, cream, salt, pepper, and nutmeg. Spoon broccoli mixture into mold. Place mold in a 13" x 9" x 2" baking pan and place on oven rack. Pour boiling water into baking pan halfway up side of mold. Bake at 350° for 35 minutes or until knife comes out clean. Remove from oven. Lift mold out of water and let stand 5 minutes. With metal spatula, loosen broccoli ring from edge of mold. Place serving plate over mold and invert mold to release broccoli ring.
In a medium saucepan, melt 3 tablespoons butter. Whisk in flour, salt, and white pepper. Cook until bubbly, about 1 minute. Gradually stir in light cream or milk. Cook, stirring constantly, until thickened, about 3 minutes. Stir in Parmesan cheese. Pour over broccoli ring.

Serves 10–12

ORIENTAL CABBAGE

1   head cabbage, shredded
1   large onion, sliced
2   bell peppers, chopped
3   tablespoons oil
½   cup chicken broth
2   tablespoons vinegar
1   tablespoon sugar

Heat 3 tablespoons oil in skillet over medium heat. Add cabbage, onions, and green peppers and stir for 5 minutes. Mix chicken broth, vinegar, and sugar. Pour over vegetables. Cover and simmer 5 minutes.

Serves 4

CARROT SOUFFLÉ

1   pound carrots, cooked
3   eggs
⅓   cup granulated sugar
2   tablespoons all-purpose flour
1   teaspoon baking powder
1   teaspoon vanilla extract
½   cup butter, melted
Dash nutmeg
Dash ground cinnamon
¼   cup crushed corn flakes
3   tablespoons light brown sugar
2   tablespoons butter
¼   cup chopped nuts

Purée cooked carrots in blender or food processor. Add eggs to puréed mixture and blend well. Add sugar, flour, baking powder, vanilla, butter, nutmeg, and cinnamon. Purée until smooth. Pour into greased 1½-quart soufflé dish. In a bowl, combine corn flakes, brown sugar, butter, and nuts. Sprinkle over casserole. Bake at 350° for 1 hour.

Serves 6

Carrots à la Crème

1 pound young, tender carrots
3 tablespoons melted butter
Salt and freshly ground pepper to taste
½ teaspoon sugar
⅓ cup heavy cream

Wash carrots. Trim off both ends, but leave whole. Blanch in boiling water for 5 minutes. Rinse under cold water and peel off skins. Place in skillet with melted butter. Sprinkle with salt, pepper, and sugar. Simmer 5 minutes. Add cream; cover and cook until carrots are tender.

Serves 6

Cheesy Carrot Casserole

2 (1 pound) bags carrots, trimmed and cleaned
¾ (10 ounces) bottle mustard-mayonnaise sauce
1 large onion, finely chopped
1 egg, beaten
Dash hot pepper sauce
1½ cups grated Cheddar cheese

Cook carrots in water until tender. Drain, but leave a small amount of water in pan with carrots. Mash carrots with potato ricer or in a food processor. Add onion, egg, pepper sauce, and 1 cup of the cheese. Pour into 1¾-quart casserole and sprinkle remaining ½ cup cheese on top. Bake at 375° for 45 minutes.

Serves 6–8

STEAMED CARROTS

Slice carrots, celery, or other long thin vegetables diagonally. Steam 8 minutes or until crisp-tender; then season with butter, lemon juice, and herbs.

Fresh Collard Greens

2 pounds collards
4 cups water
1 teaspoon sugar
1 teaspoon salt
6 strips bacon

Wash collards carefully to remove sand and grit. Put collards in pan of water with sugar and salt. Boil 45 minutes or until tender. Drain well. Cook bacon in an iron skillet, and crumble. Add greens and simmer for approximately 20 minutes. Serve with warm cornbread.

Serves 6

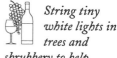

String tiny white lights in trees and shrubbery to help create a magical setting for an outdoor party.

Mexican Corn Pudding

2 cups water
½ teaspoon salt
½ cup old-fashioned grits
1 tablespoon butter or margarine
1 can (17 ounces) cream-style corn
1 cup (4 ounces) Monterey Jack cheese, shredded
½ cup stone-ground yellow cornmeal
2 large eggs
1 (4 ounce) can chopped green chilies
¼ cup skim milk
¼ teaspoon ground red pepper

Bring water and salt to a boil. Gradually stir in grits. Reduce heat to low, cover, and cook 15 to 20 minutes, stirring occasionally until thickened. Remove from heat. Stir in butter and let stand 10 minutes. Heat oven to 350˚. Lightly grease 1½-quart shallow baking dish. Stir remaining ingredients into the grits. Pour mixture into the prepared dish. Bake 1 to 1¼ hours until golden and knife inserted into center comes out clean. Let stand 10 minutes before serving.

Serves 8

As a general rule, plan on one bartender for every 50 guests. Although a bartender is not necessary for smaller parties, it's a nice touch that allows you much more time with your guests!

Sweet Corn Pudding

½   stick margarine
2   tablespoons flour
1   egg
1   (16½ ounce) can cream-style corn
1   (11 ounce) can whole kernel corn
Salt and pepper
½   cup sweetened condensed milk

Mix all ingredients. Place in a casserole dish and bake at 350° for approximately 45 minutes or until firm.

Serves 6

To measure half an egg, beat whole egg lightly, then measure two tablespoons. This will give you half an egg.

Savory Baked Eggplant

1   egg, beaten
1   (10¾ ounce) can condensed Cheddar cheese soup
¾   cup milk, divided
1   medium eggplant (1 pound)
1   cup fine dry breadcrumbs
2   tablespoons cooking oil
¼   cup sour cream
½   teaspoon crushed dried basil
⅛   teaspoon garlic powder
Several dashes ground red pepper
Grated Parmesan cheese

Combine egg, ⅓ cup soup, and ¼ cup milk. Cut eggplant into ¼" thick slices. Dip into the soup mixture, then crumbs. In a skillet, heat oil. Sauté eggplant slices, a few at a time for 2 minutes per side. Add more oil if necessary. Place cooked slices on paper towel to absorb excess oil. Arrange slices in 12" x 7½" x 2" baking dish. In a bowl, combine remaining soup, milk, sour cream, basil, garlic powder, and pepper. Spoon mixture on top of eggplant slices. Sprinkle with Parmesan cheese. Bake in 400° oven for 20 minutes.

Serves 6

A good rule of thumb: If eggplant is to be cooked for a short time, peel off the skin. If it is to be cooked longer, peeling isn't necessary.

Cheesy Eggplant Casserole

2 medium eggplant
1 onion, chopped
1 green pepper, finely chopped
1 tablespoon bacon drippings
1 egg, beaten
1 cup seasoned dry breadcrumbs
½ teaspoon salt
¼ teaspoon pepper
¾ cup mild shredded Cheddar cheese
1-2 tablespoons picante sauce
½ cup grated Parmesan cheese

Peel eggplant and cut into 1" cubes. Cook in a small amount of boiling water for 10 minutes or until tender. Drain well and mash. In a skillet, heat bacon drippings and sauté onion and green pepper until just tender. Remove from heat. Combine eggplant, egg, breadcrumbs, salt, and pepper. Mix well and add onion mixture. Spoon half of eggplant mixture into a greased 1½-quart casserole. Sprinkle with Cheddar cheese. Spoon remaining eggplant over cheese and top evenly with picante sauce. Sprinkle with Parmesan cheese. Bake at 350° for 30 minutes.

Serves 6

Southern Fried Eggplant

• *2 medium eggplant, trimmed and peeled*
• *1 egg*
• *½ cup milk*
• *1 cup flour*

Cut eggplant into bite-sized pieces. Beat 1 egg and ½ cup milk in a small bowl. Dip eggplant into egg mixture, then dredge with flour. Fry in 1" of moderately hot grease. Cook until golden brown, then drain on paper towels. Salt and serve hot.

Serves 4

DEVILED EGGS

• 1 dozen hard boiled eggs, shelled
• ⅓ cup mayonnaise
• Dijon mustard, to taste
• garlic salt, to taste
• paprika

Slice boiled eggs lengthwise. Remove yolks and mash. Add mayonnaise, Dijon mustard, and garlic salt to the mashed yolks. The more mustard used, the more tangy the flavor. Refill the egg white halves with the yolk mixture. Sprinkle lightly with paprika for color.

Serves 12

DEVILED EGGPLANT

1   cup chopped onion
2   tablespoons chopped green pepper
2   tablespoons butter or margarine
½   cup evaporated milk
½   cup water
2   eggs
1   cup breadcrumbs
¾   teaspoon salt
¼   teaspoon sugar
2   tablespoons diced pimientos
1   teaspoon baking powder
2   cups cooked, peeled, and diced eggplant
Yellow food coloring
¼   cup melted butter
Paprika

Sauté onions and pepper in 2 tablespoons butter. In a bowl, beat milk, water, and eggs. Add onions, pepper, and remaining ingredients, except paprika, to milk mixture and combine well. Place in a greased casserole. Sprinkle with paprika. Bake at 425° for 20 to 30 minutes.

Serves 8

MUSHROOMS AU GRATIN

1   pound fresh mushrooms, cleaned and quartered
2   tablespoons butter
⅓   cup sour cream
1   egg yolk
¼   cup finely chopped fresh parsley
½   cup grated Swiss cheese
Salt and pepper to taste

Heat butter in large skillet. Sauté mushrooms until lightly browned. Simmer 2 minutes. In a bowl, blend in sour cream, egg yolk, salt, and pepper until mixture is smooth. Add to mushrooms. Heat, stirring constantly, until blended. Remove from heat. Pour into shallow baking pan. Sprinkle with parsley and cheese. Before serving, bake uncovered at 425° for 10 minutes or until mushrooms are heated and cheese is melted.

Serves 6

Individual Mushroom Casseroles

6 tablespoons butter or margarine
1 tablespoon chopped parsley
2 teaspoons lemon juice
½ teaspoon salt
¼ teaspoon dried chervil
Dash pepper
4 slices French bread, cut ½" thick and toasted
1¼ pounds fresh mushrooms, stems trimmed to ½ inch
½ cup heavy cream
2 tablespoons dry sherry

In a small bowl, beat butter with chopped parsley, lemon juice, salt, chervil, and pepper. Use half of mixture to spread on 1 side of toast slices. Place slices, buttered side up, in individual casseroles or ramekins. Spread mushrooms with remaining butter mixture. Mound mushrooms over toast, and drizzle with heavy cream. Cover and bake at 375° for 20 minutes or just until mushrooms are tender. Sprinkle each serving with sherry. Serve at once.

Serves 4

Vidalia Onion Pie

1 deep-dish pie shell, baked
3 cups thinly sliced Vidalia onions
3 tablespoons butter, melted
½ cup milk
3 tablespoons flour
1½ cups sour cream
4 strips cooked bacon, crumbled
1 teaspoon salt
2 eggs, beaten

Cook onions in butter until lightly browned. Spoon into pastry shell. Combine milk, sour cream, salt, eggs, and flour. Mix well and pour over onions. Garnish with bacon. Bake at 325° for 30 minutes or until knife inserted in center comes out clean.

Serves 6–8

Marinated Onion and Tomato Slices

• *tomatoes, sliced*
• *onions, sliced*
• *bottled Italian salad dressing*

For a quick and easy side dish, arrange onions and tomatoes on platter. Pour bottled Italian dressing over vegetables and refrigerate for several hours. For variety include other colorful vegetables such as red, yellow, and green bell peppers.

Add a festive touch to your next buffet: Tie napkins and flatware together with pretty ribbons for an easy-to-pick-up "package."

ONION SOUFFLÉ

3   cups chopped Vidalia onions
1   stick butter or margarine
3   eggs, beaten
¾   cup milk
½   cup crushed saltine crackers
¾   cup grated Cheddar cheese
Salt and pepper

Sauté onions in butter until tender but not brown. In a bowl, mix 3 beaten eggs with milk and crushed crackers. Add salt and pepper to taste. Line a baking dish with sautéed onions; pour egg mixture over onions. Top with grated cheese and bake at 350° for 45 to 60 minutes. Soufflé will rise when done.

Serves 6

To give canned vegetables, such as peas and beans, a fresh vegetable taste, place a lettuce leaf in the pan while heating them.

ONIONS BAKED WITH CHEESE

1   cup peeled, thinly sliced Vidalia onions
1   (10¾ ounce) can condensed cream of mushroom soup
½   soup can milk
½   teaspoon celery salt
1½ cups shredded Cheddar cheese
Buttered breadcrumbs

Put onion rings in buttered 2-quart casserole. In saucepan, combine soup, milk, celery salt, and cheese. Heat, stirring until cheese melts. Pour over the onions. Sprinkle with buttered breadcrumbs and bake uncovered at 350° for 1 hour.

Serves 6

Savory Baked Onions

4   large onions
1½ cups chili sauce
Pinch salt
¼   cup brown sugar
¼   cup butter or margarine

Peel onions and cut in half crosswise. Place in single layer in casserole, cut side up. In a saucepan, heat chili sauce, salt, sugar, and butter. Spoon mixture over onions. Bake at 400° until onions are tender and glazed, about 30 to 45 minutes.

Serves 8

Accept help from guests when it is offered! While you may want to do all the cooking yourself, having someone uncork and pour wine, fill water glasses, and slice bread can alleviate last minute hassles.

Creamy Peas with Bacon and Mushrooms

3   cups (1½ pounds) fresh tiny green peas
3   slices bacon
5   tablespoons flour
¼   cup chopped onion
1   cup half-and-half
2   cups sliced mushrooms
Salt and pepper to taste

Cook the peas until just tender. Fry the bacon until crisp, drain on paper towel, and reserve fat in pan. Add flour to bacon fat and mix well to make a roux. Cook over medium heat, stirring constantly, until it begins to turn a caramel brown color. Add onions and cook for 3 minutes. Whisk in the half-and-half until smooth. Gently fold in the mushrooms and peas. Heat thoroughly and put in serving dish. Crumble bacon on top.

Serves 8–10

Cheesy-Chive Potatoes

4   medium potatoes, cooked and diced
1   cup sour cream
1   cup small-curd cottage cheese
1   teaspoon chives
½   teaspoon garlic powder
½   teaspoon salt
¼   teaspoon white pepper
1   cup grated sharp Cheddar cheese
Paprika

Combine all ingredients except paprika. Place in lightly greased casserole dish. Sprinkle with paprika. Bake at 350° for 30 minutes.

Serves 4

Irish Potato Casserole

1   cup milk
Salt and pepper to taste
2   tablespoons margarine
1   small onion, chopped
3   eggs
1   cup cubed Cheddar cheese
½   cup chopped green pepper
4   medium potatoes, peeled and cut into small pieces

Place all ingredients in a blender or food processor in the order listed. Blend for only 1 second. Pour into greased casserole dish and bake at 350° for 1 hour.

Serves 4-6

Swiss Cheesy Potatoes

4   eggs, separated
4   cups seasoned, hot mashed potatoes
2   cups shredded Swiss cheese
2   tablespoons finely chopped chives
2   tablespoons finely chopped green pepper
2   tablespoons finely chopped parsley
2   tablespoons diced pimientos
½   teaspoon black pepper
Dash paprika

In a bowl, beat egg whites until stiff peaks form. Set aside. In a large bowl, beat yolks, 1 at a time, into hot mashed potatoes. Stir in cheese, chives, green pepper, parsley, pimientos, and pepper. Fold beaten egg whites into mashed potato mixture until thoroughly mixed. Spoon mixture into buttered 6-cup baking dish. Bake at 375° for 40 minutes until puffed and golden. Sprinkle with paprika and serve.

Serves 6

If your raw potatoes become soft, put them in ice water for half an hour and they'll become firm again.

Guacamole Potatoes

4   baking potatoes
1   avocado
2   tablespoons sour cream
Dash salt and pepper
4   slices bacon, cooked and crumbled
1   cup grated Cheddar cheese

Wash potatoes and rub the skins with oil. Prick skins to allow steam to escape. Bake at 375° for 1½ hours. When potatoes are almost done, peel avocado, discard seed, and mash with a fork. Texture should be chunky. Mix avocado with sour cream and seasonings. Cut baked potatoes down the center and open. Spoon the avocado mixture into the potato. Sprinkle with bacon and cheese.

Serves 4

If you want baked potatoes to have a roasted flavor, don't wrap them in foil. Foil traps the moisture and steams potatoes rather than baking them.

PRALINE SWEET POTATO CASSEROLE & ORANGE SAUCE

2   (16 ounce) cans yams or sweet potatoes, drained
2   eggs
½   cup firmly packed dark brown sugar, divided
⅓   cup butter or margarine, melted and divided
Scant teaspoon salt
½   cup pecan halves
⅓   cup sugar
1   tablespoon cornstarch
⅛   teaspoon salt
1   teaspoon grated orange peel
1   cup orange juice
1   tablespoon lemon juice
2   tablespoons butter or margarine
1   tablespoon Grand Marnier
3   dashes angostura bitters

Mash potatoes in large bowl. Beat in eggs, ¼ cup brown sugar, 2 tablespoons melted butter and a scant teaspoon of salt. Pour into 1-quart casserole. Arrange pecans on top, sprinkle with remaining ¼ cup brown sugar and drizzle with remaining melted butter. Bake uncovered at 375° for 20 minutes. To make sauce, blend ⅓ cup sugar, cornstarch, and ⅛ teaspoon of salt in saucepan; add grated orange peel, orange juice, and lemon juice. Bring to a boil over medium heat, stirring constantly until sauce is thickened. Remove from heat and stir in butter, Grand Marnier, and angostura bitters. Serve warm sauce with casserole.

Serves 8

Heavenly Hash Browns

1   (2 pound) bag hash brown potatoes, thawed
1   (10¾ ounce) can cream of mushroom soup
⅓   cup finely chopped bell pepper
⅓   cup finely chopped onion
1   cup sour cream
½   cup butter, melted, divided
1½ cups grated Cheddar cheese
Breadcrumbs
6   slices bacon, cooked and crumbled

Grease a glass baking dish and add potatoes. In a bowl, mix soup, bell pepper, onion, sour cream, and ¼ cup melted butter; pour over potatoes. Bake for 1 hour at 325°. Remove from oven and top with crumbled bacon, breadcrumbs, remaining melted butter, and grated cheese. Return dish to oven and bake for an additional 15 minutes.

Serves 8

Seasoned Rice

1   stick margarine
1   (10¾ ounce) can cream of mushroom soup
1   (10¾ ounce) can beef consommé
1   envelope onion soup mix
1   cup long-grain rice

In a saucepan, heat margarine, mushroom soup, beef consommé, and onion soup mix. Stir until well blended. Place in a 1½-quart casserole with rice. Cover and place in a 350° oven for 1 hour. Stir occasionally as rice cooks.

Serves 4

One tablespoon of butter or oil added to the water before adding the rice will prevent rice from becoming gooey or sticking to the pan.

For very white rice, add a few drops of lemon juice to cooking water.

Spinach Cheese Bake

1   (10 ounce) package frozen chopped spinach, thawed and drained
4   egg whites
1   (16 ounce) container nonfat cottage cheese
4   ounces mozzarella cheese, shredded
4   tablespoons flour
¼   teaspoon garlic powder
Black pepper to taste
2   tablespoons sliced almonds (optional)

Mix together all ingredients, except almonds. Place in a lightly oiled 8" x 8" baking dish. Bake at 350° for 35 to 45 minutes or until knife placed in center comes out clean. During the last 10 minutes, sprinkle with almonds.

Serves 6

Sautéed Fresh Spinach

1   (10 ounce) bag fresh spinach
1   tablespoon olive oil
1   tablespoon butter
3   cloves garlic, minced
½   teaspoon nutmeg
Salt to taste

Wash spinach and remove stems. Lightly brown garlic in olive oil and butter. Add spinach and sauté until wilted. Add nutmeg and salt.

Serves 6

Washing spinach or other sandy greens in tepid water will remove grit more easily than cold water. Remember that 1¼ pounds of fresh spinach will yield about 1 cup cooked spinach.

Southern-Style Deviled Spinach

2   (10 ounce) packages frozen chopped spinach
5   tablespoons butter
¼   cup diced onion
3   tablespoons flour
¼   cup heavy cream
2   tablespoons milk
1-2 teaspoons crushed red pepper
1   teaspoon salt
1   teaspoon dry mustard
⅛   teaspoon celery seed
Dash Worcestershire sauce
2   cups grated Cheddar cheese, divided
2   hard boiled eggs, coarsely chopped
⅔   cup crushed buttery, round crackers
1   teaspoon paprika

Cook spinach according to directions. Drain well and reserve ½ cup cooking liquid. Set liquid and spinach aside. Melt butter in large saucepan over low heat. Add diced onion and sauté, stirring often until translucent, about 2 minutes. Stir in flour; mix until absorbed, but do not let flour brown. Stir in liquid from spinach. Still over low heat, gradually stir in cream and milk, cooking and stirring about 3 minutes, until thickened and smooth. Raise heat and bring sauce to a boil. Remove from heat. Add crushed red pepper, salt, mustard, celery seed, and Worcestershire sauce; then stir in spinach. Add 1½ cups of grated cheese, stirring until well blended. Spoon half spinach mixture into greased 1½-quart casserole or soufflé dish and sprinkle with hard boiled eggs. Cover eggs with remaining spinach mixture, then sprinkle top with crumbled crackers. Bake at 375° for 30 minutes or until crackers begin to brown. Sprinkle with remaining ½ cup of cheese and paprika.

Serves 6–8

Perfect Wild Rice

• *1 medium onion, chopped*
• *2 tablespoons butter*
• *1 cup wild rice*
• *4 cups chicken broth*

In a heavy 3-quart saucepan or skillet, sauté the onion in butter. Add wild rice and broth. Bring to a boil. Cover, reduce heat, and simmer 45 to 60 minutes or until most of the liquid has been absorbed. Fluff rice with fork. Add salt if desired. Cook uncovered to evaporate any excess liquid.

Makes 4 cups

♡ *You don't have to throw out your favorite recipes when you want to watch fat. Nor do you have to live on rice cakes and tuna fish. This popular squash casserole can easily be transformed into a healthier dish with only a few minor changes. Parmesan cheese is the leanest cheese with only 25 grams of fat per cup. Decrease it to ¾ or ½ cup and enjoy the savings. No-fat mayonnaise will work fine, providing the greatest reduction in fat. Eliminate 1 of the whole eggs by substituting 2 egg whites and reduce the margarine to 1 teaspoon or less. These 4 modifications eliminate almost 200 grams of fat. Such a big improvement for such a small change!*

Barbra Crumpacker, Registered Dietitian

Squash Parmesan

2	pounds yellow squash, sliced
1	cup mayonnaise
1	cup grated Parmesan cheese
1	small onion, chopped
2	eggs, beaten
½	teaspoon salt
¼	teaspoon pepper
½	cup soft breadcrumbs
1	tablespoon butter or margarine, melted

In a covered pot, cook squash in boiling salted water for 10 to 15 minutes or until tender. Drain and cool slightly. Combine mayonnaise, cheese, onion, eggs, salt, and pepper; stir until well combined. Add squash, stirring gently. Pour squash mixture into lightly greased 1½-quart casserole. Combine breadcrumbs and butter; spoon over squash mixture. Bake at 350° for 30 minutes.

Serves 6

Linda's Squash Soufflé

3	pounds yellow squash, diced
1	stick butter or margarine, softened
1	can evaporated milk
3	eggs
2	teaspoons flour
4	teaspoons salt
¼	cup sugar
1	rounded tablespoon baking powder
1 teaspoon pepper	
¾ cup chopped onion	

Cook squash in small amount of water until tender but not mushy. Drain well. Place in a bowl and mash lightly. Add butter. In a separate bowl, beat together remaining ingredients. Add squash. Stir well. Pour mixture into a buttered 8" x 12" glass baking dish. Bake at 425° for 30 minutes or until squash is golden brown and set.

For a change, oil then dust soufflé dish with Parmesan cheese instead of flour.

Serves 12

Butternut Squash Casserole

2 cups cooked butternut squash
3 eggs
¾ cup sugar
½ teaspoon coconut flavoring
3 cups crushed cornflakes
½ cup brown sugar
½ cup chopped pecans
⅔ cup margarine

Combine first 4 ingredients; mix well. Put in buttered casserole dish. Bake at 350° for 30 minutes. While casserole is baking, mix together remaining ingredients. Remove casserole from oven and sprinkle top with cornflake mixture. Return to oven and bake an additional 15 minutes.

Serves 6

Cheesy Tomato and Onion Casserole

4 cups (1 pound) thinly sliced onion
4 medium ripe tomatoes, peeled and sliced
1 teaspoon salt
¼ teaspoon pepper
½ teaspoon dried basil
2 cups (8 ounces) grated Cheddar cheese, divided
½ cup packaged breadcrumbs
3 tablespoons butter or margarine, melted

Lightly grease 1½-quart casserole. In 1 inch of boiling water, cook onion, covered, for 10 minutes then drain. In prepared casserole, layer in order, half of the tomatoes and onions. Sprinkle with half of salt, pepper, and basil. Top with half of cheese. Repeat. Toss breadcrumbs with melted butter and sprinkle over top of cheese. Bake uncovered at 350° for 30 to 45 minutes or until tomatoes are tender.

Serves 6

Hot Fruit Casserole

• *1 (14 ounce) can plums, drained*
• *1 (14 ounce) can pineapple chunks, drained*
• *1 (14 ounce) can apricots, drained*
• *1 (14 ounce) can sliced peaches, drained*
• *1 (10 ounce) can pitted black cherries, drained*
• *1 (14 ounce) can pear halves, drained*
• *2 bananas, sliced*
• *¾ cup brown sugar*
• *4 tablespoons butter*
• *½ cup chopped pecans*

Layer fruit in greased 3-quart casserole. Sprinkle liberally with brown sugar and dot with butter. Top with chopped pecans. Bake at 350° for 20–30 minutes until bubbly.

Serves 10–12

*Brush dirt off mush-
rooms with a soft brush
or damp cloth. If very
gritty, rinse as quickly
as possible under
running cold water so
they don't soak up
liquid.*

TOMATO PIE

1   box frozen pie crusts
3   large fresh tomatoes, unpeeled and sliced
1   pound fresh mushrooms, sliced
Salt
Pepper
Basil
Chives
½   cup chopped onions
1   cup mayonnaise
⅔   cup grated Cheddar cheese

Place 1 crust in glass pie dish. Lightly brown according to package
directions. Place sliced tomatoes around bottom and sides of
cooled crust, overlapping slices, and placing 1 or 2 slices in the
center. Sprinkle tomatoes with salt and pepper. Add a layer of
sliced mushrooms. Sprinkle basil and chives generously over
tomatoes and mushrooms. Add a light layer of chopped onions.
Repeat process, adding another layer of tomatoes, mushrooms,
seasonings, and onions. In a bowl, combine mayonnaise and
cheese and spread over the top of entire pie. Bake at 325° until
lightly browned and bubbly, about 30 minutes. Let cool for 5
minutes before serving.

Serves 6-8

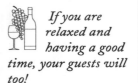

*If you are
relaxed and
having a good
time, your guests will
too!*

OCEAN POND TOMATOES

1   (16 ounce) can chopped tomatoes
1   (16 ounce) can tomato sauce
⅓   cup chopped bell pepper
½   cup chopped onion
1   cup chopped celery
½   teaspoon salt
1   teaspoon sugar
3   slices buttered toast, crumbled
1   cup shredded Cheddar cheese

Mix all ingredients, except cheese, and place in a greased baking
dish. Bake for 30 minutes at 350°. Remove from oven and top
with cheese. Bake for 20 more minutes at 350°.

Serves 6

Green Tomato Casserole

5 green tomatoes, sliced
1 cup chopped green onion
1 teaspoon salt
¼ teaspoon pepper
¼ teaspoon garlic powder
Lemon pepper
¾ cup grated Cheddar cheese
1 roll buttery round crackers, crushed
1 stick margarine or butter

Place sliced tomatoes in a buttered 13" x 9" x 2" casserole dish. Cover with green onions. Sprinkle with salt, pepper, and garlic powder. Sprinkle generously with lemon pepper. Top with grated cheese and crushed crackers. Dot with butter. Bake covered for 45 minutes at 400°. Bake uncovered an additional 10 minutes.

Serves 6-8

Marinated Vegetables

1 (17 ounce) can small baby peas, drained
1 (12 ounce) can shoe-peg corn, drained
1 (2 ounce) jar diced pimientos, drained
1 cup finely chopped onion
1 cup finely chopped celery
1 cup finely chopped green pepper
1 cup sugar
½ cup vinegar
¼ cup corn oil
1 teaspoon salt
1 teaspoon pepper
½ cup diced Cheddar cheese

In a bowl, mix together the first 6 ingredients. In a saucepan, mix together the remaining ingredients, except cheese. Bring mixture to boil and cook until sugar dissolves. Pour over vegetables. Add cheese. Refrigerate overnight.

Serves 8-10

Fried Green Tomatoes

- *green tomatoes*
- *salt*
- *black pepper*
- *cornmeal*
- *vegetable oil*

Wash tomatoes and pat dry. Cut tomatoes into ¼" slices. Sprinkle with salt and pepper. Dip each slice in cornmeal and lay on wax paper. Heat oil. Fry tomato slices until golden brown. Drain on paper towel. Serve hot.

CREAMY VEGETABLE MEDLEY

• *1 (16 ounce) package frozen cauliflower, carrots, and broccoli mix*
• *1 can cream of mushroom soup*
• *1 cup shredded Swiss cheese, divided*
• *⅓ cup sour cream*
• *¼ teaspoon pepper*
• *1 (4 ounce) jar pimientos*
• *1 (2.8 ounce) can onion rings, divided*

Cook vegetables for 5 minutes. Combine vegetables, soup, ½ cup cheese, sour cream, pepper, pimientos, and ½ can onion rings. Pour into a 1-quart casserole. Bake uncovered at 350° for 30 minutes. Top with remaining cheese and onion rings. Bake 5 minutes longer.

Serves 6

MIXED VEGETABLE CASSEROLE

1 (16 ounce) can French-style green beans, drained
1 (11 ounce) can shoe-peg corn, drained
1 cup fresh mushrooms or 1 (4-ounce) can mushrooms, drained
1 (10¾ ounce) can cream of celery soup
½ cup sour cream
½ cup chopped onions
½ cup grated Cheddar cheese
1 stick margarine, melted
1 roll buttery round crackers, crushed
½ cup sliced almonds

Combine green beans, corn, and mushrooms; place in an 8" x 12" baking dish. In a bowl, combine soup, sour cream, onions, and cheese. Pour on top of vegetables. In another bowl, combine crushed crackers, margarine, and almonds; sprinkle on top of entire dish. Bake uncovered at 350° for 40 minutes.

Serves 8

YAM PEANUT PUFFS

4 cups mashed yams
3 tablespoons butter or margarine
2 tablespoons brown sugar
½ teaspoon ground nutmeg
½ teaspoon ground cinnamon
½ teaspoon salt
⅛ teaspoon ground black pepper
1 egg, lightly beaten
2 apples, peeled, cored, and cut into 12 wedges
1 cup coarsely chopped peanuts
2 tablespoons melted butter or margarine

Combine first 8 ingredients. Mix well. Shape mixture around each of the 12 apple wedges. Roll each yam-covered apple wedge in peanuts. Place on a greased baking dish. Pour melted butter over wedges. Bake in preheated 350° oven for 25 to 30 minutes.

Serves 6

Zucchini Crescent Pie

4 cups unpeeled, thinly sliced zucchini
1 cup coarsely chopped onion
1 pound fresh mushrooms, sliced
½ cup margarine
2 teaspoons parsley flakes
¼ teaspoon oregano leaves
½ teaspoon salt
½ teaspoon pepper
¼ teaspoon garlic powder
2 eggs, beaten
8 ounces mozzarella cheese, shredded
2 teaspoons prepared mustard
1 (8 ounce) can refrigerated crescent dinner rolls

In a 10" skillet, cook zucchini, onion, and mushrooms in margarine until tender, about 10 minutes. Stir in parsley and seasonings. In a large bowl, blend eggs and cheese. Stir in vegetable mixture. Separate dough into 8 triangles. Place in ungreased 11" quiche pan or 10" pie pan. Press triangles over bottom and up sides to form crust. Spread crust with mustard. Pour vegetables evenly into crust. Bake at 375° for 18 to 20 minutes or until knife inserted in center comes out clean. Let stand 10 minutes before serving.

Serves 8

Julienne Vegetables

• ¾ pound zucchini, unpeeled and cut in ¼" julienne strips
• ¾ pound yellow squash, unpeeled and cut in ¼" julienne strips
• ¾ pound carrots, peeled and cut in ¼" julienne strips
• ½ cup unsalted butter, melted
• salt and pepper to taste

Arrange carrots in a vegetable steamer over 1" of boiling salted water. Place zucchini and yellow squash on top of carrots and steam until vegetables are tender-crisp. Place in a serving dish, toss with butter and season.

Serves 4

ZUCCHINI SAUTÉ

• 4 to 5 zucchini, sliced in ½" cubes
• 1 tablespoon olive oil or butter
• 2 large cloves garlic, minced
• 1 small onion, chopped
• 1 yellow or green bell pepper, cut into strips
• 1 tablespoon fresh lemon juice
• ½ teaspoon lemon pepper

Heat oil or butter in large skillet over medium-high heat. Add garlic, onion, and bell pepper; sauté 3 to 4 minutes. Add zucchini and sauté until crisp-tender, about 5 minutes. Add lemon juice and lemon pepper. Transfer to bowl and serve.

Serves 4–5

$\mathscr{P}$ARMESAN ZUCCHINI AND TOMATOES

1½ pounds zucchini
¼ cup all-purpose flour
1½ teaspoons salt, divided
1½ teaspoons dried oregano, divided
¼ teaspoon pepper
¼ cup olive oil
2 medium tomatoes, sliced
1 cup sour cream
½ cup grated Parmesan cheese

Lightly grease an 8" x 8" x 2" baking dish. Wash zucchini and cut crosswise into ¼" slices. In a medium bowl, combine flour with ½ teaspoon salt, ½ teaspoon oregano, and ¼ teaspoon pepper. Toss zucchini slices in seasoned flour and coat well. Heat oil in a large skillet. Sauté zucchini until golden brown, about 4 minutes on each side. Drain. Cover bottom of baking dish with zucchini. Top with tomato slices. Combine sour cream and remaining oregano; spread evenly over tomato slices. Sprinkle with Parmesan cheese. Bake at 350° for 30 to 35 minutes or until cheese is melted and zucchini is tender.

Serves 6

ENTRÉES

Melissa's Spinach Salad Quiche

1 deep-dish pie crust, baked
1 medium onion, chopped
6 slices bacon, cooked and crumbled
8 eggs, lightly beaten
½ cup sour cream
½ cup half-and-half
¼ teaspoon salt
⅛ teaspoon white pepper
Dash nutmeg
3 cups shredded fresh spinach, lightly packed
⅔ cup shredded mozzarella cheese
½ cup shredded Gruyère cheese

Cook bacon until crisp. Sauté onion in bacon drippings until tender. Remove from heat. Combine eggs, sour cream, half-and-half, salt, pepper, and nutmeg. Combine onion and spinach. Place the cheeses in the baked pie crust and top with spinach-onion mixture. Pour egg mixture evenly over the top. Bake at 300° for 45 to 50 minutes.

Serves 6–8

Menu Suggestion: Serve with seasonal fruits and Sesame Parmesan Rolls (page 120). Garnish quiche with salad tomatoes.

Don't forget music! Music can set the tone for the evening. Try different types of music at different times during the evening. For example, lively jazz may be perfect during cocktails and appetizers, while soothing classical music may be more appropriate during the meal. Make tapes to reflect these moods. Tapes and CD's are easier to manage than albums!

Tortilla Black Bean Casserole

2   cups chopped onion
1½ cups chopped green pepper
1   (14½ ounce) can chopped tomatoes
¾   cup picante sauce
2   garlic cloves, minced
2   (15 ounce) cans black beans
12   (6") corn tortillas
2   cups shredded Monterey Jack cheese, divided
2   medium tomatoes, sliced
2   cups shredded lettuce
1   green onion, sliced
½   cup sour cream

Combine onion, green pepper, undrained tomatoes, picante sauce, and garlic. Bring to boil; reduce heat and simmer, uncovered, 10 minutes. Stir in beans. Spread ⅓ of bean mixture on bottom of a 13" x 9" x 2" baking dish. Top with 6 tortillas, overlapping as necessary, and half of the cheese. Repeat layering process until all ingredients are used, saving ¼ cup of cheese for later use. Cover and bake at 350° for 30 minutes. Sprinkle remaining cheese and let stand for 10 minutes. Top with tomato slices, lettuce, green onions, and a dollop of sour cream. Cut into squares and serve.

Serves 4

Menu Suggestion: Serve with Mexican Cornbread (page 121) and Zingy Lemon Dessert (page 271).

Casseroles wrapped in aluminum foil, then in several layers of newspaper will stay hot for several hours in an insulated ice chest.

Chicken Breasts in Triple Mustard Sauce

8   skinless, boneless chicken breasts
Salt and pepper
Paprika
1   tablespoon butter
2   tablespoons vegetable oil
1   tablespoon whole grain mustard
1½ tablespoons Dijon mustard
1   teaspoon dry mustard
½   cup dry white wine
1   cup heavy cream, at room temperature

Sprinkle chicken with salt, pepper, and paprika. In a large skillet, heat butter and oil over medium heat. Cook chicken about 10 minutes, turning once. Reserve drippings, remove chicken to platter, and cover loosely with foil. Keep warm in 250° oven. In a small bowl, stir the 3 mustards together. Stir wine into drippings in skillet. Bring to boil over medium heat, scraping bottom of pan. Stir in mustards. Then whisk in cream. Bring to boil, stirring often, until thick, about 3 minutes. Pour sauce over chicken and serve.

Serves 8

Cajun Chicken

2   teaspoons salt
1   teaspoon paprika
¾   teaspoon red pepper
½   teaspoon onion powder
½   teaspoon thyme
¼   teaspoon white pepper
¼   teaspoon black pepper
¼   teaspoon garlic powder
1   whole fryer
3   medium onions, quartered

Mix together first 8 ingredients; rub on chicken, inside and out. Stuff cavity with quartered onions. Place chicken in large plastic bag and refrigerate overnight. Remove from bag and bake at 250°, uncovered, for 5 hours, basting frequently with juices. Cut into quarters and serve.

Serves 4

For a festive fall table, use a quilt for your tablecloth, a variety of antique spools for candle-holders, small pump-kins and butternut squash hollowed out for dips, and a variety of earthen-ware pottery for other foods.

Braised Chicken with Garlic and Spinach

½ pound fresh spinach
1 tablespoon olive oil
3 chicken breasts, skinned
3 chicken thighs, skinned
3 chicken legs, skinned
1 cup sliced carrots
10 cloves garlic, halved
½ cup canned salt-free chicken broth
¼ teaspoon pepper
¼ teaspoon salt
1 cup sliced yellow squash

Clean, stem, and tear spinach into bite-sized pieces. Heat oil in a large skillet over medium heat. Add chicken pieces and cook 5 minutes per side until browned, then add carrots, squash, and garlic. Cover, reduce heat, and cook 20 minutes, turning chicken once. Remove chicken, squash, and carrots with slotted spoon; set aside and keep warm. Cover and cook garlic 3 minutes more. Add broth, salt, pepper; bring to a boil. Cook uncovered 3 minutes or until reduced to ¼ cup. Blend until smooth. Set aside. Place a large Dutch oven over medium heat. Add spinach, cover and cook 3 minutes. (Do not add water.) Drain well. On serving platter, arrange chicken, squash, and carrots on top of spinach. Drizzle with garlic mixture.

Serves 6–8

CHICKEN ENCHILADAS

8   chicken breasts
1   celery stalk, chopped
1   teaspoon salt
1   (10 ounce) package frozen chopped spinach
1   medium onion, chopped
1   tablespoon butter
2   (10¾ ounce) cans cream of chicken soup
2   (8 ounce) cartons sour cream
¼   cup milk
1   cup shredded Cheddar cheese
Salt and pepper to taste
8   large flour tortillas
¾   cup shredded Colby cheese
¾   cup shredded Monterey Jack cheese
1   (4 ounce) can green chilies, drained and chopped

Place chicken, celery, and salt in a Dutch oven; cover with water
and bring to a boil. Cover, reduce heat, and simmer for 1 hour or
until tender. Bone chicken, dice, and set aside; reserve ¼ cup of
chicken broth. Cook spinach according to package directions.
Drain well and set aside. Sauté onion in butter until tender. Stir in
spinach and chicken; set aside. Combine 1 can soup, reserved
broth, 1 carton sour cream, milk, and Cheddar cheese in a large
bowl. Stir in chicken mixture, salt, and pepper; mix well. Spoon
mixture evenly down the center of each tortilla; roll up tightly.
Place tortillas seam-side down into a lightly greased 13" x 9" x 2"
baking dish. Combine remaining ingredients for sauce; spoon over
tortillas. Bake uncovered at 350° for 30 minutes.

Serves 4–6

*Menu Suggestion: A good appetizer to serve with this would be Tomato
Salsa (page 49) and tortilla chips.*

*If you do not
have enough
place settings,
borrow dishes from
friends and relatives.
Do not feel that all of
your dishes must
match! Some of the
most memorable tables
are created when the
hostess combines
different patterns and
styles. A unifying
theme or color will help
pull it all together!*

Ginger Chicken

1   teaspoon salt
1   teaspoon cornstarch
1   egg white
1   pinch pepper
2   tablespoons soy sauce
2   boneless chicken breasts, cut into small pieces
4   tablespoons oil, divided
⅓   cup diced onion
1   teaspoon ginger
1   teaspoon minced garlic
1   (8 ounce) can water chestnuts
1   (8 ounce) can bamboo shoots
1   cup fresh sliced mushrooms
1   teaspoon salt
½   cup chicken broth
4   teaspoons cornstarch
1   (10 ounce) package Chinese pea pods
½   cup cashews
Oyster sauce to taste (optional)

Combine first 5 ingredients. Place chicken in mixture and allow it to marinate for at least 2 hours or overnight. Remove chicken from marinade and stir-fry in 2 tablespoons hot oil in a wok or skillet. Remove chicken. Add 2 tablespoons of oil to pan. Brown onion, ginger, and garlic. Add remaining ingredients, including cooked chicken. Simmer until hot. Serve over rice.

Serves 2–4

Menu Suggestion: Serve with Mandarin Orange Salad (page 92), Oriental Cabbage (page 135), and Dixie Rolls (page 118).

Chicken Chutney Stir-Fry

1   tablespoon vegetable oil
4   skinless, boneless chicken breast halves, cut into strips
½   medium red bell pepper, cut into strips
1   cup thinly sliced carrots
1   tablespoon cornstarch
1   tablespoon soy sauce
½   cup chutney
6   ounces Chinese pea pods
2   cups cooked rice
¼   cup chopped peanuts

Stir-fry chicken, bell pepper, and carrots in oil for 5 to 7 minutes or until done. Mix cornstarch, soy sauce, and chutney. Stir into chicken. Cook and stir until thick. Stir in pea pods. Serve over hot rice. Sprinkle with peanuts.

Serves 4

Christmas Chicken

6   skinless, boneless chicken breasts (or whole chicken, cut up)
⅓   cup flour
1   teaspoon salt
4   tablespoons margarine
1½ cups fresh cranberries or whole berry cranberry sauce
¾   cup sugar
½   cup chopped onion
Zest of ½ orange
¾   cup orange juice
¼   teaspoon ground cinnamon
¼   teaspoon ground ginger

Pound chicken breasts and coat with mixture of flour and salt. Brown in melted margarine. Combine remaining ingredients in a separate saucepan and bring to boil. Stir to dissolve sugar. Pour over chicken. Cover and cook over low heat for 35 to 40 minutes or until chicken is tender. Serve with rice.

Serves 6

Christmas is a time when people often decide to stop watching their fat intake. There is no question that Christmas should be a joyous time of celebration and good food; but good food does not always mean high fat. This recipe offers a great opportunity to save a little fat while serving a scrumptious meal. Just substitute vegetable cooking spray for the 4 tablespoons of margarine and watch the recipe lose 4 to 6 grams of fat and 414 calories. A small change can make a big difference.

*Barbra Crumpacker,
Registered Dietitian*

Blue Cheese Chicken

4   skinless, boneless chicken breast halves
Salt and pepper
3   tablespoons butter, divided
1   tablespoon flour
½   cup chicken broth
½   cup milk
¼   cup heavy cream
¼   pound blue cheese, crumbled
4   slices cooked ham
½   cup chopped onion
½   cup dry white wine

Salt and pepper chicken to taste. Cook the chicken with 2 table-spoons butter in a skillet. Cook until golden brown. In another saucepan, heat 1 tablespoon butter with flour, broth, and milk, stirring with a whisk. Add cream and continue stirring for 5 minutes. Add cheese and stir until melted. Remove chicken from skillet, but keep warm. Heat ham on both sides. Remove ham to serving dish and place chicken on top of each piece. Keep warm. In skillet sauté onion until browned and add wine. Stir in the cheese mixture. Pour the sauce over chicken and serve.

Serves 4

Chicken with Tarragon Sauce

1   pound skinless, boneless chicken breasts, cubed
2   tablespoons margarine, divided
1   tablespoon all-purpose flour
1   cup milk
2   tablespoons chopped parsley
½   teaspoon dried tarragon
½   cup sour cream
1   tablespoon Dijon mustard
Cooked noodles

Prepared too much food? Refrigerate or freeze the excess. Buy pre-made crêpes and fill with leftover chicken. Cover with sauce and serve. Your family won't even realize they are eating leftovers!

Sauté chicken in 1 tablespoon of margarine until done. Arrange on platter and keep warm. Melt remaining margarine in skillet. Add flour, stirring constantly until smooth. Gradually add milk until thick and bubbly. Remove from heat; stir in remaining ingredients. Pour sauce over chicken. Serve over cooked noodles.

Serves 4

CARIBBEAN CHICKEN

1   hen or 2 small fryers
2   tablespoons butter
2   medium onions, finely chopped
1   clove garlic, minced
2   bell peppers, chopped
1   (4 ounce) can sliced mushrooms
1   (15 ounce) can tomato sauce
1   teaspoon curry powder
1   teaspoon thyme
Salt and pepper to taste
1   cup raisins
1   cup chicken broth (reserved from chicken)
1   cup chopped peanuts

Boil chicken until well done. Reserve broth. Remove skin and
bone. Cut into small pieces. Sauté onion and garlic in butter. Add
bell pepper, tomato sauce, mushrooms, raisins, and seasonings.
Add chicken broth; mix well. Add chicken; cover and simmer for 1
hour over low heat. Serve over rice. Garnish with chopped peanuts.

Serves 4-6

DIJON CHICKEN BREASTS

2   skinless, boneless chicken breasts, pounded thin
2   tablespoons butter or margarine
4   green onions, finely chopped
½   cup dry white wine
1   cup sour cream
2   tablespoons Dijon mustard

Melt butter; brown chicken and transfer to a warm platter. Add
green onions to skillet, stirring for 30 seconds. Add wine, stirring
to deglaze pan. Stir in sour cream and mustard; bring to a boil.
Add chicken breasts and simmer 10 to 15 minutes. Serve over
noodles.

Serves 2

*There are
many interest-
ing and stylish
alternatives to the
usual tablecloth.
Quilts, shawls, lace,
fabric remnants,
sheets, scarves, and
rugs are wonderfully
creative ways to top a
table. Look around
your home--the
possibilities are
endless!*

*Removing the skin
from chicken before
cooking is an easy way
to reduce fat and
calories.*

One teaspoon of fresh herbs equals ¼ teaspoon of dried herbs.

GARLIC AND TOMATO CHICKEN

4 skinless, boneless chicken breasts
Salt and pepper
1½ teaspoons olive oil (for brushing chicken)
1 tablespoon olive oil
1 small onion, minced
2 large cloves garlic, minced or pressed
½ cup chopped celery or ½ cup sliced fresh mushrooms
1 teaspoon chopped fresh rosemary or ¼ teaspoon dried rosemary
¼ teaspoon dried thyme
3 fresh tomatoes, peeled, seeded, and chopped or 1 can chopped tomatoes, drained
¼ cup light white wine
Zest of 1 lemon

Pound chicken breast to approximately ¼" thickness. Salt and pepper chicken, brush with olive oil and place in baking dish. Heat 1 tablespoon olive oil in a large heavy skillet and sauté onion and garlic, until onion is tender. Add celery (or mushrooms) and sauté for 3 to 4 minutes. Add herbs, tomatoes, and wine. Sauté over medium heat, stirring occasionally, for another 5 to 10 minutes. Remove from heat. Stir in lemon zest, and season to taste with salt and pepper. Spoon sauce over each breast, cover baking dish tightly with foil. Bake for 20 to 30 minutes at 375°. Serve over rice.

Serves 4

Menu Suggestion: Serve with Marinated Asparagus (page 129), crusty French bread, and Coconut Sour Cream Cake (page 241).

Southern Fried Chicken

2   cups buttermilk
2   eggs, beaten
2   tablespoons butter, melted
2   teaspoons paprika
1½ teaspoons salt
1   teaspoon pepper
1   3-pound skinned fryer, cut up
Additional pepper
All-purpose flour
Vegetable oil

Combine first 6 ingredients and mix well. Place chicken in large bowl and pour milk mixture over top. Refrigerate several hours. Remove chicken from liquid. Sprinkle lightly with additional pepper and dredge in flour. Let stand 5 minutes. In a large skillet heat 1" of oil to 325°. Add chicken and fry 30 minutes or until golden brown, turning once. Drain on paper towels.

Serves 4–6

Soaking chicken in buttermilk an hour or more before frying gives great flavor and tenderizes as well.

Chicken with Sun-Dried Tomatoes

4   skinless, boneless chicken breasts
3   tablespoons butter
Salt and pepper
1   large shallot, minced
½   cup heavy cream
½   cup dry white wine
⅛   teaspoon Cajun seasonings
¼   cup coarsely chopped sun-dried tomatoes

Heat butter in large skillet. Slice each chicken breast into 3 pieces. Sprinkle with salt and pepper, and sauté in butter until lightly browned. Remove chicken and sauté shallot until softened. Add remaining ingredients and bring to boil, stirring until sauce thickens slightly. Return chicken to skillet and simmer for about 20 minutes, coating with sauce. Serve with green fettuccine or other pasta.

Serves 4

Baskets can make wonderful serving pieces. Line with aluminum foil or plastic wrap to prevent leakage and then drape with pretty cloths.

GREEK LEMON CHICKEN

6 skinless, boneless chicken breasts
3 tablespoons olive oil, divided
1 teaspoon oregano
1 teaspoon marjoram
1 teaspoon lemon pepper
1 teaspoon parsley
1 teaspoon garlic salt
½ cup fresh lemon juice

Brush chicken on both sides with 2 tablespoons of olive oil. Mix together dry spices and herbs and sprinkle over both sides of chicken. Pour lemon juice over chicken and marinate for about 30 minutes, turning chicken occasionally. Heat remaining olive oil in ovenproof skillet. Remove chicken from marinade and brown, about 3 to 4 minutes per side. Pour remaining marinade over chicken and place skillet in 300° oven for 30 to 45 minutes.

Serves 6

PINKY'S CHICKEN

1 3-pound chicken, cut up
Salt and pepper
3 tablespoons butter
¼ pound sliced fresh mushrooms
¼ cup chopped onion
1 teaspoon minced garlic
2 tablespoons flour
1 cup dry red wine
½ cup chicken broth
1 bay leaf
1 teaspoon parsley
½ teaspoon thyme

Salt and pepper chicken. In a large skillet, cook the chicken pieces in butter for 15 minutes, turning after about 7 minutes. Cook until brown. Add mushrooms, onion, and garlic and stir. Sprinkle flour evenly over chicken. Add wine and broth. Bring to boil, stirring constantly. Cover and simmer 30 minutes. Transfer chicken to serving platter and garnish with mushrooms. Pour desired amount of sauce over chicken and serve.

Serves 4

CULTURAL CENTER CHICKEN CASSEROLE

1 small onion, diced
½ cup mayonnaise
2 (10¾ ounce) cans cream of chicken soup
½ cup drained and chopped water chestnuts
4 cups diced cooked chicken
1¾ cups chicken stock (reserved from chicken)
1 box wild rice with herbs
1 (2 ounce) jar pimientos, drained

Mix together all ingredients, except pimientos. Place in a greased 9" x 13" x 2" casserole. Sprinkle ingredients with pimientos. Bake for 1 hour at 350˚.

Serves 6

One pound of cooked meat equals 3 cups of diced meat. One 5 pound chicken equals 4 cups diced, cooked chicken. Use 1 teaspoon salt to season 1 pound of meat.

ORIENTAL VEGETABLES AND CHICKEN

3 pounds skinless, boneless chicken breasts, cut into strips
Vegetables (celery, mushrooms, snow peas, etc., about ½ cup each)
½ cup chicken broth
4 teaspoons cornstarch
1 teaspoon sugar
1 teaspoon sherry
2 teaspoons soy sauce
1 clove garlic, minced
2 tablespoons vegetable oil
¼ cup finely chopped green onions
Dash red pepper

Blend the broth with cornstarch, sugar, sherry, soy sauce, and garlic. Set aside. Heat oil in skillet or wok and add chicken. Stir fry on high heat until meat is no longer pink in center. Push chicken to side and add vegetables. Cook all ingredients for 1 minute. Stir broth mixture and add to chicken and vegetables. Cook another 5 minutes or until vegetables are crisp-tender. Serve over rice and sprinkle with green onions and red pepper.

Serves 6

Don't chop vegetables with the same knife just used on raw chicken. To prevent the spread of bacteria, any utensils or preparation surfaces that have come in contact with raw chicken need to be washed thoroughly with soap and water before using again.

CLARIFYING BUTTER
Our favorite way is to put the butter in a stainless steel bowl in a 200° oven. After an hour, skim off the crust on top. Put the bowl in the refrigerator. When the butter has resolidified, turn it out of the bowl. Scrape off and discard the white layer of milk solids (this is what burns during frying). Wrap and refrigerate the yellow layer of clarified butter until needed. One pound of butter yields about 14 ounces of clarified butter.

CHICKEN FLORENTINE WITH MORNAY SAUCE

⅓ (10-ounce) bag fresh spinach
½ cup butter, divided
¼ cup flour
2¾ cups milk
¾ teaspoon salt
¾ teaspoon pepper
⅛ teaspoon nutmeg
⅛ teaspoon cayenne pepper
½ cup grated Parmesan cheese
2 large tomatoes
1 pound fresh spinach pasta
2 tablespoons olive oil, divided
8 skinless, boneless chicken breast halves
½ cup flour seasoned with 1 teaspoon each: salt and pepper
¼ cup clarified butter (see instructions at left)
½ teaspoon salt
¼ teaspoon pepper

Wash spinach and cook in water until wilted. Rinse under cold water and drain. Squeeze dry and finely chop. Set aside. Melt ¼ cup butter. Whisk in ¼ cup flour and stir over low heat for 3 minutes. Slowly whisk in milk. Simmer until thick. Add the next five ingredients. Whisk until smooth, then add spinach and set aside. Cut tomatoes into 8 thick slices; set aside. Cook pasta, drain, and toss with 1 tablespoon olive oil. Set aside. Coat chicken breasts with seasoned flour and shake off excess. Heat the clarified butter in large skillet. Sauté the chicken over medium heat for 5 minutes, then turn and sauté for 3 to 5 minutes more. Remove chicken and keep warm in 200° oven. Melt remaining ¼ cup butter in a saucepan. Add pasta, salt, and pepper and combine well. Cover and reheat, stirring occasionally. Reheat spinach sauce separately. In another saucepan, briefly sauté both sides of tomato slices in remaining olive oil. To serve, arrange each chicken breast on a bed of pasta, cover with sauce and top with sautéed tomato slice.

Serves 8

Honey Mustard Chicken with Wine

4   skinless, boneless chicken breasts
Salt and pepper to taste
1   tablespoon olive oil
1   teaspoon butter
2   large cloves garlic, minced, or 1 teaspoon chopped garlic
1   teaspoon crumbled thyme
¼   cup white wine
1   tablespoon cornstarch or flour
¼   cup honey
¼   cup Dijon mustard

Salt and pepper chicken. Heat oil and butter in skillet. Rub chicken with garlic and thyme and brown in oil. Remove chicken. Deglaze skillet with wine and add cornstarch or flour. Combine honey and mustard; add to the skillet. Return chicken to skillet and simmer 25 minutes. Serve chicken with sauce.

Serves 4

Mediterranean Chicken

1   3-pound chicken, cut up
5   tablespoons olive oil
5   cloves garlic, minced
3   yellow onions, chopped
3   cups chopped tomatoes
1   (6-ounce) jar sliced green olives with pimientos, drained
1   tablespoon oregano
1   cup dry red wine
Salt and pepper

In a large skillet, brown chicken in oil. Drain and set aside on platter. In same skillet, sauté garlic and onions. Add tomatoes and olives and sauté until tomatoes are soft. Return chicken to skillet and add remaining ingredients. Salt and pepper to taste. Cover and simmer about 25 minutes.

Serves 4-6

For versatility, lean poultry is hard to beat. Three ounces of skinless, boneless chicken or turkey breast has ⅓ less fat than the same amount of lean beef. Like fish, chicken can be converted to low-fat dishes simply by the method used to prepare it. Compare this Honey Mustard Chicken recipe with 3 grams of fat and 140 calories to a fried chicken breast with 11 grams of fat and 221 calories.

To lower fat in a recipe, always start by asking if the fat is essential. In the Honey Mustard Chicken recipe, try vegetable cooking spray when browning instead of using oil or butter. The results will fool your taste buds but not your scale!

Barbra Crumpacker, Registered Dietitian

CHICKEN AND SAUSAGE JAMBALAYA

1	pound smoked sausage, thinly sliced
3	tablespoons olive oil
⅔	cup chopped green pepper
2	cloves garlic, minced
¾	cup chopped fresh parsley
1	cup chopped celery
2	(16-ounce) cans tomatoes
2	cups chicken broth
1	cup chopped green onions
1½	teaspoons thyme
2	bay leaves
2	teaspoons oregano
⅓	teaspoon red pepper
⅓	teaspoon black pepper
⅓	teaspoon chili powder
⅓	teaspoon garlic powder
2	cups raw long grain converted rice, washed
4	chicken breasts, cooked and cut into small pieces

In a large pot, sauté sausage until firm and remove with slotted spoon. Add olive oil to drippings and sauté green pepper, garlic, parsley, and celery for 5 minutes. Chop tomatoes and reserve the liquid. Add tomatoes, tomato liquid, chicken broth, and green onions. Stir in all spices. Add the rice and sausage. Cook over low heat for approximately 30 minutes until liquid has been absorbed by the rice. Occasionally stir so the rice does not stick. Stir in the chicken. Transfer to a 3-quart casserole dish. Bake at 350° for approximately 25 to 30 minutes.

Serves 10

Menu Suggestion: Serve with a Green Garden Salad, Garlic Italian Bread (page 102), and Bread Pudding with Whiskey Sauce (page 267).

Parmesan Chicken

4 skinless, boneless chicken breasts
8 green onions, chopped (½ tops, ½ onion)
8 ounces Monterey Jack cheese, shredded
⅓ cup butter, melted
1 tablespoon Worcestershire sauce
1 teaspoon chopped fresh garlic or ⅛ teaspoon garlic powder
¾ cup breadcrumbs
¼ cup grated Parmesan cheese
½ teaspoon salt
½ teaspoon pepper
4 tablespoons chopped fresh parsley
¼ teaspoon garlic salt

Pound chicken breasts flat and place a small portion of the onions in the center of each. Roll chicken up and secure with toothpicks. Add Worcestershire sauce and chopped garlic to melted butter and Monterey Jack cheese. Set aside. Mix breadcrumbs with Parmesan cheese, salt, pepper, parsley, and garlic salt. Dip chicken rolls in butter sauce and roll in bread crumbs mixture. Place chicken rolls in a greased baking dish. Pour remaining butter mixture over chicken. Bake at 350° for 40 minutes.

Serves 4

 Consider this alternative to place cards at your next luncheon or brunch: Top individual jars of home-made preserves with lacy doilies and secure with rubber bands. Calligraphy each guest's name on a decorative label and attach to each jar. Place the jars at each place setting according to your desired seating arrangement. Your guests will love it, and they will have a nice gift to take home.

Look for specials on plain clear glass or white plates; they will mix and match with almost any china and glassware.

Spicy Southwestern Oven-Fried Chicken

3 slices soft white bread, cut into 1" pieces
2 large cloves garlic, peeled
2 tablespoons yellow cornmeal
2 tablespoons pine nuts
3 tablespoons chopped fresh cilantro leaves
1½ teaspoons ground cumin
½ teaspoon dried oregano
½ teaspoon salt
¼ teaspoon cayenne pepper
Pinch ground cloves
2 teaspoons egg white, stirred
4 chicken breasts, halved and skinned
2 tablespoons Dijon mustard
1 tablespoon water
2 teaspoons honey
Salt and pepper to taste

Lightly grease a 15" x 10" jelly roll pan. Mix bread, garlic, corn-meal, pine nuts, cilantro, cumin, oregano, salt, cayenne, and cloves in a food processor until finely crumbled. Add egg white. Mix to moisten crumbs. Transfer crumbs to shallow pie plate. Combine mustard, water, and honey in small bowl. Spread mustard mixture over each piece of chicken. Season with salt and pepper. Dip in crumb mixture to coat with crumbs. Gently pat crumbs in place. Place chicken in prepared pan. Bake at 400° until crisp and brown, about 30 minutes.

Serves 4

Orange-Glazed Cornish Hens

¾ cup orange juice
½ cup orange honey
¼ cup soy sauce
2 tablespoons Grand Marnier or brandy
2 tablespoons minced orange peel
3 large cloves garlic, minced
1 tablespoon minced fresh ginger
2 teaspoons sesame oil
2 (1½-pound) Cornish hens
3 oranges, peeled and sectioned
Sesame seeds

Mix first 8 ingredients in large bowl. Add hens, skin side down. Cover and refrigerate 24 hours. Transfer hens to shallow baking pan. Pour marinade in small, heavy saucepan and boil for 12 minutes, stirring constantly. Brush hens entirely with reduced marinade. Arrange hens, skin side up, in baking pan. Roast 50 minutes at 400°. Baste. Cook 10 minutes longer. Reduce oven heat to 350°. Baste. Sprinkle with sesame seeds and roast 10 minutes longer. Serve with orange sections.

Serves 2–4

Stuffed Cornish Hens

2   tablespoons finely chopped onion
⅓   cup long-grain rice, uncooked
6   tablespoons butter or margarine, melted
1   tablespoon lemon juice
½   cup cream of celery soup, undiluted
1   teaspoon chives
1   teaspoon parsley flakes
¾   cup water
1   chicken bouillon cube
2   (1 to 1¼ pound) Cornish hens
Salt and pepper

Sauté onion and rice in 2 tablespoons butter until onion is transparent and rice is golden, about 5 minutes. Add lemon juice, soup, chives, parsley, water, and bouillon cube; bring to boil. Cover, reduce heat to medium-low, and cook for 25 minutes. Remove giblets from hens. Rinse hens and pat dry. Sprinkle cavities with salt and pepper. Stuff hens with rice mixture and close cavities; secure with wooden toothpicks. Place hens breast side up in shallow pan, brush with melted butter. Cover and bake 1 hour at 375°. Uncover and bake 30 minutes more, basting frequently with butter.

Serves 2

Menu Suggestion: Serve with Tomato Aspic (page 84), Artichoke and Spinach Casserole (page 129), and Butter Dips (page 120).

Jazzy Chicken Livers

1½ pounds chicken livers
2 tablespoons olive oil
¾ cup chopped onion
½ cup chopped celery
¾ cup diced green peppers
½ cup chopped shallots
2 cups canned tomatoes
1 bay leaf
1 tablespoon pepper flakes
Salt and pepper to taste
⅔ cup oil
1 tablespoon butter
½ teaspoon rosemary
Cooked rice

Sauté onion, celery, peppers, and shallots in olive oil until onion is transparent. Add tomatoes, bay leaf, pepper flakes, salt, and pepper. Boil 10 minutes. Set aside and keep warm. Heat oil in large skillet; add livers. Fry until crisp, about 2 to 3 minutes. Drain on paper towels. Clean out skillet. Add butter, livers, and rosemary and heat 1 minute. Place rice on plate, add livers, then cover with sauce.

Serves 4

 You can pour six to eight glasses of wine from a normal-sized bottle (750 ml). Many guests might only want a glass or two, but over the course of dinner some guests might consume 5 or 6 glasses from aperitif to dessert wine. To be sure to have enough, plan on ½ to 1 bottle per person.

Breaded Veal with Lemon and Mushrooms

1   pound fresh mushrooms, sliced
1   clove garlic, chopped
1   stick butter, melted
3   tablespoons grated Parmesan cheese
1   cup Italian breadcrumbs
½   teaspoon salt
¼   teaspoon pepper
3   tablespoons olive oil
6   veal cutlets
Juice of 2 large lemons

Sauté mushrooms and garlic in 3 tablespoons of melted butter and set aside. Mix Parmesan cheese, breadcrumbs, salt, and pepper. Dip veal in remaining melted butter and roll in bread crumb mixture. Brown veal in skillet with olive oil. Transfer veal to baking dish; top with mushrooms. Pour lemon juice over veal and mushrooms. Bake at 350° for 20 to 30 minutes.

Serves 6

Veal Chops Provençal

3   tablespoons olive oil
4   1" veal loin chops (about 2 pounds)
1   green bell pepper, cut into strips
1   large clove garlic, minced
1   (16 ounce) can Italian plum tomatoes, chopped, with juice
     reserved
½   cup dry white wine
6   large oil-packed sun dried tomatoes, drained and chopped
1½   teaspoons oregano
Salt and pepper

Heat oil in large skillet over high heat. Season veal with pepper on both sides. Cook veal until brown, about 5 minutes per side. Transfer to a plate. In same skillet, sauté green pepper and garlic for about 1 minute. Add tomatoes, reserved juice, wine, sun-dried tomatoes, and oregano. Bring to a boil, scraping up browned bits. Cook until thickened, about 10 minutes; stir occasionally. Return veal to skillet and heat through. Season with salt and pepper. Place veal on platter and spoon sauce over.

Serves 4

Sauce Tips

• *If a sauce or gravy is lumpy, process in a blender until smooth.*
• *If a sauce is too thick, gradually add a little more liquid, stirring constantly.*
• *If the sauce is too thin, add 2 beaten egg yolks to which a small amount of the hot sauce has been added, and cook for another 2 minutes.*
• *If an egg-based sauce begins to separate, add a tablespoon of ice water and whisk vigorously.*

Veal with Shrimp and Crabmeat

12 veal cutlets
1 teaspoon salt
1 teaspoon pepper
3 tablespoons flour
1 stick butter
1 tablespoon olive oil
2 tablespoons chopped green onions
½ cup dry white wine
1 cup heavy cream
½ pound fresh mushrooms, sliced
2 tablespoons lemon juice
2 tablespoons chopped parsley
¼ pound shrimp, cooked and peeled
½ pound fresh lump crabmeat

Pound veal until ¼" thick. Combine salt, pepper, and flour. Dredge cutlets. Heat 3 tablespoons of butter with olive oil. Sauté cutlets 2 minutes on each side. Remove veal; keep warm. Sauté green onions in pan. Remove from heat and add wine. Scrape brown bits from bottom. Add cream. Return to heat and let sauce thicken about 4 minutes. Add mushrooms and simmer for 3 minutes. Add lemon juice and parsley. Pour over veal. In another skillet, heat remaining butter, shrimp, and crabmeat. Spoon over veal.

Serves 6

THE THERMOMETER KNOWS

Cooking timetables are simply guides; actual cooking time will vary with individual cuts. Use the internal temperature to determine doneness.

BEEF, LAMB
140° F.
(rare - bacterial risk)

160° F. (medium)

170° F. (well-done)

PORK
160° F.
Crown roast
160-170° F.
Boston Butt

POULTRY
180° F.

170° F.
Poultry Breasts

SMOKED PORK/ HAM
160° F.

VEAL
170° F.

GROUND MEAT & MEAT MIXTURE
Chicken, Turkey
170° F.

Beef, Pork, Veal, Lamb
160° F.

Sausage Pizzas

2   tablespoons olive oil
1   small zucchini, diced
¾   cup diced Kielbasa sausage (about 4 ounces)
4   mushrooms, sliced
¼   cup oil-packed sun-dried tomatoes, drained and chopped
1   teaspoon dried basil
1   teaspoon oregano
2   small pre-made pizza crusts, fresh or frozen
¼   cup pizza sauce
¼   cup shredded Parmesan cheese
¼   cup shredded mozzarella cheese
2   ounces goat cheese, crumbled

Heat oil in skillet over medium-low heat. Add zucchini, sausage, and mushrooms. Sauté until tender, about 5 minutes. Add tomatoes and sauté 3 minutes longer. Remove skillet from heat, stir in basil and oregano. Arrange pizza crusts on cookie sheet. Spread half of pizza sauce on each crust. Sprinkle each crust with half of Parmesan cheese. Divide vegetables and sausage mixture between the 2 crusts. Top each with half of the mozzarella and goat cheeses. Bake at 450° until cheese is melted, about 8 to 10 minutes.

Serves 2

Sausage and Apple Casserole

2   pounds ground sausage
9   slices bread
2   apples, sliced
¾   teaspoon dry mustard
9   eggs, beaten
1½ cups grated sharp Cheddar cheese
3   cups milk

Brown sausage in skillet; drain, saving drippings. Place sausage in lightly greased 13" x 9" x 2" casserole dish. Remove crusts from bread and cut into cubes. Sauté apple slices in reserved sausage drippings. Combine apples and other ingredients. Pour over sausage. Cover dish and refrigerate overnight. Bake, covered, at 350° for 30 minutes. Remove cover and bake another 30 minutes.

Serves 8

BANKER'S RED BEANS AND RICE

1 pound red beans
2 quarts water
1 meaty ham bone or a thick slice of pork
1 pound hot sausage, thinly sliced
2 cups chopped onion
2 celery stalks, chopped
1 bunch green onions, chopped
1 green pepper, chopped
4 bay leaves
Pinch of thyme
Salt and pepper to taste
Hot sauce
Rice

Rinse beans thoroughly. Place in a Dutch oven and add water to cover. Place over medium heat and add next 8 ingredients. Bring to a boil, reduce heat, and simmer 3 hours. Using wooden spoon, mash ⅓ to ½ of beans against side of pan until smooth. Season with salt, pepper, and hot sauce to taste. Serve over freshly cooked rice.

Serves 8–10

For a pretty, simple center-piece, float a candle in a pretty crystal bowl. Purchase clear plastic discs with wicks from a florist or craft store. Fill your bowl with water and top with ½" clear oil. Add the candle. It's also pretty to float flowers in with the candle!

BLACK-EYED PEAS AND SAUSAGE

1   (16 ounce) package dried black-eyed peas
1   ham hock or ham bone
1   cup diced celery
1   cup diced onion
1   tablespoon savory seasoning
3   large cloves garlic, diced
Salt and pepper to taste
2   pounds mild or hot sausage
4   large bell peppers, coarsely chopped
4   large tomatoes, chopped
10 cups cooked rice
Red vinegar
Hot pepper sauce
Soy sauce

Let peas soak overnight. Bring peas to a full boil, then pour peas in a colander, and rinse. Fill a large stock pot ¾ full of water. Add peas, ham hock or bones, celery, onion, savory seasoning, garlic, salt, and pepper. Cook until tender. While peas are cooking, brown the sausage and cook rice. To serve, make a bed of rice on a large platter, hollowing out the middle. Place drained peas in the bed of rice. Spoon the sausage on top of peas. Cover the remaining rice with the bell pepper and place tomatoes on the top, covering the peas and sausage. Sprinkle with green onions. Offer remaining ingredients as condiments when serving.

Serves 16

MANICOTTI WITH BEEF

1   (15 ounce) container ricotta cheese
1   (8 ounce) package shredded mozzarella cheese
¼   cup grated fresh Parmesan cheese
2   tablespoons chopped parsley
⅛   teaspoon black pepper
1   pound ground beef
1   (8 ounce) box manicotti shells
1   (15 ounce) bottle marinara sauce
¼   cup grated Parmesan cheese

Mix first 5 ingredients; set aside. Brown ground beef, drain and cool. Add to cheese mixture; set aside. Prepare manicotti shells according to package directions. Stuff shells with beef and cheese mixture and place in baking dish. Cover with sauce and sprinkle with Parmesan cheese. Bake at 350° for 25 minutes or until bubbly.

Serves 6

MARTINI STEW

2   pounds stew meat, dredged in flour
2   onions, sliced in rings
1½ cups sliced fresh mushrooms
1½ cups canned tomatoes
2   cloves garlic, pressed
1   (10¾ ounce) can consommé
1   teaspoon oregano
½   cup gin
⅓   cup dry vermouth

Layer meat and vegetables in a roasting pan. Combine remaining ingredients; pour over meat and vegetables. Cover and bake at 325° for 2½ hours. Serve over buttered noodles or pasta.

Serves 6

When you think Italian, you think cheese--and that means FAT. But with the availability of lower fat and non-fat cheeses, it is easy to transform almost any Italian dish into a heart-healthy alternative. Using non-fat ricotta and part-skim mozzarella cheese will leave you feeling satisfied without the fat. The new ultra-lean ground beef has only 8 grams of fat per 4 ounces versus 12 grams for the same amount of ground round. Decrease the amount of meat in a recipe by adding some fresh mushrooms. The consistency will go unchanged but the calories will not.

Barbra Crumpacker, Registered Dietitian

Texas Hash

• *1 pound ground beef*
• *1 cup chopped onions*
• *½ cup chopped bell pepper*
• *1 (16 ounce) can tomatoes, undrained*
• *3 tablespoons uncooked rice*
• *salt and pepper to taste*

Brown ground beef, onion, and bell pepper in skillet; drain fat. Add tomatoes, rice, salt, and pepper. Stir together and cut up tomatoes. Transfer ingredients to a covered casserole dish and bake at 350° for 30 to 40 minutes or until rice is tender.

Serves 4

Chili Bean Tacos

1 pound ground beef
½ cup chopped green peppers
¼ cup chopped onion
1 (1 pound) can red kidney beans, drained
1 tablespoon Worcestershire sauce
1 tablespoon chili powder
½ cup mayonnaise
Shredded lettuce
6 English muffins, split and toasted
Cheddar cheese, shredded

Brown first 3 ingredients in skillet; drain fat. Add beans, Worcestershire sauce, chili powder, and mayonnaise. Heat thoroughly. Arrange lettuce over toasted muffins. Spoon meat mixture onto lettuce and sprinkle with cheese.

Serves 6

Mama's Famous Meat Loaf

1 pound ground beef
½ pound ground pork
2 slices white bread, torn into small pieces
2 eggs, beaten
½ cup milk
¼ cup finely chopped onion
¼ cup finely chopped bell peppers
Salt and pepper to taste
3 bacon strips, uncooked
1 (18 ounce) bottle smoked barbecue sauce

Mix meats with bread. In a separate bowl, combine eggs, milk, onion, peppers, salt, and pepper. Pour into meat mixture and mix together with hands. Shape into loaf and place in casserole dish. Lay several strips of bacon over loaf; cover with barbeque sauce. Bake at 350° for 1 hour.

Serves 4–6

CHILI ST. GEORGE

1½ pounds ground chuck
1 pound sausage
½ pound bacon, chopped
¼ cup whiskey
1 tablespoon olive oil
1 tablespoon butter
3 medium onions, chopped
3 cloves garlic, pressed
1 bell pepper, chopped
2 (4 ounce) cans mild green chilies, chopped and drained
2 (14½ ounce) cans tomatoes
1 (10¾ ounce) can tomato purée
¼ cup peanut butter
1 tablespoon grape jelly
5 tablespoons cumin seed, ground
1 tablespoon oregano
1 tablespoon Worcestershire sauce
2 tablespoons pickapeppa sauce
1 teaspoon bottled brown bouquet sauce
2 teaspoons salt
2 teaspoons ground pepper
1 (15½ ounce) can kidney beans, drained

Brown the first 3 ingredients separately and drain fat. Deglaze skillets with whiskey and combine all meats in a large pot. In separate pan, sauté the next 6 ingredients and add to the large pot. Add remaining ingredients and simmer slowly for several hours.

Serves 6–8

When preparing bacon for a large family or crowd, place it in a pan and bake it at 300° to 350° for about 10 minutes. It will be evenly crisp and delicious.

Dress up a plain hamburger! Shape hamburger patties around a flattened ball of cheese (use soft cheese like Roquefort or cottage cheese mixed with chopped chives) or put cooked vegetables in the center of patty. Cook hamburger patties as usual, deglazing the skillet after patties are cooked with water or wine. Pour sauce over patties and serve.

Beef Medallions in Sherry Mushroom Sauce

6   slices beef tenderloin, ½" thick
½   teaspoon salt
⅛   teaspoon pepper
1   stick butter
¼   pound fresh mushrooms, sliced
2   tablespoons chopped green onion
½   cup dry sherry
1   tablespoon brandy

Season tenderloin with salt and pepper. In a skillet, melt butter over high heat. Add tenderloin and cook until done, about 2 minutes per side. Remove to a platter and keep warm. Add mushrooms and green onions to skillet and sauté for 2 minutes. Add sherry and cook over high heat until liquid is reduced to ¼ cup. Add brandy; pour over meat. Serve.

Serves 4

Beef Tenderloin with Mustard Sauce

5   pounds beef tenderloin
Soy sauce
Worcestershire sauce
Garlic salt
4   tablespoons Dijon mustard
1   teaspoon dry mustard
3   tablespoons sugar
2   tablespoons white vinegar
½   cup light vegetable oil
1   small bunch fresh chopped dill

Rub tenderloin with soy sauce, Worcestershire sauce, and garlic salt. Let marinate for at least 1 hour. Bake uncovered for 15 minutes at 450°. Turn oven down to 350° and bake another 15 minutes. Remove from oven, cover with foil then bake for another 15 minutes. While meat is cooking, prepare mustard sauce by mixing together remaining ingredients. Spoon sauce over tenderloin and serve.

Serves 10

Boeuf Bourguignon

¼ pound bacon
3 pounds stewing beef
Peanut oil
4 cups dry red wine
2 cups beef broth
2 tablespoons tomato paste
5 cloves garlic, pressed
½ teaspoon thyme
2 bay leaves
Salt
1 pound fresh mushrooms, sliced, sautéed in butter
24 pearl onions, peeled, chopped, and browned in butter
Roux (½ cup flour browned in ½ cup butter)
8 baby carrots
Parsley, chopped for garnish

Sauté bacon lightly and remove from skillet. Discard drippings. Add the beef and a dash of oil; brown rapidly. Place meats in a large casserole dish. Add wine, broth, tomato paste, garlic, thyme, bay leaves, and a dash of salt to casserole dish. Deglaze skillet with a shot of red wine and add this to casserole. Bake at 350° for 2 to 3 hours. When beef is tender, add mushrooms, onions, and carrots. Continue to cook for 30 minutes. Thicken with roux.

Serves 8–10

Menu Suggestion: Serve with Garden Vegetable Rice Salad (page 85), Broccoli Balls (page 133), Quick Mayonnaise Rolls (page 120), and Aunt Ginger's Chocolate Pie (page 278).

After meat or other food has been cooked in a sauté pan or skillet, a lot of flavor is trapped in the browned bits which stick to the pan. Deglazing is a method of capturing that flavor by heating a small amount of liquid in the pan, then stirring and scraping to release the browned bits. This can then be used as a base for sauce or gravy.

A good way to reduce calories in meat dishes is to trim away visible fat before cooking the meat.

Wrap lettuce leaves around rare beef before reheating to keep it rare.

FILET MIGNON WITH RED WINE SAUCE

3 cups dry red wine
3 tablespoons cognac
3 green onions, chopped
1 teaspoon thyme
6 (6 ounce) filet mignon steaks
4 cups beef stock or canned broth
4 tablespoons olive oil
5 tablespoons butter, cut into pieces
Salt and pepper to taste

Combine first 4 ingredients in a large bowl. Place steaks in 2 glass baking dishes. Pour marinade over meat, cover dishes, and refrigerate overnight. Remove steaks from marinade and pat dry. Transfer marinade to a heavy, large saucepan. Boil until reduced to 1 cup, about 20 minutes. Add beef broth and boil about 20 minutes; set aside. Divide olive oil between 2 large skillets and place over high heat. Season steaks with salt and pepper. Add 3 steaks to each skillet and brown on both sides. Reduce heat to medium-high and cook to desired doneness. Transfer steaks to plates and keep warm. Add half of sauce to each skillet and bring to a boil, scraping up brown bits. Add butter and stir until melted. Spoon sauce over steaks and serve.

Serves 6

HOW MUCH MEAT TO BUY PER SERVING

• *Boneless meat – ¼ pound per serving*
• *Medium amount of bone – ⅓ to ½ pound per serving*
• *Large amount of bone – ¾ to 1 pound per serving*

Bourbon and Praline Ham

8 pounds pre-cooked ham
1½ cups bourbon
2 tablespoons butter
1 cup maple syrup
½ cup brown sugar
½ cup finely chopped pecans
½ cup pecan halves

Remove fat from ham and score the skin; rub with bourbon. Marinate for 3 hours, basting every ½ hour, if possible. Pour off excess bourbon, reserving it for sauce. Bake ham, skin-side up, for 2 hours at 325°. In a saucepan, melt butter. Stir in reserved bourbon marinade, syrup, sugar, and chopped pecans; bring to a boil. Pour over ham. Decorate with pecan halves and bake an additional 15 to 20 minutes.

Serves 12

South Carolina Chopped Barbecue

4 pounds pork shoulder with bone
4 cloves garlic, whole and peeled
3 cups apple cider vinegar, divided
12 peppercorns
1 teaspoon cayenne pepper
½ teaspoon salt

In a Dutch oven, combine the pork, garlic, 1 cup vinegar, and peppercorns. Add enough water to cover. Bring liquid to boil over moderately high heat, skimming the froth as it rises to the surface. Simmer, partially covered, for about 3 hours, or until very tender. Meanwhile, prepare the sauce by combining the remaining vinegar, salt, and cayenne pepper in a covered container, shaking vigorously to blend. Remove pork from liquid to a roasting pan (on a rack) and baste thoroughly with sauce. Roast meat for about 3 hours at 350°. Continue basting every 15 minutes and turn the meat after 1½ hours. Remove pork from oven and chop very fine. Baste with more sauce. Mixture should be moist, but not juicy.

Serves 4–6

Easy Garlic Pork Roast

• *2 pounds boneless pork loin roast*
• *3 tablespoons minced or chopped garlic*
• *garlic pepper to taste*

Rub garlic over entire roast. Sprinkle with garlic pepper. Place in baking dish, uncovered. Insert meat thermometer and roast in 350° oven until thermometer reads 155° to 160°, about 45 minutes to 1 hour. Let stand 5 minutes before serving.

Serves 6

Roasted Pork

1   (4 pound) boneless pork loin roast
1   tablespoon minced garlic
½   cup chopped bell pepper
½   cup chopped onion
1   tablespoon oil
3   tablespoons butter
2   teaspoons black pepper
1½ teaspoons salt
1   teaspoon white pepper
1   teaspoon cayenne pepper
1   teaspoon paprika
1   teaspoon thyme
½   teaspoon dry mustard

Combine and sauté all ingredients, except pork roast, in butter and oil for about 4 minutes. Place roast in baking pan fat side up. Using a sharp knife, make several deep slits in the meat to form pockets. Stuff pockets with garlic mixture, saving some to rub over roast by hand. Bake uncovered at 275° for 3 hours. Turn heat to 425° and bake an additional 15 minutes to brown roast on top.

Serves 6

Spicy Chops

4   lamb chops, at least 1" thick
¼   cup lemon juice
¼   cup olive oil
2   tablespoons grated onion
2   teaspoons chili powder
1   teaspoon ground ginger
1½ teaspoons curry powder
1   teaspoon salt
1   clove garlic, crushed

Mix lemon juice with other ingredients and pour over chops. Place in airtight container; refrigerate 3 hours. Remove chops from marinade and place in shallow roasting pan. Broil for 20 minutes, or until done, turning once. Baste frequently.

Serves 4

Lamb Chops Made Simple

• *2 loin lamb chops*
• *black pepper*
• *Dijon mustard*
• *bread crumbs*
• *1 teaspoon rosemary*

Sprinkle lamb chops with pepper. Coat both sides of chops with Dijon mustard. Combine bread crumbs with rosemary. Roll lamb chops in crumbs. Bake at 400° for 20 minutes.

Serves 2

Pork Medallions in Creamy Peppercorn Sauce

1½ pounds pork tenderloin, cut into 1" thick medallions
Salt and pepper to taste
3 tablespoons butter, divided
3 shallots, minced
½ cup dry vermouth
1½ cups chicken broth
1 tablespoon green peppercorns in brine, drained
½ teaspoon dried thyme
2 teaspoons Dijon mustard
⅓ cup whipping cream

Flatten pork with palm of hand; sprinkle with salt and pepper. In a large skillet, melt 2 tablespoons butter over medium high heat. Add pork and cook until brown, about 3 minutes per side. Transfer to a plate and set aside. In same skillet, melt remaining 1 tablespoon butter. Add shallots and sauté 2 minutes. Add vermouth and boil about 5 minutes. Add broth, peppercorns, and thyme. Boil until reduced to ¾ cup, about 10 minutes. Whisk in mustard, then cream. Season with salt and pepper. Return pork to skillet and simmer about 3 minutes.

Serves 4

Rack of Lamb with Mustard Sauce

1 (5 pound) rack of lamb
Salt and pepper to taste
4 tablespoons Dijon mustard
½ teaspoon salt
½ teaspoon pepper
4 tablespoons brown sugar
2 tablespoons soy sauce
2 tablespoons olive oil
⅓ cup lemon juice

Salt and pepper lamb. Set aside. Combine remaining 7 ingredients in a small saucepan and heat. Baste lamb with sauce. Bake at 325° in a Dutch oven until meat thermometer reads 160°, approximately 3½ hours. Baste lamb with sauce frequently.

Serves 10

Mint Sauce

• *1 cup sugar*
• *½ cup sherry vinegar*
• *1 tablespoon raspberry vinegar*
• *5 tablespoons chopped fresh mint leaves*
• *2 tablespoons hot pepper jelly*

Combine sugar and vinegars and bring to a boil over medium heat. Reduce heat and cook 5 minutes, stirring occasionally. Remove from heat; add chopped mint leaves, cover and let stand 5 minutes. Add pepper jelly. Serve warm with lamb.

Try making your own "pastry scallop shells" to use for serving seafood dishes. Lightly oil 4" or 5" scallop shells and line with your favorite homemade pastry--or use a prerolled pastry from the refrigerator case. Cover dough with pie weights. Bake at 375° for 10 minutes. Two crusts will make 6 pastry shells. Fill as desired.

CRABMEAT IN PASTRY SHELLS

½   pound sliced mushrooms
3   tablespoons butter
3   tablespoons flour
1   cup chicken broth
½   cup cream
1   pound lump crabmeat
½   cup grated Parmesan cheese
½   teaspoon salt
¼   teaspoon pepper
¼   teaspoon paprika
2   tablespoons sherry
6   pastry shells

Sauté mushrooms in butter. Remove mushrooms and set aside. Stir flour into butter until well blended. Stir in chicken broth and cream. When sauce is boiling, add crabmeat and mushrooms. Bring to boil again; add seasonings and Parmesan cheese. Remove from heat, add sherry and serve in pastry shells.

Serves 6

BLUE CRAB BROCCOLI CASSEROLE

1   pound crabmeat (fresh or frozen)
16 ounces chopped broccoli (fresh or frozen)
3   tablespoons chopped pimientos
1   egg
¼   cup mayonnaise
1   tablespoon prepared mustard
½   cup crushed corn flakes

Remove all shell particles from crabmeat. Spread broccoli and pimientos in bottom of greased 2-quart casserole dish. Beat egg, mayonnaise, and mustard together. Stir crabmeat into mixture and pour over broccoli. Top with corn flakes. Bake in 375° oven for approximately 20 minutes or until bubbly and golden brown.

Serves 4

CRAB FRITTERS

1 shallot, peeled and minced
1 stick butter
1 tablespoon flour
2 eggs, lightly beaten
1 pound lump crabmeat, shell bits removed
3 scallions, chopped
1 cup breadcrumbs
1 tablespoon parsley
1 tablespoon dill
1 tablespoon salt
1 tablespoon pepper

Sauté shallot in 1 tablespoon butter. Gently mix all remaining ingredients, except remaining butter, in large bowl. In large frying pan, heat remaining butter until foamy. With hands, form crabmeat mixture into small, thick pancakes. Sauté in butter 3 to 4 minutes on each side. Serve with lime wedges and cocktail sauce.

Serves 4

CRAB IMPERIAL

1 green pepper, finely chopped
2 pimientos
2 eggs or ½ cup cholesterol-free substitute
1 cup mayonnaise
1 tablespoon salt
1 tablespoon mustard
½ teaspoon white pepper
3 pounds fresh lump crabmeat
Dash paprika

In a bowl, combine all ingredients, except crabmeat and paprika. Mix well. Add crabmeat. Stir gently so as not to break up pieces of crab. Spoon mixture into 8 cleaned and rinsed crab shells or 8 individual casseroles. Spread top with a thin layer of additional mayonnaise. Sprinkle with paprika. Bake at 350° for 15 to 18 minutes. Serve hot or cold.

Serves 4-6

 Consider serving your next seafood supper alfresco by the pool. Scatter round tables for 4 and cover with blue and white table cloths. Place a large round glass bowl at the center of each table. Add gravel, pretty seashells, water and 3-4 goldfish to each bowl. Scatter additional seashells, starfish, and coral around the bowls and at each place setting. Add votive candles and serve the meal on simple pottery plates.

CHINESE CRABMEAT WITH CELERY CABBAGE

1   pound head of celery cabbage
4   tablespoons oil
½   teaspoon salt
1   cup chicken broth
1   slice ginger root, finely chopped
1   scallion, finely chopped
1   cup fresh crabmeat, cooked
1   tablespoon sherry
1   tablespoon light soy sauce
¼   teaspoon sugar
1   tablespoon cornstarch, dissolved in 1 tablespoon water
Pepper

Wash and cut cabbage into quarters. Discard heart. Cut quarters
into pieces 2 inches long. Heat 2 tablespoons of oil in wok over
high heat. Stir-fry cabbage until soft. Add salt and ½ cup of broth.
Cook 3 minutes and remove. Heat 2 tablespoons of oil in wok
over medium heat. Add ginger and scallion. Stir fry until there is
an aroma (about 1 minute). Increase heat to high. Pour in
crabmeat. Stir-fry 1 minute. Add sherry, soy sauce, and sugar.
Remove from wok. Return cabbage to wok. Pour crabmeat mixture over cabbage. Add ½ cup broth thickened with dissolved
cornstarch. Sprinkle with pepper to taste.

Serves 4-6

FISH AND VEGETABLE DINNER

4   orange roughy fillets (about 1½ pounds)
½   teaspoon salt
¼   teaspoon pepper
½   cup buttermilk salad dressing
2   cups broccoli flowerets
1   medium sweet red pepper, cut into strips
1   small onion, cut into strips

Place orange roughy fillets on a 12" square piece of heavy-duty
aluminum foil. Sprinkle with salt and pepper. Spread 2 tablespoons
buttermilk salad dressing on each fillet. Arrange vegetables over
fish. Fold foil over, sealing edges securely. Bake at 450° for 20 to
25 minutes, or until fish flakes easily when tested with a fork.

Serves 4

Lemon Steamed Fish

4   fish fillets
Salt and pepper
4   teaspoons soy sauce
Juice of 1 lemon
Dried parsley
Dried dill
Thin lemon slices
Paprika

Salt and pepper fish. Put in a shallow glass dish. Spread 1 teaspoon of soy sauce over each fillet, then the juice of 1 lemon over all 4 fillets. Sprinkle dried parsley and dried dill over each fillet. Cover each with thin lemon slices and sprinkle with paprika. Cover dish and refrigerate several hours. Heat water until boiling in vegetable steamer. Put fish in top of steamer, cover and cook 20 minutes. Do not over cook.

Serves 4

Light Mexican-Style Fish

2   cups unpeeled tomatoes, chopped (¾ pound)
¼   cup chopped green onions
3   tablespoons fresh lime juice
2   tablespoons chopped green chili peppers
1   tablespoon chopped fresh parsley
⅛- ¼ teaspoon garlic salt
Dash pepper
4   (4 ounce) red snapper fillets or any lean fish fillets

Combine all ingredients except fish in large skillet. Stir well. Bring to a boil, reduce heat and simmer, uncovered, for 10 minutes. Add fish, cover and cook an additional 11 minutes or until fish flakes easily when tested with a fork. Place fish on a serving platter and spoon tomato mixture on top of fish, using a slotted spoon.

Serves 4

Steamed Florida Lobster

Although broiling cooked lobster is common practice, steaming is the preferred method for heating cold, cooked lobster. Steaming retains the natural moisture and delicate texture of the meat. To steam cooked cold lobster meat, thaw if frozen, then clean and rinse body cavity thoroughly. Place whole lobster or lobster tails on a rack in a covered saucepan or steamer containing a small amount of boiling water. Do not immerse rack in water. Steam just long enough to heat. Serve with your favorite sauce.

FISH FILLETS ITALIANO

4   white fish fillets
4   cloves garlic, crushed
Basil
1   stick margarine
1   onion, thinly sliced
1   (16 ounce) can tomato sauce
Parmesan cheese, freshly grated

Rinse fish fillets well and pat dry. Place each fillet on a large piece of heavy aluminum foil. Rub each fillet with 1 crushed garlic clove. Sprinkle fish liberally with basil. Place 3 pats margarine on top of each fillet. Top each fillet with several onion ring slices. Coat entire top of fish with tomato sauce. Fold aluminum over each fish and pinch ends together to form a tight foil packet. Place in oven and bake for 30 minutes at 350°. Remove packets from oven, open, and sprinkle fillets generously with Parmesan cheese. Return to oven, leaving foil wrap open, and broil for 5 minutes longer, or until cheese is melted.

Serves 4

OYSTER STEW

Oyster stew makes a warming winter meal with grilled cheese sandwiches.

1½ pints oysters, medium to large, liquid reserved
2   cups half and half
10 cups milk
½   stick butter
Salt and pepper to taste

Cook oysters with butter and some of the reserved oyster liquid in a 4-quart pot. Stir constantly until oysters curl up. Don't overcook. Add half and half, milk, and dash salt and pepper. Refrigerate overnight to enhance flavor. Reheat gently before serving.

Serves 4

Stuffed Flounder

¼ cup chopped onion
¼ cup plus 2 tablespoons butter or margarine
7½ ounces crabmeat
½ cup coarse cracker crumbs
1 (3 ounce) can chopped mushrooms, drained, liquid reserved
2 tablespoons parsley
¾ teaspoon salt, divided
Dash pepper
2 pounds flounder fillets
3 tablespoons all-purpose flour
Milk
⅓ cup dry white wine
4 ounces Swiss cheese, shredded
½ teaspoon paprika

In skillet, cook onion in ¼ cup butter until tender but not brown. Stir mushrooms into skillet with crab, cracker crumbs, parsley, ½ teaspoon salt, and pepper. Spread evenly over fillets. Roll fillets and place seam side down in a 13" x 9" x 2" baking dish. In a saucepan, melt 2 tablespoons butter. Blend in flour and ¼ teaspoon salt. Add enough milk to mushroom liquid to make 1½ cups and add to sauce. Add wine to sauce. Cook and stir until thickened and bubbly. Pour over fillets and bake at 400° for 25 minutes. Sprinkle with cheese and paprika. Return to oven and bake 10 minutes longer.

Serves 8

Oysters Lizbeth

1 pint stewing oysters, liquid reserved
8 large mushrooms
1 teaspoon salt
⅛ teaspoon pepper
½ cup cracker crumbs
¼ cup butter
½ cup milk

Place oysters and mushrooms in a 1½-quart baking dish. Sprinkle with salt, pepper, cracker crumbs, and pat with butter. Pour milk and reserved oyster liquid over casserole. Bake at 375° for about 20 to 25 minutes or until bubbly.

Serves 4

Votive candles scattered throughout the home will create instant atmosphere. Purchase them by the case so you have plenty on hand. Select a brand that burns slowly--they should last the entire evening.

SHRIMP
ST. GEORGE

• *½ teaspoon salt*
• *½ teaspoon white pepper*
• *1½ teaspoons paprika*
• *3 to 4 tablespoons butter*
• *1 pound shrimp*

Coat shrimp in salt, pepper, and paprika. Heat butter in sauté pan. Sear shrimp until done. Do not overcook.

Serves 4

SHRIMP SALAD

1	pound large shrimp, boiled, peeled, and cut into pieces
1	pound small shrimp, boiled and peeled
3	cups uncooked shell macaroni
2	tablespoons instant minced onion
1	tablespoon salt
1	tablespoon crushed sweet basil
½	cup French dressing
¼	teaspoon garlic powder
¼	teaspoon black pepper
¼	cup mayonnaise
1	teaspoon lemon juice
1	whole green pepper, finely chopped
2	sticks celery, finely chopped

Romaine lettuce

Cook and drain macaroni. Add all other ingredients, except lettuce, and mix well. Chill overnight. Line salad bowl with romaine lettuce or place lettuce leaves on individual serving plates. Top with shrimp mixture.

Serves 8–10

MENU SUGGESTION: Perfect dish for luncheons! Serve with Pat's Applesauce Muffins (page 110) and sliced honeydew.

CAJUN BARBECUED SHRIMP

2	pounds headless shrimp
2	sticks butter or margarine
1½	teaspoons salt
½	teaspoon black pepper
1	teaspoon garlic powder
½	tablespoon lemon juice
½	teaspoon oregano
2	teaspoons liquid crab boil

Place shrimp in a 13" x 9" x 2" baking dish. Melt butter in sauté pan and add rest of ingredients. Stir to combine, then remove from heat. Pour over shrimp. Bake in 350° oven for 15 minutes.

Serves 4

Seafood Primavera with Basil Sauce

½   cup white wine vinegar
3   tablespoons dry sherry
2   cloves garlic, crushed
1   teaspoon salt
⅔   cup olive oil
10 thin asparagus spears, cut into 1½" lengths
1½ cups broccoli flowerets
½   cup julienne carrots
1½ cups cauliflower flowerets
1½ cups frozen tiny green peas, thawed
1   pound scallops, cooked
1   pound medium shrimp, cooked and peeled
½   pound spinach fettuccine
3   scallions, minced
10 ounces fresh spinach leaves
Salt and pepper to taste
1   cup cherry tomatoes, halved
Basil Sauce (see recipe at right)

To prepare dressing, combine wine vinegar, sherry, garlic, and salt in a quart jar. Shake to combine. Add olive oil and shake again. Set aside. Steam asparagus, broccoli, carrots, and cauliflower separately until tender-crisp. Do not overcook. Rinse each vegetable with cold water to stop the cooking. Drain. Combine steamed vegetables with peas and refrigerate. Toss scallops and shrimp with ½ cup of the dressing. Cover and chill. Cook pasta in 4 quarts boiling, salted water until tender. Drain, rinse in cool water, and drain again. To assemble, arrange spinach leaves around outer edge of a large platter. Toss pasta with the vegetables and arrange in the center of the platter. Make a well in the center of the pasta. In a bowl, toss together the scallops, shrimp, and scallions. Season to taste with salt and pepper. Mound seafood mixture in the center of the pasta. Distribute cherry tomatoes over the salad. Serve with Basil Sauce on the side.

Serves 6–8

Basil Sauce

• *3 tablespoons white wine vinegar*
• *1 tablespoon Dijon mustard*
• *6 tablespoons fresh basil or 2 tablespoons dried basil*
• *1 large clove garlic*
• *3 tablespoons olive oil*
• *½ cup sour cream*
• *¼ cup heavy cream*
• *4 tablespoons chopped parsley*

Combine vinegar, mustard, basil, and garlic in a food processor and process until smooth. With machine running, slowly add oil. Add sour cream and parsley; purée. Season with salt and pepper. Cover and chill.

Makes 1–1½ cups

Shrimp and Green Noodles

1   (8 ounce) package spinach noodles or fresh angel hair pasta
2   pounds shrimp, peeled and deveined, or 1 pound shrimp and 1
    pound scallops
1   (10¾ ounce) can cream of mushroom soup
1   cup sour cream
1   cup mayonnaise
½   teaspoon Dijon mustard
¼   cup dry sherry
¾   cup grated sharp Cheddar cheese
½   cup butter

Cook noodles 5 minutes. Drain. Line a 13" x 9" x 2" casserole with
noodles. Sauté shrimp in butter until pink and tender, about 5
minutes. Cover noodles with shrimp. Pour any liquid remaining in
the sauté pan over the shrimp. Combine soup, sour cream, mayonnaise, mustard, and sherry. Pour sauce over shrimp and sprinkle
with cheese. Dish can be refrigerated at this point and baked later.
Bake at 350° for about 30 minutes, until bubbly.

Serves 8–10

Shrimp Curry

1   pound shrimp, shelled and deveined
2   (10¾ ounce) cans cream of shrimp soup
1   cup sour cream
1   teaspoon curry powder
Cooked rice
Optional toppings: chopped peanuts, chopped hard boiled eggs,
    chutney, chopped crisp bacon, grated coconut, chopped green
    onions

Cook shrimp in boiling, salted water for 3 minutes. Drain and cut
into pieces. Heat soup and add sour cream, curry powder, and
shrimp pieces. Cook mixture, but do not boil. Serve over rice and
top with assorted toppings.

Serves 4–6

If rice is overcooked and gummy, use it in soups, combine with ground beef in casseroles, use in a custard, or add to an omelet.

Shrimp and Spinach Pasta

1   (14-16 ounce) package spinach linguine
4   pounds shrimp, shelled and deveined
1   cup butter
2   (10¾ ounce) cans cream of mushroom soup
1   cup mayonnaise
2   cups sour cream
2   tablespoons chives
1   cup Dijon mustard
8   tablespoons dry sherry
1   cup shredded sharp Cheddar cheese

Cook noodles as directed on package. Layer two 13" x 9" x 2" baking dishes with noodles. Sauté shrimp in butter approximately 5 minutes. Cover noodles with shrimp. Combine soup, mayonnaise, sour cream, chives, mustard, and sherry. Pour sauce over shrimp and sprinkle with cheese. Bake 30 minutes at 350°.

Serves 14–16

Offer a variety of cheese, breads, and fresh fruits. They act as "filler" for the main menu and make a buffet table look bountiful.

Shrimp Carolyn

6   green onions, chopped
1   tablespoon butter or margarine
1   (4 ounce) jar mushrooms, drained
1   pound shrimp, peeled
¼   teaspoon salt
¼   teaspoon red pepper
10 ounces sour cream
Fettucine, cooked

Cook onion in butter until tender. Add mushrooms, shrimp, salt, and red pepper. Cook until shrimp turns pink, about 5 minutes. Stir in sour cream. Cook over low heat until hot and bubbly. Serve over fettuccine.

Serves 4

SHRIMP AND SAUSAGE GUMBO

• 1 medium onion, chopped
• 1 green pepper, chopped
• butter
• 2 (16 ounce) cans black-eyed peas with jalapeño peppers
• ⅓ cup uncooked rice
• ⅔ cup Bloody Mary mix
• 1 pound shrimp, peeled and deveined
• ½ pound Polish sausage, cooked

Sauté onions and peppers in butter. Add peas, rice, and Bloody Mary mix. Cook on low for 25 minutes. Add shrimp. Add sliced cooked sausage. Cook another 5 to 10 minutes.

Serves 4–6

SHRIMP CASSEROLE

2-3 pounds shrimp, cooked and peeled
1   (5.2 ounce) box long-grain white and wild rice, cooked
1   cup grated Cheddar cheese
1   cup grated Swiss cheese
1   (10¾ ounce) can cream of mushroom soup
1   cup chopped onion
1   cup diced green pepper
1   cup chopped celery
6   tablespoons butter
1   lemon, sliced thin
Salt
Pepper
Paprika

Mix together the first 5 ingredients. Set aside. Sauté onions, peppers, and celery in butter and add to shrimp mixture. Place in 3-quart casserole dish. Season with salt and pepper. Place thin slices of lemon down the center of the casserole and sprinkle with paprika. Cover dish with foil and bake at 350° until heated through, about 30 minutes.

Serves 8–10

SHRIMP AND CHEESE CASSEROLE

6   slices white bread
½   pound sharp processed cheese spread
1   pound shrimp, cooked, peeled, deveined
4   tablespoons butter, melted
3   eggs, beaten
½   teaspoon dry mustard
Salt to taste
2   cups milk

Tear bread into pieces about the size of a quarter. Break cheese into bite-sized pieces. Place a layer of shrimp in a greased 2-quart casserole dish. Follow with a layer of bread and then cheese. Repeat process, until you have several layers in the dish. Pour melted butter over entire mixture. Combine eggs, mustard, and salt. Mix in milk. Pour mixture over layers in casserole dish. Cover and refrigerate at least 3 hours, preferably overnight. Cover and bake 1 hour at 350°.

Serves 4–6

Shrimp with Lemon-Garlic Sauce

1   pound shrimp, peeled and deveined
¾   stick butter
2   tablespoons fresh lemon juice
⅓   cup white wine
½   teaspoon garlic salt
1   teaspoon dried basil
1   teaspoon grated Parmesan cheese

In large skillet, melt butter over medium-high heat until bubbly but not brown. Add lemon juice, garlic salt, basil, and Parmesan cheese. Cook for about 2 minutes. Add wine and cook another 4 minutes or until alcohol evaporates, stirring constantly. Add shrimp and continue to stir constantly until shrimp turn pink. Serve hot with sauce reserved for spooning or dipping. Serve with steamed artichokes.

Serves 4

Shrimp and Artichoke Casserole

½   cup butter
¼   pound fresh mushrooms, sliced
⅓   cup flour
1   cup heavy cream
1   cup milk
⅓   cup white wine
1   tablespoon Worcestershire sauce
Salt and pepper to taste
1   (14 ounce) can artichoke hearts, halved and drained
1   pound medium shrimp, cooked, shelled, and deveined
⅓   cup freshly grated Parmesan cheese

Melt butter, add sliced mushrooms and cook for 2 minutes. Stir in flour until blended. Add cream and milk. Stir constantly with a wire whisk until thickened. Add wine and Worcestershire sauce. Season with salt and pepper. Arrange artichokes in a 2-quart baking dish and cover with shrimp. Pour sauce over shrimp and artichokes. Top with Parmesan cheese. Bake at 375° for 20 to 30 minutes.

Serves 6

Shrimp Butter Cream Sauce

5½ tablespoons butter, divided
2   tablespoons all-purpose flour
½   cup finely chopped eggplant pulp
¼   cup finely chopped onion
1½ cups reserved stock
¾   teaspoon salt
½   teaspoon ground red pepper
¼   teaspoon white pepper
½   cup heavy cream
12 small shrimp, boiled, stock reserved

In a 1-quart saucepan, melt 4 tablespoons butter. Whisk in flour with a metal whisk until well blended. Remove from heat and set aside. Place the remaining 1½ tablespoons butter, eggplant pulp, and onion in a 2-quart saucepan. Sauté over high heat until onions are tender, about 2 minutes. Add the stock and bring to a boil. Whisk in the salt and red and white peppers, then the butter-flour mixture. Cook over high heat for 4 minutes, whisking frequently. Add the cream and continue cooking 1 minute, whisking constantly. Add the shrimp. Continue cooking and stirring just until the shrimp turn pink, about 30 seconds. Remove from heat.

Serves 3

Fried Shrimp

2   cups milk
1   egg
⅛ teaspoon salt
⅛ teaspoon pepper
2   pounds shrimp, cleaned, shelled, and deveined
1   cup flour
1   tablespoon baking flour
Oil for frying

Mix first 4 ingredients in bowl. Add shrimp and soak for 5 minutes. Drain off liquid. Mix flours in a plastic bag or in a pie plate. Add shrimp and coat well. Fry in hot vegetable oil until golden brown. Remove and drain.

Serves 4

Seafood Frying Batter

- ¾ cup flour
- pinch salt
- 1 egg, beaten
- ½ cup beer
- 1 tablespoon melted butter
- 1 egg white, stiffly beaten

Sift flour and salt into mixing bowl. Stir in butter and egg. Add beer gradually. Stir until mixture is smooth. Let batter stand in warm place one hour. Fold in beaten egg white. Dip shrimp or onion rings a few at a time in batter. Deep fry until golden brown. Drain on paper towel.

ORIENTAL SHRIMP

1   pound fresh shrimp, shelled and deveined
½   teaspoon salt
1½ teaspoons cornstarch
2   cups oil plus 2 tablespoons, divided
¼   cup finely chopped onions
2   scallions, finely chopped
2   tablespoons finely chopped fresh ginger
¼   cup ketchup
¼   cup chicken broth
1   tablespoon sugar
1   tablespoon sherry
1   tablespoon chili paste with garlic

Cut shrimp into halves lengthwise. Place in bowl. Add salt and cornstarch. Mix well with hand. In wok, heat 2 cups of oil over high heat. Deep-fry shrimp 1 minute. Remove from oil, drain, and set aside. Remove oil from wok. Heat 2 tablespoons of oil in wok over medium heat. Stir-fry onion, scallions, and ginger for 1 minute. Add ketchup, broth, and sugar. Bring to a boil. Add the fried shrimp, sherry, and chili paste to the onion-ginger mixture. Stir-fry briskly for 1 minute over high heat. May be served over steamed or fried rice.

Serves 2–4

FRIED RICE

•1 tablespoon vegetable oil
• 1 egg, beaten
• 2 cups cold steamed rice
• ½ (10 ounce) package frozen peas
• 2 green onions with tops, chopped
• soy sauce

In a wok, heat oil over medium-high heat. Fry egg lightly and cut into small pieces with spatula. Add rice, peas, and onions. Stir-fry until light brown. Add soy sauce to taste.

Serves 2–4

When boiling shrimp, add fresh celery leaves to minimize odor.

Seafood Casserole

1 (4¼ ounce) can shrimp, drained or 1½ cups fresh shrimp, cleaned and deveined
1 (4¼ ounce) can white crabmeat, drained
1 cup chopped celery
1 cup chopped green pepper
1 cup chopped onion
¾ cup mayonnaise
1 teaspoon Worcestershire sauce
Salt to taste
Pepper or lemon pepper to taste
Breadcrumbs
¼ cup butter or margarine, melted

Mix together all ingredients, except bread crumbs and butter. Place in 3-quart casserole dish. Top with bread crumbs. Pour melted butter over crumbs. Bake at 375° until golden brown and bubbly.

Serves 4–6

Have a progressive dinner in your own home. Serve each course in a different room or area. Not only is it fun, but by setting up each area in advance, you will avoid the noise and clutter of clearing plates and resetting places.

Hot Seafood Salad

1 pound shrimp, shelled, cooked, and deveined
1 pound claw crabmeat
4 tablespoons chopped green onions
½ cup chopped green pepper
2 cups chopped celery
1 (8 ounce) can water chestnuts, drained and chopped
2 (10 ounce) packages frozen peas, thawed
2 cups cooked wild rice or 1 (5.2 ounce box) long-grain wild rice
2 teaspoons Worcestershire sauce
Dash cayenne pepper
2 cups mayonnaise
1 teaspoon pepper
3 cups croutons or dry roasted cashews

Combine all ingredients except croutons. Pour into greased 13" x 9" x 2" glass baking dish. Top with croutons. Bake uncovered at 325° for 30 minutes.

Serves 8

Royal Seafood Casserole

2   (10½ ounce) cans cream of shrimp soup
½   cup mayonnaise
1   small onion, finely chopped
¾   cup milk
Salt and white pepper
Seasoned salt
Ground nutmeg
Cayenne pepper
3   pounds shrimp, cooked and cleaned
1   (7½ ounce) can crabmeat, drained
1   (5 ounce) can water chestnuts, drained and sliced
1½ cups diced celery
½   cup minced fresh parsley
1⅓ cups cooked white long grain rice
Paprika
Slivered almonds

Blend soup with mayonnaise in a large bowl. Stir until smooth.
Add onion, then milk. Season to taste with salt, white pepper,
seasoned salt, nutmeg, and cayenne pepper. Add other ingredients,
except paprika and almonds, and mix. Add more milk if mixture
seems dry. Turn into greased 9" x 13" casserole dish. Sprinkle with
paprika and almonds. Bake uncovered for 350° for 30 minutes or
until hot and bubbly.

Serves 10

Broiled Tuna

2   tuna steaks
½   teaspoon lemon pepper
¼   teaspoon garlic powder
¼   teaspoon salt

Sprinkle steaks with lemon pepper, garlic powder, and salt. Place
steaks on broiler pan and broil for 5 to 10 minutes on each side,
depending on thickness of steak fillet.

Serves 2

*Fish should be as fresh as
possible when purchased,
kept ice cold during
storage, and cooked only
Briefly. Fish is done
when it flakes easily
with a fork. Serve
immediately.*

POACHED FISH

To poach any whole fish, tie fish in cheesecloth, lower into boiling water to which a bouquet garni of onion, celery rib, parsley sprigs, bay leaf, sprig of thyme, 2 whole cloves and 2 black peppercorns, has been added. Simmer fish 6 to 10 minutes per pound, depending on thickness of fish.

Zesty Scalloped Oysters

1 quart oysters
2 tablespoons butter
1 cup cracker crumbs
¼ teaspoon pepper
1 teaspoon salt
2 eggs
1 tablespoon Worcestershire sauce
1 teaspoon hot pepper sauce
1 scant cup milk

Drain oysters and reserve liquid. In a 2-quart baking dish, layer half of the oysters. Sprinkle with salt and pepper. Dot with butter, then sprinkle with ½ cup of cracker crumbs. Make another layer of oysters, salt, pepper, and crackers. Dot with butter. In a medium mixing bowl, beat eggs; add milk and 1 cup of reserved oyster liquid. Add Worcestershire and hot pepper sauce. Pour mixture over casserole. Bake in a 375° oven for 25 to 30 minutes or until bubbly.

Serves 6

Salmon Florentine

2 cups canned salmon
Milk
¼ cup butter
¼ cup flour
½ teaspoon dry mustard
¼ teaspoon salt
¼ teaspoon pepper sauce
1½ cups grated mild Cheddar or Monterey Jack cheese, divided
2 cups spinach, cooked and drained

Drain and flake salmon, reserving liquid. Add enough milk to salmon liquid to make 1½ cups. In saucepan, melt butter and add flour. Stir until blended. Slowly add milk mixture to butter-flour mixture. Stir briskly until smooth and thick. Season with mustard, salt, pepper sauce, and 1 cup of cheese. Place spinach in greased casserole dish, top with salmon, sauce, and remaining cheese. Baked uncovered for 15 minutes at 425°.

Serves 4

Salmon Loaf

1 (1 pound) can red or pink salmon
3 eggs
1 cup milk
½ cup chicken broth
¼ cup diced celery
¼ cup diced onion
3 tablespoons chopped mushrooms
2 tablespoons butter
2 cups breadcrumbs
Salt and pepper
Melted butter
Paprika

Drain salmon. Reserve juice. Remove bones and skin. In a separate bowl, beat eggs and milk. Measure salmon juice and add enough chicken broth to make 1½ cups. In a skillet, sauté celery, onion, and mushrooms in 2 tablespoons butter. Remove from heat. Add salmon, egg mixture, and measured liquid to sautéed celery, onion, and mushrooms. Fold in breadcrumbs. Season to taste with salt and pepper. Place in greased 2-quart casserole. Top with melted butter and paprika. Bake at 350° for 45 minutes. Cut into squares.

Serves 6–8

Salmon Croquettes

1 (1 pound) can pink salmon, drained
¼ cup finely chopped onion
1 teaspoon salt
⅛ teaspoon pepper
2 eggs, beaten
2 tablespoons flour
Vegetable oil

Mix all ingredients together. Shape into 2" patties. Fry patties in vegetable oil over medium heat until golden brown.

Serves 4

To improve the flavor of canned seafood, soak in diluted lemon juice at least 30 minutes before using with a recipe.

SALMON RING

RING:

1   (1 pound) can pink salmon, drained and flaked
1   cup fine dry breadcrumbs
½   cup chopped celery
¼   cup chopped green bell pepper
2   tablespoons minced onion
1   tablespoon lemon juice
1   cup evaporated milk
1   egg, beaten

SAUCE:

¼   cup mayonnaise
1   tablespoon all-purpose flour
¼   teaspoon salt
⅔   cup evaporated milk
½   cup water
¼   cup sliced stuffed green olives
¼   cup salted almonds

In a bowl, combine salmon, breadcrumbs, vegetables, and lemon juice. In another bowl combine milk and egg. Add milk-egg mixture to salmon mixture; mix together gently. Turn into well greased 5-cup ring mold. Bake at 350° for 30 minutes. To prepare sauce, combine mayonnaise, flour, and salt in a saucepan; blend until smooth. Combine milk and water, and slowly add to mayonnaise mixture. Cook over medium heat, stirring until thick; add almonds and olives. While salmon ring is still hot, invert onto a serving platter. Pour sauce over salmon ring.

Serves 6

Menu Suggestion: Serve with Broccoli Mushroom Salad (page 89) and Dill Muffins (page 118).

Salmon and Noodles Romanoff

2   large salmon steaks, fresh or thawed (¾-1 pound total)
¼   cup water
1   tablespoon red wine vinegar or any berry vinegar
6   ounces green spinach noodles
1   tablespoon vegetable oil (flavored with some sesame oil, if
    available)
6   ounces fresh mushrooms, sliced
1   bunch green onions, sliced with tops
½   (1.1 ounce) package dry ranch style dressing mix
¼   teaspoon dill weed
Dash garlic salt
Several dashes hot pepper sauce
1   (8 ounce) carton plain, low-fat yogurt
3   tablespoons mayonnaise

Place salmon steaks in large, deep saucepan. Poach in water and
flavored vinegar. Heat to boil. Cover and reduce heat. Simmer 10
minutes for 1" thick steaks. Most of the liquid should be evaporated
at end of cooking time. Remove salmon to a plate and cool. Cook
noodles in boiling water. Drain in a colander. Set aside. When
salmon is cool, remove skin and bones. Flake meat into large
chunks. Set aside. In a deep saucepan, heat oil on high. Add sliced
mushrooms and cook, stirring often. No liquid will escape into pan
if heat is high enough. Add onions, toss with mushrooms. Reduce
heat. Stir in dry ranch mix, dill, garlic salt, and hot sauce. Stir in
yogurt and mayonnaise. Toss in noodles and salmon. Heat through
and serve.

Serves 4

Escargot with Scallops

12 small mushroom caps
¼ pound bay scallops
1 can small escargot
2 teaspoons crushed garlic
4 slices bacon
Grated Parmesan cheese
Garlic salt
Margarine

Wash mushroom caps and place in bottom of 4 scallop dishes with margarine. Place 2 or 3 small bay scallops or 1 large scallop on top of mushrooms. Add 1 small escargot. Add enough garlic to cover the top of the entire dish. Cut bacon to cover the top. Sprinkle with Parmesan cheese and garlic salt. Broil 4 to 5 minutes.

Serves 4

Shrimp and Scallop Sauté

3 tablespoons butter
3 tablespoons olive oil
6 large cloves garlic, minced
1 pound mushrooms, sliced (optional)
2 tablespoons tomato paste
¼ cup dry white wine
¼ cup fresh lemon juice
1 pound medium shrimp, peeled and deveined
1 bunch green onions, sliced
1 pound bay scallops
⅓ cup chopped fresh parsley or 1½ teaspoon dried parsley
Salt and pepper

In large skillet, over medium heat, melt butter and olive oil. Add garlic and sauté approximately 1 minute. Increase heat to high, add mushrooms, and sauté approximately 5 minutes. Add tomato paste and stir until ingredients are well blended. Add wine and lemon juice and bring mixture to a boil. Add shrimp and sliced green onions and stir for 1 minute. Add scallops and cook 3 to 4 more minutes. Season to taste with salt and pepper. Sprinkle with parsley. Serve immediately.

Serves 4-6

BROILED SCALLOPS

• *1 pound fresh bay scallops*
• *1 pound bacon, thinly sliced (about ½ bacon slice per scallop)*

Place scallops on a large baking sheet. Cut strips of bacon in half and wrap a strip around each scallop. Broil for about 7 minutes or place on hot grill for 5 minutes. Sprinkle lightly with parsley.

Serves 4

CAJUN SPICED OYSTERS

24 medium oysters
⅛ pound salted butter
¾ cup finely chopped onion
½ cup finely chopped celery
⅛ cup finely chopped bell pepper
1 teaspoon minced garlic
¼ teaspoon red pepper
¼ teaspoon white pepper
2 chicken bouillon cubes
½ cup heavy cream
½ cup grated Parmesan cheese, divided
½ cup Italian breadcrumbs
1 tablespoon finely chopped parsley
¼ cup finely chopped green onions
½ pound crabmeat

Drain oysters in a colander and set aside. To prepare stuffing, sauté ¾ cup onion, celery, bell pepper, and garlic in the butter until the onions are translucent. Add the red pepper, white pepper, and bouillon cubes. Stir until all ingredients are well mixed. Add the heavy cream and continue cooking until mixture is bubbling. Add ¼ cup cheese and remove from heat. Fold in the bread crumbs; allow the stuffing to cool. Place oysters in a 9" x 9" x 2" baking dish. Cover oysters with crabmeat. Spread the stuffing over the crabmeat and oysters, and top with remaining ¼ cup Parmesan cheese. Bake at 350° for 20 minutes or until golden brown. Garnish with chopped parsley and green onions before serving.

Serves 4-6

SAUTÉED SHRIMP

- *½ stick butter or margarine*
- *1 (0.7 ounce) envelope of Italian dressing mix*
- *2 pounds fresh or frozen shrimp, peeled and deveined*

Melt butter in a sauce pan. Blend in dressing mix, add shrimp, and sauté over medium heat until done. Serve over rice.

Serves 4

For a simple cocktail sauce that's great with the recipe above, combine ½ cup chili sauce, ½ cup ketchup, 4 tablespoons horseradish, ¼ teaspoon salt, dash pepper, ½ teaspoon Worcestershire sauce, and a few drops hot pepper sauce.

Smoked Turkey

1   whole turkey, thawed, with neck and gizzard removed
2   apples, sliced
1   (12 ounce) can frozen apple juice
4   tablespoons sage
1   tablespoon garlic powder
1   tablespoon black pepper
2   cups white wine

Prepare smoker with a heaping pan of charcoal. Fill water pan of smoker with apple juice, one cup wine, and enough hot water to fill halfway. Stuff turkey cavity with apples sprinkled with 1 tablespoon of sage and remaining cup of wine. Sprinkle sage, garlic powder, and pepper over the outside of the turkey. Place two large hickory wood chips—soaked in water 30 minutes—on charcoal when you begin cooking. Place turkey on rack and cook about 12 hours. Check water pan every three to five hours.

Serves 8–10

Smoked Cheese

• *1 (8–16 ounces) block of cheese, such as Monterey Jack with jalapeño peppers*

Prepare smoker with ⅓ pan of charcoal. Spray an aluminum pan with non-stick cooking spray. Place cheese on pan. Smoke cheese over warm, but not hot, coals. Place one chunk of unsoaked hickory wood on the coals. Smoker's water pan should be ⅔ full. Cook the cheese 15 to 20 minutes until it begins to melt.

Serves 4–6

Wild Turkey with Oyster Pecan Dressing

This recipe would make a wonderfully different holiday turkey.

1   wild turkey
4   tablespoons finely chopped shallots
½   stick margarine
1   cup chopped fresh parsley
1   cup coarsely chopped celery
1   cup fresh mushrooms, washed and cut in half
1½ cups coarsley chopped pecans
8   slices bread with crusts, toasted and torn in pieces
1   teaspoon tarragon
1   teaspoon paprika
¼   teaspoon nutmeg
Turkey giblets, chopped
1   pint oysters and juice
1   heaping tablespoon flour
¼   cup Worcestershire sauce
1   tablespoon poultry seasoning
1   tablespoon lemon pepper
¾   stick margarine
1   can beef broth
1   cup white wine

Sauté shallots in margarine until slightly brown. Add parsley, celery, mushrooms, pecans, and toast pieces. Stir. Continue to simmer over low heat. Stir in tarragon, paprika, and nutmeg; add giblets, oysters, and oyster juice. Remove from heat. Put 1 heaping tablespoon flour in browning bag; shake. Place the turkey in the bag and stuff the turkey with the oyster pecan dressing. Douse the turkey with Worcestershire sauce, dust heavily with poultry seasoning and lemon pepper. Smear the bird with ¾ stick margarine. Add beef broth and white wine into the bag. Tie up bag, punch 5 small holes in top of bag. Cook about 3 hours at 350˚.

Serves 6–8

$\mathscr{V}$ENISON SAUSAGE GUMBO

3   cups diced cooked chicken
1   pound venison sausage
⅓   cup cooking oil
½   cup flour
1   pound okra, chopped
1   cup chopped onion
¾   cup chopped celery
½   cup chopped green pepper
2   tablespoons minced garlic
¼   cup chopped parsley
¾   teaspoon thyme
2   bay leaves
½   teaspoon basil
1   (28 ounce) can tomatoes
4   cups chicken broth
1   teaspoon Worcestershire sauce
Salt, pepper, cayenne pepper, and hot sauce to taste.

In a large pot, heat oil, stir in flour and cook, stirring over medium-low heat until roux is medium-brown color—about 30 minutes. Add okra, onion, celery, and green pepper. Cook over medium heat until okra is no longer stringy. Add garlic, parsley, thyme, bay leaves, basil, and tomatoes with their juice. Add chicken and broth, adding more broth if needed. Slice sausage and fry. Drain and add to gumbo. Simmer slowly 1½ to 2 hours, stirring often to prevent sticking. Season with Worcestershire sauce, salt, pepper, cayenne pepper, and hot sauce. Serve over rice.

Serves 10–12

Hunter's Pie

1 pound ground venison or ground beef
1 large onion, chopped
1 (1.1 ounce) package hunter sauce mix
1 (12 ounce) package frozen carrots and peas
2 cups mashed potatoes
1 can French-fried onions
½ cup grated Parmesan cheese

Cook hunter sauce mix, frozen peas and carrots according to their package directions. In a skillet, brown venison and chopped onion. Add hunter sauce mix and cooked vegetables. Place in a greased 8" x 8" casserole dish. Top with mashed potatoes. Sprinkle with French-fried onions and Parmesan cheese. Cook at 300° for 30 minutes or until heated.

Serves 4

Venison Chili

2 tablespoons vegetable oil
2 pounds venison, coarsely chopped
2 medium onions, chopped
1 (16 ounce) can tomatoes, undrained
1 cup water
¾ cup red wine
3 large green chilies, diced
1 clove garlic, minced
3 tablespoons chili powder
¾ teaspoon oregano
½ teaspoon cumin seeds, crushed

Heat oil in a Dutch oven over medium heat. Add venison and onion; cook, stirring frequently, until meat is browned. Stir in remaining ingredients. Reduce heat and simmer, uncovered, for 1 hour, stirring occasionally.

Makes 2 quarts

Venison Beef Jerky

• *3 pound venison roast, cut with the grain into strips like bacon*
• *½ cup soy sauce*
• *½ cup Worcestershire sauce*
• *2 teaspoons meat tenderizer*
• *2 teaspoons seasoned salt*
• *1 teaspoon garlic powder*
• *2 teaspoons onion powder*
• *1 teaspoon black pepper*
• *½ teaspoon chili powder*
• *¼ cup liquid smoke*
• *¼ cup lemon juice*

Mix ingredients for sauce. Add meat and marinate for at least 24 hours in the refrigerator. Remove meat from marinade and drain. Line bottom of oven with foil and spray racks with non-stick vegetable spray. Preheat oven to 150°. Place venison strips directly on oven racks and bake for 8 hours.

Serves 10-12

Venison in Red Wine

1½ pounds venison tenderloin
½ cup red wine
1 stick butter
1 clove garlic, minced
1 tablespoon olive oil
4 shallots, minced
½ cup port
Salt and pepper

Slice venison into ¼" slices. Season with salt and pepper. Cover venison with red wine. Set aside for at least 1 hour. Melt ½ stick butter (¼ cup) in a large skillet. Add garlic, shallots, and olive oil. When shallots and garlic are tender, add butter and venison slices. Add wine marinade as necessary to keep ingredients moist. Add port. When bubbling, add rest of butter. Serve immediately.

Serves 4-6

Woodfield Springs Plantation Venison Stew

3 pounds venison, cut into medium-sized pieces
2 (10¾ ounce) cans cream of mushroom soup
1 envelope dry onion soup mix
1 teaspoon freshly ground black pepper
¼ cup sherry

Soak venison in salt water overnight to tenderize. Mix remaining ingredients together. Drain meat and place in a well-buttered, covered 9" x 12" casserole dish. Top with soup mixture. Bake at 300° for 3 hours.

Serves 8

Baked Duck Beverly

Teal or big duck (amount will depend on servings needed—plan ½ to 1 duck per person)

Onions
Green pepper
Celery
Margarine
Oregano leaves
Garlic salt
Lemon pepper
Celery salt
1 stick margarine
1 cup chicken broth
5 ounces white wine

Cut onion and green pepper in wedges. Cut celery in 3" to 4" pieces. Rub duck inside and out with margarine. Rub garlic, salt, oregano leaves, lemon pepper, and celery salt inside and out of duck. Stuff cavity of duck with onion, green pepper, and celery sticks. Place duck in a large roaster or baking pan. In a saucepan, melt 1 stick margarine. Add chicken broth and wine. Simmer a few minutes. Pour sauce in bottom of pan; do not pour sauce over duck. Cover pan tightly with lid or heavy aluminum foil. Bake at 325° for 2 to 2½ hours until tender. Skim fat off sauce and discard. Serve sauce in gravy boat.

Serves 1–2

Wild game is usually a very lean choice. Duck, however is an exception. While chicken and duck may look similar, they are very different when it comes to fat content. One pound of chicken has 15 grams of fat and 385 calories. The same portion of duck has 109 grams of fat and 1,215 calories. The numbers speak for themselves. You may want to serve duck only for those very special occasions.

*Barbra Crumpacker,
Registered Dietitian*

Anitra Alle Olive

1 (4-5 pound) oven-ready duck
Salt to taste
Black pepper, freshly ground, to taste
1½ teaspoons sage or oregano
3 tablespoons oil
1 bay leaf
1 large onion, peeled and quartered
1 large carrot, peeled and quartered
2 celery stalks, sliced
1 tablespoon flour
1½ cups red wine
2 cups chicken broth
1½ cups black and green olives, pitted and mixed (Green stuffed olives may be used)

Prick duck skin well with fork. Sprinkle inside and outside of duck with salt, pepper, and herbs. Heat oil in a large Dutch oven. Fry duck briskly until browned all over. Remove. Add bay leaf, onion, carrot, and celery. Sauté gently for 5 to 6 minutes. Sprinkle in flour and stir. Cook for 1 to 2 minutes. Stir in wine, bring to a boil, allow to bubble several minutes. Add chicken broth and simmer. Add duck to pan. Cover and simmer gently 2 hours or until duck is tender. Baste occasionally. Add more broth if necessary. Place duck in a clean covered casserole dish and keep hot. Skim fat from sauce remaining in pan; discard bay leaf. Add olives to sauce; adjust seasoning and pour over duck.

Serves 4

Duck and Wild Rice Casserole

4 cups cubed duck meat (see recipe at right for cooking duck)
½ cup margarine
½ cup chopped onion
¼ cup flour
1 (4 ounce) can sliced mushrooms, drained with liquid reserved
¾ cup half-and-half
1 tablespoon chopped parsley
1 (6 ounce) package wild rice
1½ teaspoons salt
¼ teaspoon pepper
Slivered almonds

Cook rice according to package directions. Melt margarine; add onion and sauté. Stir in flour. Add mushrooms to onion-flour mixture and stir to combine. Pour reserved mushroom liquid into a large measuring cup, add enough duck broth (reserved from cooking duck) to make 2¼ cups of liquid. Stir liquid into onion mixture. Add remaining ingredients, except almonds. Pour into a 2-quart casserole dish. Sprinkle almonds on top. Baked covered at 350° for 15 to 20 minutes. Uncover and bake an additional 5 to 10 minutes or until very hot.

Serves 8

Roast Duck

• 4 ducks
• ½ cup salt
• 2 medium oranges, halved
• 2 medium onions, quartered
• 2 teaspoons salt
• 2 teaspoons pepper

Place ducks in a plastic container. Soak in ½ cup salt water for 6 hours in refrigerator. Remove ducks from container. Stuff cavities with oranges and onions. Place ducks in roasting pan. Add water, about ¾ way up the duck. Sprinkle with 2 teaspoons salt and pepper. Cover and cook at 250° for 5½ hours. Reserve duck broth for Duck and Wild Rice Casserole (at left).

Serves 4

Serve with your favorite barbecue sauce. This recipe also makes a wonderful hors d'oeuvre.

CHARCOALED MARINATED DUCK BREASTS

8   whole duck breasts, split, boned, and skinned
4   tablespoons salt
1½ cups bottled Italian salad dressing
3   tablespoons Worcestershire sauce
¾   teaspoon garlic powder
¾   teaspoon ground cloves
Juice of 3 lemons
16 slices bacon

Cover duck breasts with water. Add salt and soak for about 3 hours. Wipe with paper towels and place in a shallow pan. Combine next 5 ingredients and pour over duck breasts. Place in refrigerator. Marinate at least three hours or overnight. Remove duck breasts from marinade, wrap each in a bacon slice and secure with a toothpick. Grill over slow coals seven minutes on each side or until bacon is done. Slice duck breasts very thin.

Serves 12-16

To freeze dove and small game birds, pack them in milk cartons and fill with water. Seal tightly. They will keep in the freezer for 1 year.

GRILLED DOVE

8   dove
8   bacon slices
White wine Worcestershire sauce

Wrap dove in bacon. Marinate for 6 hours in white wine Worcestershire sauce. Grill over medium-hot coals for 10 minutes each side.

Serves 4

Menu Suggestion: Serve with Quick Mayonnaise Rolls (page 120), Broccoli Surprise (page 133), Perfect Wild Rice (page 149), and Spiced Pears (page 275).

DOVE STEW

You may substitute quail in this recipe if dove is not available.

15 dove
Water to cover
1 large onion, chopped
2 potatoes, chopped
2 (1 pound) cans stewed tomatoes, chopped
1 (16 ounce) package frozen lima beans
1 (16 ounce) can corn
1 (16 ounce) package frozen cut okra
Salt, pepper, and hot pepper sauce, to taste

Place dove in a large cook pot. Cover with water and cook until tender. Cool dove in liquid. Remove dove from pot and bone meat. Strain cooking liquid and pour back into pot. To the liquid, add onion, potatoes, tomatoes, and frozen lima beans. Simmer for 1 hour. Add corn and okra. Cook until corn and okra are tender. Add salt, pepper, and hot pepper sauce. Add more water if stew is too thick.

Serves 12

• *The USDA
recommends marinat-
ing meat in the
refrigerator.*
• *Reserve a portion of
the marinade for
basting before adding
raw meat.*
• *Remove visible fat
before grilling to
avoid charring and
flare-ups.*
• *Don't place cooked
meat in the same
container used to hold
the raw meat unless
the container has been
washed with soap and
hot water.*

Merrily Plantation Deep Dish Dove Pie

12 dove
1   teaspoon thyme
1   teaspoon parsley
2   bay leaves
2   cups dove broth
2   carrots, chopped
3   stalks celery, chopped
1   medium white potato, cubed
1   teaspoon salt
1   pastry crust (see Basic Pastry recipe on page 281)

Place dove into a saucepan, cover with water, and bring to a full boil. Add thyme, parsley, and bay leaves. Simmer 45 minutes uncovered. Remove from heat and let cool. Remove dove and reserve 2 cups of broth. Bone dove. In a clean, large saucepan, boil 2 cups dove broth, carrots, celery, potatoes, salt, and pepper until vegetables are tender. Place dove meat in a 2-quart casserole dish. Place cooked vegetables on top of dove. Place pastry crust over the whole dish and pierce 4 holes with a fork. Bake at 375° for 30 minutes.

Serves 6

*To tenderize and
bring out flavor of
quail, rub with lemon
before cooking.*

Tallokas Quail

10-12 quail
Herb and garlic marinade or teriyaki marinade

Split quail down the back at the breast bone. Refrigerate and marinate overnight or for up to 3 days, if time allows. Remove quail from marinade and pat dry. Grill over medium hot coals seven to eight minutes per side.

Serves 6

Stuffed Quail

12 quail
Salt and pepper
1¾ sticks butter
1 pound bulk venison sausage (may substitute pork)
1 cup chopped onion
1 cup chopped green pepper
1 pound fresh mushrooms, sliced
1 (10 ounce) jar mayhaw jelly

Wash and dry quail. Season with salt and pepper. Preheat oven to 425˚. In a large skillet, brown sausage; drain and set aside. Sauté onion, green pepper, and mushrooms in 4 tablespoons butter. Combine vegetables and sausage. Stuff quail with sausage mixture. Rub outside of quail with 6 tablespoons softened butter. Place in a shallow roasting pan. (Quail may be covered and refrigerated at this point). Roast 1 hour. Baste with remaining 4 tablespoons melted butter until well browned. Melt jelly in a small sauce pan. Pour over quail.

Serves 6–8

Southern Fried Quail with Cream Gravy

6-8 quail
4 cups whole milk
1 cup flour
1 teaspoon Cajun poultry seasoning
2 cups oil
1 tablespoon butter

Marinate quail in 4 cups milk for 1 hour. Drain and reserve milk. Heat oil and butter together in a skillet. Season flour with Cajun seasoning. Dust quail in flour and fry in oil and butter, turning occasionally until golden brown. Can be served alone or with cream gravy (see recipe at right).

Serves 4

Menu Suggestion: Serve with Fresh Collard Greens (page 137) and Garlic Cheese Grits (page 230).

Cream Gravy

- *2 tablespoons oil*
- *2 tablespoons flour*
- *2 cups chicken broth*
- *4 cups milk or reserved milk from Southern Fried Quail recipe*

Make a roux by heating oil and adding flour. Add chicken broth. Then add milk, stirring constantly until desired consistency. May add additional milk if needed. Serve with Southern Fried Quail.

Makes 6 cups

SMOKED OYSTERS

1   (12 ounce) can beer
3   dozen oysters
1   cup butter
Juice of 2 lemons
1   teaspoon salt
1   teaspoon pepper
3   tablespoons Worcestershire sauce

Prepare a ½ pan of charcoal. Place beer in water pan then add enough water to fill halfway. Place all ingredients in an aluminum pan or on aluminum foil sheet with edges formed to make a pan. Place on smoker rack. Smoke over medium heat for two hours.

Serves 4-6

SMOKED SALMON

4   pounds salmon steaks, thickly cut
2   cups white wine
1   cup soy sauce
1   cup lemon juice
1   tablespoon black pepper
⅓   cup butter, melted

Prepare smoker. Fill charcoal pan ¾ full and add two wood chunks. Fill water pan ¾ full. Marinate salmon overnight in wine, soy sauce, lemon juice and pepper. Make a pan with aluminum foil. Place on top rack of smoker. Place salmon on foil and pour enough marinade to have approximately ½" of liquid in the pan. Add remaining marinade to smoker's water pan. Pour melted butter over fish. Smoke 2 to 2½ hours or until fish flakes easily with a fork.

Serves 8

Grilled Salmon Steaks with Caper Dill Sauce

6   (1½" thick) salmon steaks
½   cup butter
2   tablespoons Dijon mustard
4   tablespoons lemon juice, divided
1   tablespoon fresh dill or 1 teaspoon dried dill
2   tablespoons capers

Marinate steaks in 2 tablespoons lemon juice 1 to 2 hours before cooking. Melt butter, add Dijon mustard, 2 tablespoons lemon juice and dill. Simmer 2 to 3 minutes. Divide sauce in half. Set one half aside to baste fish. Add capers to remaining half of sauce and use to accompany fish when served. Grill salmon 10 minutes per side over medium-hot coals, basting frequently with sauce. Fish will flake when done.

Serves 6

Menu Suggestion: Serve with Parsley New Potatoes (recipe at right) and fresh corn.

Grilled Sesame Trout

6   (8-12 ounce) pan-dressed rainbow trout
½   cup lemon juice
¼   teaspoon salt
1   teaspoon pepper
¼   teaspoon parsley
¼   cup sesame seeds
¾   cup butter

With a sharp knife, make 3 light slashes on each side of fish. In 9" x 13" baking dish, combine lemon juice, parsley, salt, and pepper. Place fish in dish turning to coat with mixture; cover and refrigerate for several hours. In medium saucepan over medium heat, toast sesame seeds until golden; add butter and heat until melted. Drain lemon juice mixture from baking dish into sesame seed mixture. Cook fish over medium-hot coals for about 5 minutes on each side or until fish flakes easily when tested with a fork. Baste frequently with sesame seed mixture.

Serves 6

Parsley New Potatoes

• *20 small new potatoes, precooked in microwave or oven until fork tender*
• *¼ cup butter, melted*
• *2 tablespoons chopped fresh parsley*
• *1 tablespoon Cajun seasoning*

Quarter cooked potatoes. Place in aluminum foil. Drizzle butter over potatoes and sprinkle with parsley and Cajun seasoning. Close aluminum foil tightly over potatoes and place on grill while cooking salmon.

Serves 6

GARLIC-CHEESE GRITS

- *1 cup grits*
- *4 cups water*
- *¼ cup butter*
- *2½ cups grated sharp Cheddar cheese*
- *3 egg yolks, beaten with 1 tablespoon milk*
- *1 tablespoon Worcestershire sauce*
- *1 teaspoon garlic powder*
- *dash hot sauce*
- *3 egg whites, stiffly beaten*
- *paprika*

Add grits to boiling water. Cook until thick (quick grits may be used). Remove from heat. While hot, add 2 cups cheese, egg yolk mixture, Worcestershire sauce, garlic powder, and hot sauce. Cool mixture. Fold in egg whites. Pour in greased 2-quart casserole. Sprinkle with remaining cheese then top with paprika. Bake at 400° for 30 minutes.

Serves 6-8

SPRINGWOOD PLANTATION GRILLED AMBERJACK

2	amberjack fillets
¼	cup olive oil
2	tablespoons white wine vinegar
2	tablespoons water
1	teaspoon basil
1	teaspoon oregano

Place fish in a shallow dish. Mix together next 5 ingredients. Pour over fish. Marinate in refrigerator 2 to 4 hours. Remove fish from marinade. Cook over hot coals according to thickness of fish, approximately 15 minutes or until fish flakes.

Serves 4

GRILLED FISH AND VEGETABLES

½	pound fresh mushrooms, sliced
3	medium tomatoes, peeled and cut in wedges
2	medium yellow squash, sliced
2	medium green peppers, sliced
1	medium zucchini, sliced
1	medium onion, sliced
½	cup butter or margarine
2	pounds grouper fillets
½	cup soy sauce
1	clove garlic, finely chopped
¼	teaspoon pepper

Prepare grill. Make a pan out of heavy duty foil. Place on grill. Place vegetables on foil. Arrange fish over vegetables. Top with soy sauce, garlic, and pepper. Seal edges of foil together securely. Grill over hot coals for 30 minutes or until fish flakes and vegetables are done. Serve immediately.

Serves 8

Great Grouper

4-6 grouper steaks, 1" thick
¼ cup fresh lemon juice
½ cup olive oil
Salt and freshly ground pepper
1 tablespoon tarragon
Lemon wedges

Place fish in a shallow baking dish. Combine lemon juice, olive oil, salt, pepper, and tarragon. Pour over fish; marinate at room temperature for 30 minutes. Place fish in a grill basket. Grill over hot coals for 5 to 6 minutes per side until fish flakes. Serve with lemon wedges.

Serves 4-6

Grilled Scallops

1 bunch green onions, chopped
½ cup vegetable oil
Juice of 1 lemon or lime
½ teaspoon minced garlic
¼ teaspoon salt
½ teaspoon pepper
2 pounds scallops

Combine first 6 ingredients in a large shallow dish. Add scallops to marinade and refrigerate 2 hours. Thread scallops on skewers. Grill 10 to 12 minutes over hot coals, turning and basting occasionally.

Serves 4

Menu Suggestion: Serve with Angel Hair Pasta with Tomato Basil Sauce (page 99), Mandarin Orange Salad (page 92), and Cookie Cheesecake Squares (page 293).

The grill is particularly kind to fish high in oil—those with a pink, orange, red, or brown tint to their flesh, such as salmon, bluefish, and mackerel. These fish retain their moisture in the high, dry heat of grilling and their flavors are enhanced by smoke.

SPINACH-STUFFED TOMATOES

- *4 medium tomatoes*
- *½ (12 ounce) frozen spinach soufflé*
- *grated Parmesan cheese*

Scoop out 4 medium tomatoes. Fill with ½ (12 ounce) frozen spinach soufflé. Sprinkle with Parmesan cheese. Bake at 350° for 20 to 25 minutes.

Serves 4

KEY WEST SHRIMP

¼ cup olive oil
¼ cup fresh lime juice
½ teaspoon chili powder
½ teaspoon ground turmeric
2 teaspoons dried rosemary leaves
1 teaspoon minced garlic
2 pounds large or jumbo shrimp, peeled

Combine all ingredients, except shrimp, in a large glass dish. Add shrimp and marinate 4 hours, stirring occasionally. Remove shrimp from marinade and place on skewers. Grill approximately 7 to 10 minutes, until shrimp are opaque, turning occasionally. Brush with marinade.

Serves 4

Menu Suggestion: Serve with yellow rice, Spinach-Stuffed Tomatoes (recipe at left), and Key Lime Pie (page 277).

GRILLED BEEF TENDERLOIN

¼ cup vegetable oil
2 tablespoons soy sauce
1 tablespoon cider vinegar
1 tablespoon honey
1 tablespoon chopped green onions
1 teaspoon ground ginger
1 small clove garlic, minced
4-6 pounds beef tenderloin

Trim excess fat and membrane from beef tenderloin. Marinate overnight. Prepare charcoal fire, allow coals to burn down to white color. (On a gas grill use a medium heat setting.) Remove tenderloin from marinade, drain carefully (reserve marinade for basting) and place on center of grill. Place cover on grill, making sure fire has some ventilation, using vents to maintain slow, even heat. Turn meat approximately every 5 to 7 minutes, basting lightly, until tenderloin has cooked 20 to 25 minutes. Remove from fire and allow to cool for 5 minutes before carving. Outside will be well done, center rare to medium rare depending on preference, cooking time and strength of fire.

Serves 10–12

GRILLED STEAK WITH RUM BUTTER

4   steaks of your choice
3   tablespoons rum
1   tablespoon chopped green onions
3   tablespoons butter
2   tablespoons fresh lime juice
1   tablespoon chopped parsley
Salt and pepper to taste

Pour rum into pan. Stir in green onions. Season with salt and pepper. Bring to a boil and simmer until ⅔ reduced. Allow to cool slightly. While still warm, stir in butter, lime juice, and parsley, beating well to blend. Allow to cool then refrigerate. Grill steaks to desired doneness over medium hot coals. Top with rum butter.

Serves 4

MARINATED SIRLOIN KABOBS

2   pounds (1½" thick) boneless sirloin steak, cut into 1" chunks
½   pound fresh medium mushroom caps
1   pint cherry tomatoes
2   medium onions, cut into wedges
2   green peppers, cut into 1" pieces
½   cup olive oil
¼   cup red wine vinegar
¼   cup lemon juice
¼   cup soy sauce
¼   cup Worcestershire sauce
2   cloves garlic, minced
1   tablespoon sugar

Combine all marinade ingredients, mixing well. Place meat in a large shallow plastic container with lid. Cover with marinade mixture for 12 hours in the refrigerator, turning container over occasionally. Remove meat from marinade, reserving marinade. Alternate meat and vegetables on skewers. Grill over medium hot coals for 10 to 15 minutes or until desired degree of doneness. Brush lightly with marinade twice while grilling.

Serves 4-6

GRILLING TIPS:
1. Keep steaks from curling by cutting the edge fat at 2" to 3" intervals, but only cut the fat just up to the meat.
2. Turn your steaks with tongs or a spatula. A fork pierces the meat and allows juices to escape.
3. Use a spray bottle filled with water to extinguish any flare-ups.
4. Salt steaks <u>after</u> cooking. Salting before draws the juices out during cooking.

How To Add Zip To Plain 'Ole Hamburgers

1½ pounds ground chuck
Salt and pepper to taste

Shape hamburger into patties. (Try one of the tasty variations below.) Place patties on grill 3" to 4" above hot coals. Grill until well browned, turning frequently to cook evenly. Cook until done as desired. (Rare-12 minutes, Medium-15 minutes, Well done-18 to 20 minutes)

Serves 4-6

VARIATIONS:

BLUE CHEESE BURGER
Make a well in the center of hamburger patty. Add 1½ tablespoons of blue cheese. Seal. Grill to taste. Place on a toasted English muffin. Top with chili sauce or ketchup.

CHILI-CHEESE BURGER
Grill hamburger according to directions above. Just before burger is done, top with a slice of cheese. Melt cheese on burger. Place burger on toasted sesame seed bun. Smother with chili. Top with slices of tomato, onion, and pickle.

MEXICAN BURGER
Cook hamburger according to directions above. Place on a hamburger bun. Top with guacamole, lettuce, tomatoes, onions, salsa, and black olives.

ONION BURGER
Mix French-fried onions with your ground beef. Add enough ketchup to hold mixture together. Form patties. Cook until done.

$\mathcal{P}$INEAPPLE GARLIC PORK CHOPS

4 boneless pork loin chops, 1" thick
1 cup unsweetened pineapple juice
⅔ cup dry sherry
2 tablespoons brown sugar
½ teaspoon dried rosemary leaves, crushed
1 clove garlic, minced
2 tablespoons soy sauce

Combine all ingredients except pork chops, mix well. Place chops in a shallow dish, pour marinade over chops. Cover and refrigerate overnight. Remove chops from marinade. Grill over medium hot coals for 20 minutes basting with marinade and turning frequently.

Serves 4

$\mathcal{G}$RILLED PORK TENDERLOIN

1 pork tenderloin (approximately 1½-2 pounds)
¼ cup bourbon
¼ cup brown sugar
¼ cup soy sauce

Combine bourbon, brown sugar, and soy sauce. Add tenderloin, marinate 4 to 6 hours or overnight. Prepare fire. Remove pork from marinade (reserving marinade) and place on grill 3" to 4" from fire. Cover grill. Baste with marinade occasionally. Grill over medium hot coals about 45 minutes. Pour remaining marinade in a saucepan. Heat to boiling. Remove from heat. To serve, cut pork into thin slices and arrange on platter. Serve with heated reserved marinade.

Serves 4

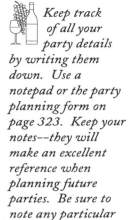

Keep track of all your party details by writing them down. Use a notepad or the party planning form on page 323. Keep your notes--they will make an excellent reference when planning future parties. Be sure to note any particular problems or successes!

Processed pork and fresh pork have very different nutritional profiles. Bacon, sausage, cold cuts, and hot dogs contain so much fat, cholesterol and sodium that it is difficult to include them in a healthy diet. Fresh pork, like tenderloin, center loin, pork leg, or lean ham, are healthy choices when limited to no more than 3 ounces daily. The saturated fat content of lean pork is usually even less than that of lean beef.

Barbra Crumpacker,
Registered Dietitian

GRILLED BOSTON BUTT

1 pork butt, approximately 5-6 pounds
Dry rub of equal amounts of salt, pepper, and paprika

Rub seasonings into pork using your hands, coating entire exterior surface. Prepare a small fire, arranging coals around a drip pan placed in the bottom of the grill. (For gas grill, use low setting.) Place meat on grill rack over drip pan and cover, making sure fire has adequate ventilation to maintain low steady heat. Turn meat every 25 to 30 minutes, adding a handful of charcoal briquets to fire each time to maintain low fire. After 2 hours, begin basting heavily every 20 minutes (for 60 to 80 minutes) with barbecue sauce of your choice. Meat should begin to fall apart. Meat should be completely cooked by this time. Remove from fire and slice or chop as desired.

Serves 6–8

Menu Suggestion: Serve with Grilled Vegetables (recipe at left), Paul's Baked Beans (page 237), and white bread or buns.

VEAL CHOPS À LA PALMER

4 veal chops
¼ pound Fontina cheese, diced
4 sun-dried tomatoes, diced
2 slices prosciutto, diced
½ teaspoon rosemary
Salt and pepper to taste

Mix together cheese, tomatoes, and prosciutto. Make a pocket in each veal chop. Place ¼ of the mixture in each veal chop pocket. Close with a toothpick. Sprinkle each chop with salt, pepper, and rosemary. Prepare grill. Cook chops 8 minutes per side.

Serves 4

GRILLED VEGETABLES

Prepare grill. Fire should be medium hot. It is best to use a vegetable rack. While cooking vegetables, brush them once or twice with BBQ sauce or an herb salad dressing or oil to prevent vegetables from drying out. Turn occasionally.
Onions
Slice onions ½" thick. Grill 15 to 20 minutes until tender.
Eggplant
Cut small eggplant in half lengthwise or a regular-sized eggplant into ½" rounds. Grill 10 to 12 minutes.
Tomatoes
Slice tomatoes ½" thick. Grill 3 to 5 minutes.
Yellow Squash or Zucchini
Cut small squash or zucchini into half lengthwise. Grill 8 to 12 minutes.
Mushrooms
Wash mushrooms. Grill whole mushrooms 12 to 14 minutes.
Artichoke Bottoms
Drain canned artichoke bottoms. Grill 12 to 14 minutes.

GRILLED LEG OF LAMB

1   cup olive oil
½   cup red wine vinegar
2   tablespoons lemon juice
½   cup chopped onion
2   tablespoons minced garlic
1   bay leaf
1   tablespoon Dijon mustard
1   tablespoon rosemary
1   tablespoon marjoram
1   teaspoon basil
1   teaspoon thyme
Salt and pepper
1   (7-9 pound) leg of lamb, butterflied

Combine all ingredients, except lamb, in a 9" x 13" casserole dish. Trim all excess fat and membrane from meat. Place in casserole dish and marinate overnight in refrigerator. Remove lamb from marinade, reserving marinade. Place meat on grill over medium heat and turn every 6 to 8 minutes, basting frequently with reserved marinade. Total cooking time will be approximately 25 to 30 minutes. Allow to cool 5 minutes before carving. Outside will be well done. Center medium rare to medium. Heat remaining marinade to boiling in a small saucepan and serve with meat.

Serves 8

PAUL'S BAKED BEANS

• *1 (48 ounce) can pork and beans*
• *2 tablespoons yellow mustard*
• *2 tablespoons ketchup*
• *1 cup chopped onion*
• *1 cup chopped bell pepper*
• *2 tablespoons molasses or brown sugar*
• *4 slices lean bacon*

Combine beans, mustard, ketchup, molasses, onion, and bell pepper in a 9" x 13" casserole dish and mix thoroughly. Top with bacon slices. Bake at 350° for 40 to 45 minutes. Just prior to removing from oven, turn on broiler for 3 to 5 minutes to crisp bacon and glaze top.

Serves 6–8

This is an all-afternoon project, but worth every minute. This recipe can also be used substituting beef or pork ribs for chicken.

Barbecued Chicken

6 whole chickens (2-2½ pounds each), split down the back
4 cups salt water
½ cup lemon juice
¼ cup Worcestershire sauce
½ cup butter or margarine

Wash chickens. Place chickens skin side up on grill rack over a slow fire. To keep chickens moist, baste with salt water for 1½ hours, turning chickens frequently to keep from burning. Combine lemon juice, Worcestershire sauce, and butter over low heat until butter is melted. Continue cooking chicken for 1½ hours basting with sauce frequently.

Serves 12

Grilled Lemon Chicken

3 pounds chicken, cut into 8 pieces
¼ cup fresh lemon juice
¼ cup olive oil
3 tablespoons oregano
1 teaspoon parsley
¾ teaspoon pepper
2 teaspoons lemon zest

Place chicken in a glass baking dish. Combine ingredients for marinade. Pour over chicken, refrigerate 6 hours or overnight. Remove chicken, reserving marinade. Cook chicken, skin side down with grill covered, over medium hot coals for 45 minutes or until done, turning frequently and brushing with marinade.

Serves 6-8

GOOD FOOD

GOOD COMPANY

DESSERTS

Coconut Sour Cream Cake

1   (18½ ounce) package regular white cake mix (not pudding)
¼   cup vegetable oil
3   eggs
1   (8½ ounce) can cream of coconut
1   (8 ounce) carton sour cream
Flaked coconut

Combine first five ingredients and beat on high for 2 minutes. Reduce speed to low and beat 1 minute. Pour batter into 3 greased and floured 8" cake pans. Bake at 350° for 40 minutes. Let cake cool completely in pans. Frost with Seven Minute Icing (see recipe at right) and sprinkle with coconut.

Serves 16–18

Dicey's Chocolate Cake

1   (14 ounce) can chocolate syrup
12 regular-size milk chocolate bars
2   teaspoons vanilla
2   sticks butter
2   cups sugar
4   eggs
½   teaspoon baking soda
2½ cups cake flour
1   cup buttermilk
1   tablespoon butter

Melt 8 milk chocolate candy bars with syrup in a double boiler. Add vanilla and cool. Cream butter and sugar. Add eggs; mix well. Add chocolate mixture and blend well. Set aside. Mix together baking soda and flour. Add this to chocolate mixture alternately with buttermilk, blending well after each addition. Bake in greased and floured tube pan at 350° for 1 to 1½ hours. To make glaze, melt 4 chocolate candy bars with 1 tablespoon butter. Cool slightly. Drizzle over cake.

Serves 14–16

Seven Minute Icing

• *2 egg whites, unbeaten*
• *1½ cups sugar*
• *¼ teaspoon cream of tartar*
• *⅓ cup cold water*
• *dash of salt*
• *1½ teaspoons vanilla*

Combine all ingredients, except vanilla, in top of double boiler. Beat together 1 minute before cooking. Place over boiling water and beat until stiff peaks form, beating constantly. Remove from heat. Add vanilla. Beat until mixture reaches spreading consistency.

Brown Sugar Chocolate Cake

2½ cups cake flour, sifted
1   teaspoon baking soda
1   cup butter or margarine, softened
2¼ cups firmly packed light brown sugar
3   eggs, slightly beaten
1   teaspoon vanilla
2   squares unsweetened chocolate, melted
1   cup milk

Sift flour with baking soda. Cream butter and sugar until light and fluffy. Add eggs and vanilla. Beat well. Stir in chocolate. Alternately add flour mixture and milk, beating after each addition until smooth. Pour into 3 greased and floured 8" layer pans. Bake at 350° for 30 to 35 minutes. Cool in pans 10 minutes. Frost. (See frosting recipe at left.)

Serves 16–18

Chocolate Chip Cake

1   package yellow cake mix
1   (3 ounce) package instant chocolate pudding
1   (8 ounce) carton sour cream
½   cup oil
½   cup warm water
1   teaspoon vanilla
4   eggs
1   (12 ounce) package chocolate chips
1   cup chopped pecans (optional)

Mix all ingredients together with electric mixer, except nuts and chocolate chips. After all ingredients are mixed well, gently fold in chips and nuts. Pour batter into a greased and floured Bundt pan. Bake at 350° for 50 to 55 minutes.

Serves 16–18

FROSTING
FOR
BROWN SUGAR
CHOCOLATE
CAKE

• *4 squares unsweetened chocolate*
• *½ cup butter*
• *4½ cups confectioners' sugar, sifted*
• *⅓ cup milk*
• *2 egg whites*
• *1 teaspoon vanilla*

Melt squares of unsweetened chocolate. Mix in butter, confectioners' sugar, milk, egg whites, and vanilla. Place mixing container in bowl of ice and water. Beat at low speed until frosting reaches spreading consistency. Spread frosting over Brown Sugar Chocolate Cake.

Cocoa Chocolate Pound Cake

2 sticks margarine
½ cup shortening
3 cups sugar
1 cup milk
5 eggs
3 cups all-purpose flour
½ cup cocoa
½ teaspoon baking powder
½ teaspoon salt
½ teaspoon vanilla

Cream margarine, shortening, sugar, and milk until smooth. Add eggs, one at a time, mixing well after each. In another bowl, sift together flour, cocoa, baking powder, and salt. Add by large spoonfuls to first mixture. Add vanilla. Mix at least 4 minutes with an electric mixer on medium speed. Pour into greased and floured large tube pan or Bundt pan. Bake at 325° for 1 hour and 15 minutes.

Serves 16–18

Sprinkle the cake platter with confectioners' sugar to prevent cake from sticking.

Chocolate Ice Box Cake

¼ pound butter
1 cup sugar
4 squares unsweetened chocolate, melted
4 eggs
½ tablespoon vanilla
1 pint heavy cream, whipped
½ cup chopped nuts
12 lady fingers or pound cake, sliced lengthwise and soaked in sherry

Cream butter and sugar. Add melted chocolate. Add eggs one at a time, blending well after each. Add the vanilla. Line a loaf pan with wax paper so the paper extends over the sides. Line the bottom with halved lady fingers or pound cake already soaked in sherry. Layer chocolate mixture, nuts, and whipped cream; top with lady fingers or cake. Freeze. Slice thin to serve, as it is very rich. Serve with whipped cream or hot chocolate sauce.

Serves 10–12

If a cake is too soggy, slice and toast before serving. If a cake is too dry, cut it into cubes and serve with chocolate fondue or use to make a trifle.

When making frosting or glaze, melt chocolate in a double boiler, over simmering, not boiling water. When water boils, the escaping steam moistens the chocolate and frosting won't dry properly.

APPLESAUCE CAKE

1½ cups applesauce
½ cup shortening
1 cup sugar
1 cup raisins
2 cups all-purpose flour
½ teaspoon cloves
1 teaspoon nutmeg
1 teaspoon cinnamon
½ teaspoon salt
2 teaspoons baking soda
¾ cup chopped nuts

In a saucepan over medium heat, stir together the first 4 ingredients until shortening and sugar are melted and blended. Allow to cool. Sift together the next 6 dry ingredients. Add liquid mixture to dry ingredients. After combining, add chopped nuts. Pour into well-greased tube pan or Bundt pan. Bake at 350° for 30 minutes. (This recipe may be doubled for making a large cake. Cook large cake for 1 hour.)

Serves 8–10

CARAMEL CAKE

CAKE
1   (8 ounce) carton sour cream
⅓   cup milk
1   cup butter, softened
2   cups sugar
4   eggs
2¾ cups all-purpose flour
2   teaspoons baking powder
½   teaspoon salt
1   teaspoon vanilla

Combine sour cream and milk. Set aside. Cream butter, gradually adding sugar. Beat well at medium speed with an electric mixer. Add eggs, beating after each addition. Combine flour, baking powder, and salt; add to creamed mixture alternately with sour cream mixture, beginning and ending with flour. Mix after each addition. Add vanilla. Pour batter into 2 greased and floured 9" round cake pans. Bake at 350° for 35 minutes. Cool in pans 10 minutes. Remove from pans and cool completely on racks. Frost with Caramel Frosting (recipe below).

CARAMEL FROSTING
3   cups sugar, divided
1   teaspoon all-purpose flour
1   cup milk
¾   cup butter
1   teaspoon vanilla

Sprinkle ½ cup sugar in a shallow heavy Dutch oven. Cook over medium heat until sugar melts and syrup is golden brown. Remove from heat. In another large saucepan, mix together remaining 2½ cups sugar with flour, stirring well; add milk and bring to boil stirring constantly. Gradually pour ¼ of hot mixture into caramelized sugar, stirring constantly. Add remaining hot mixture. Mixture will be lumpy, but continue stirring until smooth. Return mixture to heat. Cover and cook on low for 2 minutes. Uncover and cook, without stirring, until temperature on candy thermometer reaches 238°. Add butter and stir to blend. Remove from heat and cool until temperature reaches 100°, about 1 hour. Add vanilla and beat at medium speed until spreading consistency, about 20 minutes.

Serves 16–18

When icing a cake, dip the spatula in hot water occasionally to make frosting smoother.

Margarine products do not always substitute well for butter.

Corn oil margarine makes a softer cookie dough, therefore the dough should be chilled 3 hours before slicing or at least 5 hours before rolling.

Usually 1½ cups whipped margarine equals 1 cup regular margarine.

Reduced-calorie margarine has more water than regular margarine so it isn't always suitable for baking.

Place fresh flowers on top of an otherwise plain cake to make a pretty birthday cake.

RED VELVET CAKE

CAKE

1½ cups sugar
1½ cups vegetable oil
1   teaspoon vanilla
2   large eggs
1   teaspoon white vinegar
2   (1 ounce) bottles red food coloring
1   teaspoon cocoa
1   teaspoon baking soda
1   cup buttermilk
2½ cups self-rising flour

Mix together all ingredients in order given. Spray three 9" round cake pans with non-stick coating. Pour batter equally into the three pans and bake at 350° for 20 minutes. Test for doneness with a toothpick. Cool layers in pans for 10 minutes. Frost with Cream Cheese Icing (see below).

CREAM CHEESE ICING

1⅓ sticks butter, softened
10 ounces cream cheese, softened
1   (1 pound) box confectioners' sugar
2   cups chopped pecans (optional)

Combine butter, cream cheese, and confectioners' sugar. Beat until fluffy, then fold in 1½ cups pecans. Spread frosting between layers and on top and sides of cake. Decorate top of cake with remaining ½ cup pecans.

Serves 16–18

FRESH APPLE CAKE

CAKE

4	cups unpeeled Rome or Granny Smith apples, chopped
2	cups sugar
2	cups all-purpose flour
2	teaspoons baking soda
2	teaspoons cinnamon
1	teaspoon salt
2	eggs
½	cup oil
2	teaspoons vanilla
1	cup chopped nuts

Mix together apples and sugar. Let stand about 30 minutes. Sift together flour, soda, cinnamon, and salt. Beat eggs, oil, and vanilla. Add flour mixture alternately with apples to egg mixture. Fold in nuts. Pour batter into 9" x 13" greased and floured pan. Bake at 350° for 35 to 40 minutes. Cool before adding topping (recipe below).

TOPPING

½	cup butter
¼	cup evaporated milk
1	cup brown sugar
1	teaspoon vanilla

Melt butter in a saucepan. Add milk and sugar. Bring to a boil and cook for 3 minutes. Add vanilla. Pour topping over cake.

Serves 10–12

This fresh apple cake is a perfect prospect for substituting applesauce for oil. The same amount of applesauce takes the place of oil in any cake recipe, but it is usually most satisfactory in a cake that already has some fruit included. The savings are 112 grams of fat and 100 calories. Just reduce the nuts and margarine and use evaporated skim milk and you have a heart-healthy apple cake.

*Barbra Crumpacker,
Registered Dietitian*

Strawberry Patch Cake

Cake

1   box white cake mix
4   eggs
¾   cup vegetable oil
1   (3 ounce) box strawberry gelatin
1   cup frozen strawberries, thawed

Mix together cake mix, eggs, oil, and gelatin. Add 1 cup strawberries and beat well. Pour into 2 greased and floured cake pans. Bake at 350° for 30 minutes or until done. Let cool before frosting with recipe below.

Frosting

1   (1 pound) box confectioners' sugar
1   stick margarine, softened
½   cup frozen strawberries, thawed

Mix together confectioners' sugar, margarine, and strawberries until well blended. Frost cooled Strawberry Patch Cake.

Serves 16–18

Oh So Good Oatmeal Cake

Cake

1¼ cups boiling water
1 stick margarine
1 cup quick oats
1 cup sugar
1 cup firmly packed brown sugar
2 eggs
1½ cups all-purpose flour
1 teaspoon cinnamon
½ teaspoon salt
1 teaspoon nutmeg
2 teaspoons soda
1 teaspoon vanilla

Combine boiling water, margarine, and oats. Cover and let set for 20 minutes. Combine remaining ingredients, mixing well. Stir in oats mixture. Pour into a greased 9" x 13" pan. Bake at 350° for 30 to 40 minutes. Remove from oven; let cool slightly. Add topping below.

Topping

6 tablespoons margarine
1 (3½ ounce) can coconut
½ cup brown sugar
1 cup chopped nuts
¼ cup evaporated milk
1 teaspoon vanilla

Combine all ingredients in saucepan. Heat until margarine is melted. Spread on top of slightly cooled oatmeal cake. Place cake under broiler until brown.

Serves 8-10

Warm cake pans with hot water before greasing – the shortening will go on more easily and the flour will stick evenly.

Grandmother Watt's Orange Cake

5   large (or 6 small) egg yolks
2   cups sugar
½   cup fresh orange juice
Grated rind and pulp of 1 orange
2   cups all-purpose flour, sifted 3 times
1   teaspoon baking powder
3   egg whites, stiffly beaten

Grease and flour two 9" cake pans or a 9" x 13" pan. Slightly beat egg yolks. Add sugar and beat again. Add juice, rind, and pulp. Fold in flour, baking powder, and egg whites. Bake at 350° in the 9" pans for 30 minutes or 45 minutes in the 9" x 13" pan. Top sheet cake or cake layers with filling (see Orange Cake Filling at left); frost entire cake with Seven Minute Icing (page 241).

Serves 16–18

Orange Cake Filling

• 1 (8 ounce) can crushed pineapple
• 1 cup sugar
• 1 tablespoon flour
• juice, rind and pulp of 1 orange

Combine pineapple, sugar, flour, and the juice, rind, and pulp of 1 orange in a saucepan. Cook over medium heat until very thick, stirring constantly. Cool. Spread between round cake layers or on top of sheet cake.

Orange Blossoms

1   box lemon supreme cake mix
Juice of 4 lemons
Juice of 4 oranges
Rind of 2 lemons (optional)
Rind of 2 oranges (optional)
2   (1 pound) boxes confectioners' sugar, sifted

Prepare cake mix as directed on package. Grease and flour tiny muffin tins (approximately 1¾" in diameter), even if non-stick pans are used. Fill each muffin tin with about 1 tablespoon of batter. Bake at 350° until lightly golden. To make glaze, freshly squeeze oranges and lemons, discarding seeds, but saving pulp, juice, and rind. Mix in confectioners' sugar. When tiny cakes come out of oven, remove from pan and dip in glaze while hot. Place on wax paper to drain.

Makes 12 dozen

CREAMY LEMON CAKE

CAKE

2¼ cups cake flour, sifted
1½ cups sugar
4   teaspoons baking powder
1   teaspoon salt
½   cup vegetable oil
1   cup milk, divided
1   teaspoon vanilla
4   egg whites

Sift together the cake flour, sugar, baking powder, and salt. Add vegetable oil, ⅔ cup milk, and vanilla. Beat vigorously for 2 minutes. Add ⅓ cup milk and egg whites. Beat 2 minutes. Pour into 3 buttered 8" pans lined with wax paper. Bake at 350° for 25 to 30 minutes. Cool cake and top layers with Creamy Lemon Filling (below); frost entire cake with Seven Minute Icing (page 241).

CREAMY LEMON FILLING

1   stick butter, softened
1   cup sugar
6   egg yolks, well beaten
Juice of 2 large lemons or 3 small lemons

Cream together butter and 1 cup sugar. Add egg yolks and lemon juice. Cook in a double boiler, stirring constantly until filling is thick enough to spread between the layers of cake.

Serves 16–18

Test layer cakes and cupcakes for doneness by lightly touching the center. When pressed, it should spring back. The cake should also begin to pull away from the sides of the pan.

HOMEMADE BAKING POWDER:

Combine 6 ounces cream of tartar, 2⅔ ounces bicarbonate of soda, and 4½ ounces flour in bowl and mix well. Store in tightly covered container.

ℬLUEBERRY GINGER CUPCAKES WITH LEMON FROSTING

CUPCAKES

1   cup fresh or frozen blueberries
½   cup butter or margarine
¾   cup sugar
1   egg
¼   cup molasses
2   cups all-purpose flour, sifted
1   teaspoon baking powder
½   teaspoon baking soda
½   teaspoon salt
1   teaspoon ground cinnamon
1   teaspoon ground ginger
1   cup buttermilk

Thaw and drain blueberries, if frozen. In large mixing bowl, cream together butter and sugar until light and fluffy. Add egg; beat well. Stir in molasses. Sift together flour, baking powder, soda, salt, cinnamon, and ginger. Add alternately to creamed mixture with buttermilk, mixing well. Fold in blueberries. Line muffin pan with paper baking cups. Fill cups ⅔ full. Bake at 350° for 20 to 25 minutes. Cool. Frost with Lemon Butter Frosting (see below).

LEMON FROSTING

4   tablespoons butter
2   cups confectioners' sugar, sifted
1   teaspoon grated lemon peel
1   tablespoon lemon juice
1   teaspoon milk

Cream butter; gradually add sifted confectioners' sugar, blending until smooth. Add grated lemon peel and lemon juice. Beat until mixture is smooth. Stir in milk to make the frosting the proper spreading consistency (add more milk if necessary).

Makes 16

BLUEBERRY TEACAKE

CAKE
¾ cup sugar
¼ cup vegetable shortening
1 egg
½ teaspoon lemon or orange rind
½ cup milk
1 cup self-rising flour
1 cup all-purpose flour
1 teaspoon baking powder
2 cups blueberries, fresh or frozen and thawed

CRUMB TOPPING
½ cup sugar
⅓ cup all-purpose flour or oatmeal
½ teaspoon cinnamon
¼ cup butter, softened
½ cup broken pecans, if desired

Mix together first 8 ingredients until well blended. Carefully fold in blueberries. Spread batter evenly in 9" x 13" greased pan or into 2 dozen muffin cups. In another bowl, mix together the Crumb Topping ingredients. Sprinkle crumb mixture on top of batter and bake at 350° for 40 minutes for large pan or 30 minutes for muffins.

Serves 12

For the best cakes, let eggs, butter, and milk reach room temperature before mixing.

To remove cake layers from pans easily, place the pans on a damp cloth immediately after taking them from the oven.

Mocha Almond Torte

1½ teaspoons instant coffee
1   tablespoon milk
⅔   cup butter or margarine, softened
3   cups confectioners' sugar, sifted and divided
1½ (1 ounce) squares of unsweetened chocolate, melted and cooled
2   egg yolks
1   frozen loaf pound cake, thawed
½   cup of almond paste
3   tablespoons of water
Almonds, sliced and toasted

Dissolve coffee in milk. In a mixing bowl, beat the butter for 30 seconds, beat in 1½ cups of confectioners' sugar, and the melted chocolate. Add egg yolks and the dissolved coffee, beating until the mixture is well blended. Add the remaining confectioners' sugar and additional milk if needed to make a fluffy frosting. Slice the pound cake into three horizontal layers. Beat almond paste and 3 tablespoons of water together. Spread the almond mixture on the layers. Stack the layers and then frost; sprinkle with sliced toasted almonds.

Serves 6–8

Chocolate Meringue Torte

Torte

5 egg whites
Pinch cream of tartar
¾ cups granulated sugar
1¾ cups confectioners' sugar
⅓ cup unsweetened cocoa

Beat 5 egg whites with cream of tartar until they hold soft peaks. Add granulated sugar, 2 tablespoons at a time and continue beating until whites are very stiff. Sift confectioners' sugar and cocoa together and fold into egg white mixture. Using an 8" square pan as a guide, trace and cut 3 squares from parchment paper. Place paper on baking sheets. Divide meringue mixture evenly among the squares, spreading it to the edges. Bake at 300° for 1 hour and 15 minutes. Transfer meringues to racks. Cool. Prepare mousse (recipe below). To assemble torte, place one meringue square on a cake stand and spread thickly with mousse. Top with a second meringue and spread with more mousse. Top with remaining meringue. Using remaining mousse mixture and reserved whipped cream, pipe scrolls onto meringue in an alternating pattern using pastry tubes with decorative tips. Be sure scrolls overlap to cover meringue completely.

Serves 10-12

Mousse

13 ounces semi-sweet chocolate
7 egg whites, beaten with ¼ teaspoon cream of tartar
3 cups chilled heavy cream, whipped with 1½ teaspoons vanilla
   until stiff

Melt chocolate in top of a double boiler. Cool to lukewarm. Fold carefully into the 7 beaten egg whites. Fold in ⅔ of whipped cream. Mix carefully to blend. Reserve remaining cream. Refrigerate mousse and remaining cream until ready to use.

Eggs separate easily when still cold from the refrigerator, but whites should be at room temperature for maximum whipping.

Freeze dollops or piped
rosettes of sweetened
whipped cream on wax
paper. When hard, place
them into a plastic bag
and freeze until needed.
Use to garnish cakes,
puddings, and other
desserts.

CHOCOLATE CHEESECAKE

1   (10 ounce) box chocolate graham crackers or thin chocolate
    wafer cookies
½   stick butter, melted
1   tablespoon sugar
3   (8 ounce) packages cream cheese, room temperature
1   cup sugar
1½ cups sour cream
2   eggs
1   tablespoon unsweetened cocoa powder
1   teaspoon vanilla
10 ounces semisweet chocolate chips, melted

In a food processor, finely grind chocolate graham crackers. Add
butter and sugar and blend well. Press mixture onto bottom and
sides of a 9" springform pan. With electric mixer, blend cream
cheese and sugar until smooth. Add sour cream, eggs, cocoa powder, and vanilla; blend well. Add melted chocolate chips and mix in
slowly. Pour filling into crust, smooth top. Bake at 350° on center
oven rack until center is just set and cheesecake begins to crack at
edges, about 50 minutes. Cool completely, cover and chill overnight.

Serves 10–12

White Chocolate Cheesecake

¾   cup ground blanched almonds
¾   cup quick-cooking oats, uncooked
¾   cup graham cracker crumbs
¼   cup sugar
¼   cup plus 2 tablespoons butter, softened
2   (8 ounce) packages cream cheese, softened
1   cup sugar
1   (16 ounce) carton sour cream
1   teaspoon vanilla
8   ounces white chocolate, melted
4   egg whites, at room temperature
⅛   teaspoon cream of tartar
1   tablespoon confectioners' sugar

Combine first 5 ingredients in a medium bowl; blend well. Press into bottom and 2" up sides of a 10" springform pan. Bake at 350° for 5 minutes. Cool on wire rack. Combine cream cheese and 1 cup sugar. Using an electric mixer, beat at medium speed until fluffy. Add sour cream and vanilla. Mix well. Stir in melted white chocolate. Beat egg whites with electric mixer on high until foamy. Add cream of tartar, beating until soft peaks form. Add confectioners' sugar; beat until stiff peaks form. Fold egg whites into cream cheese mixture; spoon into crust. Bake at 325° for 55 minutes; turn off oven. Leave cheesecake in oven 30 minutes. Partially open oven door and leave cheesecake in oven an additional 30 minutes. Cool. Chill 8 hours before serving.

Serves 10–12

For perfect chocolate curls, place chocolate bar on a cutting board. Pull a vegetable peeler the full length of the bar at a 30° angle. Use a toothpick to pick up the curl. Store in the refrigerator or freezer.

CHOCOLATE GLAZE

• 6 (1 ounce) squares semisweet chocolate
• ¼ cup butter
• 2 tablespoons water
• ¾ cup confectioners' sugar
• 1 teaspoon vanilla

Combine chocolate and butter in top of a double boiler; bring water to a boil. Reduce heat to low and cook until chocolate melts. Remove from heat and stir in remaining ingredients. Stir until smooth. Spread over cheesecake while glaze is warm.

TRIPLE LAYER CHOCOLATE CHEESECAKE

2   cups chocolate cookies, crushed (preferably wafers)
¾   cup sugar, divided
¼   cup plus 1 tablespoon butter, melted
2   (8 ounce) packages plus 5 ounces cream cheese, softened and divided
3   eggs
1   teaspoon vanilla, divided
2   (1 ounce) squares semisweet chocolate, melted
1⅓ cups sour cream, divided
⅓   cup dark brown sugar, firmly packed
¼   cup chopped pecans
1   tablespoon all-purpose flour
¼   teaspoon almond extract
Chocolate glaze (see recipe at left)

Combine cookie crumbs, ¼ cup sugar, and butter; blend well. Press onto bottom and 2" up sides of 9" springform pan. Set aside. Combine one 8 ounce package cream cheese and ¼ cup sugar; beat at medium speed until fluffy. Add 1 egg and ¼ teaspoon vanilla; beat well. Stir in melted chocolate and ⅓ cup sour cream. Spoon over chocolate crust. Combine remaining 8 ounce package cream cheese, brown sugar, and flour. Beat until fluffy. Add 1 egg and ½ teaspoon vanilla; beat well and stir in pecans. Spoon over chocolate layer. Combine 5 ounces cream cheese and remaining ¼ cup sugar; beat until fluffy. Add remaining egg and beat well. Stir in remaining 1 cup sour cream, ¼ teaspoon vanilla, and almond extract. Spoon gently over pecan layer. Bake at 325° for 1 hour. Turn oven off and leave cheesecake for 30 minutes; open door of oven and leave cheesecake for an additional 30 minutes. Cool. Cover and chill at least 8 hours. Remove from pan and spread warm chocolate glaze over cheesecake.

Serves 10–12

Chocolate Turtle Cheesecake

2 cups vanilla wafer crumbs
6 tablespoons butter
1 (14 ounce) bag of caramels
1 (5 ounce) can evaporated milk
1 cup chopped pecans, toasted
2 (8 ounce) packages cream cheese, softened
½ cup sugar
1 teaspoon vanilla
2 eggs
½ cup semisweet chocolate morsels, melted

Combine crumbs and butter, press into bottom and sides of a 9" springform pan. Bake at 350° for 10 minutes. In a heavy 1½-quart saucepan, melt caramels with milk over low heat, stirring frequently until smooth. Pour over crust. Top with pecans. Combine cream cheese, sugar, and vanilla, mixing at medium speed with an electric mixer until well blended. Add eggs one at a time, mixing well after each addition. Blend in chocolate. Pour over pecans. Bake at 350° for 40 to 50 minutes. Loosen cake from rim of pan and chill. Garnish with whipped cream, chopped pecans, and maraschino cherries, if desired.

Serves 10–12

To cut cheesecake easily, dip the knife in warm water or coat it with vegetable cooking spray.

Miniature Cherry Cheesecakes

18 vanilla wafers
2 (8 ounce) packages cream cheese
¾ cup sugar
1 teaspoon lemon juice
1 teaspoon vanilla
2 eggs
1 (16 ounce) can cherry pie filling

Place paper liners in 18 muffin cups. In the bottom of each, place one vanilla wafer. Mix cream cheese, sugar, lemon juice, vanilla, and eggs. Spoon into lined muffin cups. Bake at 375° for 15 to 20 minutes. Cool. Top each cheesecake with 1 teaspoon pie filling. Refrigerate.

Makes 1½ dozen

Plan your menu and shop for all except the most perishable ingredients at least one day before the party.

Chocolate Sauce

• 1 (16 ounce) package semisweet chocolate morsels
• 1 (12 ounce) can evaporated milk
• 2 cups confectioners' sugar, sifted
• ½ teaspoon vanilla

Combine chocolate morsels and evaporated milk in a heavy saucepan. Cook over medium heat, stirring constantly, until chocolate melts. Stir in confectioners' sugar. Cook over medium heat, stirring frequently, 5 minutes or until sauce thickens. Stir in vanilla extract.

Frozen Peppermint Cheesecake

1½ cups crushed chocolate sandwich cookies
¼ cup sugar
¼ cup butter, melted
1 (8 ounce) package cream cheese, softened
1 (14 ounce) can sweetened condensed milk
2 teaspoons peppermint extract
2 cups whipping cream, whipped

Combine cookie crumbs, sugar, and butter; press on bottom and halfway up sides of 9" springform pan. In a large mixing bowl, beat cream cheese until fluffy. Slowly add sweetened condensed milk. Stir in peppermint flavoring. Fold in whipped cream. Pour into prepared pan. Cover and freeze 6 hours or until firm. Serve with warm chocolate sauce (recipe at left). Store in freezer.

Serves 10–12

Robin's Caramel Flan

1 cup sugar
5 eggs, separated
1 quart milk
¼ cup plus 1 tablespoon sugar
1 teaspoon vanilla

In a clean, dry cast-iron skillet, heat 1 cup sugar over moderate heat, stirring frequently, until melted and darkened. Pour hot syrup into clean, dry 2-quart mold or Bundt pan. Swirl until bottom and sides are coated. Scald milk and allow to cool slightly. In a large bowl, cream egg yolks and sugar. In a separate bowl, whip egg whites until stiff but not dry. Add milk in steady slow stream to egg yolk mixture, whisking constantly. Fold in egg whites. Stir in vanilla. Pour into prepared mold. Place mold in casserole filled with hot water to the depth of the caramelized sugar. Bake at 350° for 1 hour or until knife blade comes out clean. Chill thoroughly. Turn out on serving plate.

Serves 6–8

DECADENT CHOCOLATE SOUFFLÉ

3   tablespoons unsalted butter
3   tablespoons all-purpose flour
½   cup milk
1   pound bittersweet chocolate, cut into pieces
¾   cup strong coffee, brewed
1   teaspoon vanilla
½   cup sugar, divided
5   egg yolks
7   egg whites, room temperature
Pinch cream of tartar

Melt butter in saucepan over low heat. Whisk in flour; gradually stir in milk. Cook, stirring constantly, until thick and smooth. Add chocolate until it melts. Stir in coffee; remove from heat. Stir in vanilla and ¼ cup sugar. Add egg yolks, one at a time, whisking well after each addition. Preheat oven to 375°. Butter a 2-quart soufflé dish and coat with granulated sugar. Beat the egg whites with cream of tartar until foamy. Beat in the remaining ¼ cup sugar, 1 tablespoon at a time. Beat until the peaks are stiff and glossy. Gently fold the egg whites into the soufflé base. Pour the batter into the prepared dish. Bake for 40 minutes. Serve immediately with whipped cream. Cream may be flavored with liqueur.

Serves 12

Refrigerate or freeze the buttered soufflé dish to help the soufflé rise straight up.

Praline Soufflé with Raspberry Sauce

SOUFFLÉ
1   cup egg whites (about 6), at room temperature
10 tablespoons granulated sugar
½   cup Praline Powder (recipe below)
Whipping cream, whipped
Fresh raspberries
Raspberry Cardinal Sauce (recipe at left)

Beat egg whites until frothy. Gradually beat in sugar until mixture is stiff and glossy. Do not over beat. Fold in ½ cup praline powder (recipe follows). Spoon meringue mixture into a buttered 2-quart soufflé dish lightly coated with granulated sugar. Set dish in a deep pan and pour boiling water halfway up the sides of the soufflé dish. Place on middle rack of oven. Bake in preheated 350° oven for 40 minutes or until a cake tester inserted into the center of the soufflé comes out clean. Remove dish from water and run a spatula carefully around the soufflé to loosen the edge. Soufflé will sink as it cools. When soufflé reaches room temperature, transfer to serving plate by turning a plate upside down over soufflé dish and inverting. Spoon Raspberry Cardinal Sauce (recipe at left) over soufflé and garnish with whipped cream and fresh raspberries.

Serves 6

PRALINE POWDER
½   cup sugar
¼   cup water
½   cup chopped pecans

Place sugar and water in small, heavy saucepan. Heat, stirring until sugar dissolves. Continue to heat without stirring until mixture turns a pale caramel color. Stir in pecans and pour immediately onto an oiled cookie sheet. Cool completely. Break up candy into rough pieces; place a small amount at a time in a blender or food processor and pulverize until chunks are reduced to a powder.

Makes 1¼ cups

Raspberry Cardinal Sauce

• 2 (10 ounce) boxes frozen raspberries, thawed
• 6 fresh strawberries (optional)
• 1 tablespoon cornstarch
• 2 tablespoons lemon juice
• 2 tablespoons kirsch or amaretto

Purée raspberries and their juice with strawberries, if desired, in blender or food processor. Force mixture through a sieve to remove seeds. Mix cornstarch with lemon juice and add to raspberry mixture. Bring to a boil and cook until slightly thickened . Add kirsch. Sauce will keep in refrigerator for weeks.

Makes 2¼ cups

Normandy Chocolate Mousse

12 ladyfingers, split
¾ cup margarine
1¾ cups confectioners' sugar, sifted
6 eggs, separated
¼ cup milk
1½ teaspoons vanilla
1 teaspoon rum extract
4 ounces unsweetened chocolate, melted
1½ cups chopped nuts
Whipped cream

Line a 9" x 5" pan with wax paper. Arrange ladyfingers around sides and bottom of pan. In a mixing bowl, cream margarine; gradually add sugar, creaming until light and fluffy. Add egg yolks, one at a time; beating until smooth after each addition. Blend in milk, vanilla, and rum extract. Blend in melted chocolate. Beat egg whites until stiff but not dry and fold into chocolate mixture. Fold in nuts. Pour into pan containing ladyfingers. Refrigerate overnight. To serve, invert on a plate and remove wax paper. Cut into thin slices and top with whipped cream.

Serves 8-10

Ginger Mousse Trifle

1 quart heavy whipping cream
½ cup sugar
2 teaspoons ginger
8 ounces shredded coconut
2 cups chopped walnuts
9 tablespoons Drambuie
2 tablespoons Scotch
1 (7½ ounce) box ginger cookies, such as ginger snaps

Whip cream and sugar until stiff. Add next 5 ingredients, one at a time, ending with Scotch. Mix well. In a trifle dish or large serving bowl, place a generous layer of ginger cookies and top with a generous layer of cream. Repeat until all the cream mixture is used. The last layer should be whipped cream. Refrigerate for several hours or overnight before serving.

Serves 8

Forgery

• *1 quart vanilla ice cream, slightly softened*
• *½ dozen macaroons, broken in pieces*
• *1½ ounces bourbon*
• *1 package frozen strawberries or peaches, thawed*

Fold macaroons into softened ice cream; add bourbon and thawed strawberries. Freeze. Set out 15 minutes before serving. Serve in compote dishes.

Serves 8

ℒuscious Chocolate Mousse

3 cups chocolate wafer crumbs
1 stick unsalted butter, melted
1 pound semisweet chocolate
2 eggs
4 egg yolks
4 cups whipping cream, divided
6 tablespoons confectioners' sugar
4 egg whites at room temperature
Sugar to taste

Make crust by combining wafer crumbs and butter. Press mixture on the bottom and completely up the sides of a 10" springform pan. Refrigerate 30 minutes or chill in freezer. To make filling, soften chocolate in top of double boiler over simmering water. Let cool to lukewarm, about 95°. Add whole eggs and mix well. Add yolks and mix until thoroughly blended. Whip 2 cups cream with confectioners' sugar until soft peaks form. Beat egg whites until stiff, but not dry. Stir a little of the cream and whites into chocolate mixture to lighten. Fold in remaining whipped cream and whites until completely incorporated. Turn into crust and chill at least 6 hours or overnight until firm. Before serving, whip remaining 2 cups cream with sugar until very stiff. Using a sharp knife, loosen crust on all sides; remove springform. Top cake with whipped cream and decorate with chocolate leaves (see recipe at right).

Serves 10–12

CHOCOLATE LEAVES

• *8 ounces semisweet chocolate*
• *1 tablespoon vegetable shortening*
• *camellia, lemon, rose, or other waxy leaves*, washed and dried*

Melt chocolate and shortening in top of double boiler. Using spoon, generously coat underside of leaves. When hardened, loosen leaves gently from chocolate.

*Make sure the leaves you use are free from pesticides. Washing leaves may not remove all pesticide residue.

RASPBERRY CREAM

1   small package of raspberry gelatin
½   cup boiling water
¾   cup crushed ice
1   cup heavy cream
Cookies or fresh raspberries

Put the raspberry gelatin and boiling water into food processor or blender. Blend on high for 15 seconds. Add the crushed ice. When the ice is blended, pour in one cup of heavy cream and whip. Pour into individual glasses and chill until serving time. Add cookies or raspberries for garnish.

Serves 4

VANILLA CREAM WITH RASPBERRIES

2   cups whipping cream
¾   cup sugar
1   envelope unflavored gelatin
½   cup cold water
2   cups sour cream
1   teaspoon vanilla extract
2   cups fresh raspberries or other sliced fresh berries
¼   cup amaretto

In a small saucepan, cook the cream over low heat until warm but not hot. Gradually add the sugar and stir until dissolved; remove from heat. In another small saucepan, soften the gelatin in ½ cup of cold water. Bring to a boil, stirring to dissolve the gelatin; remove from heat. Blend into the cream mixture. Slowly add the sour cream. Pour the mixture into an ungreased 4-cup ring mold or into individual serving cups. Cover and refrigerate overnight, until firm. Shortly before serving, toss the berries with the amaretto and let stand for 15 to 30 minutes. Unmold vanilla cream, slice, and top with berries. If serving in individual cups, do not slice. Just top with berries. Serve slightly chilled.

Serves 6

If you wish, you can make a second layer of pineapples and bananas.

Banana Split Dessert

3 sticks margarine
2 cups graham cracker crumbs
1 (1 pound) box confectioners' sugar
2 eggs
1 (8 ounce) can crushed pineapple, drained
4 bananas
1 envelope whipped topping mix
Chopped nuts
Cherries

Melt 1 stick margarine. Add graham cracker crumbs and mix together well. Press mixture into a 9" x 13" glass baking dish. In a bowl, cream 2 sticks of margarine. Add confectioners' sugar, then eggs. Beat 15 minutes. Spread mixture in dish over cracker crumbs. Drain pineapple and spread over sugar and egg mixture. Slice bananas over pineapple. Prepare whipped topping according to package instructions and spread over layers. Sprinkle with nuts and cherries.

Serves 8

Cookies 'n Lime Fluff

Raspberry gelatin also works well in this recipe. Remember to substitute red food coloring for the green coloring.

30 chocolate sandwich cookies, crushed
¼ cup butter, melted
1 (3 ounce) package lime gelatin
1¾ cups hot water
1 cup sugar
¼ cup lemon juice
1 (13 ounce) can evaporated milk, well chilled
Green food coloring

Always dissolve gelatin completely before adding to any recipe – it will prevent lumps from forming.

Line a 9" x 13" pan with cookies and butter, reserving ⅓ cup of crumbs. Dissolve gelatin in hot water. Refrigerate until almost set, then whip 15 to 20 minutes with electric mixer on high setting. Add sugar, lemon juice, and green food coloring. In a separate bowl, pour chilled milk and whip until stiff. Add to gelatin mixture and whip. Pour into crust. Sprinkle with remaining cookie crumbs and chill.

Serves 10–12

BREAD PUDDING WITH WHISKEY SAUCE

1   loaf French bread, broken into small pieces
1   quart milk
3   eggs
2   cups sugar
2   tablespoons vanilla
1   cup raisins
3   tablespoons margarine, melted

Soak bread in milk. In a separate bowl, mix together eggs, sugar, vanilla, and raisins. Pour melted margarine into the bottom of a 9" x 13" x 2" pan. Top with bread mixture. Pour egg mixture over bread. Bake at 350° for 50 minutes to 1 hour. Cool. Serve with warm Whiskey Sauce (recipe at right).

Serves 8–10

BAKED BRAZILIAN

8   large, round chocolate wafers
8   scoops coffee ice cream
4   egg whites
¼   cup cream of tartar
¼   cup sugar

Place the eight wafers on 2 baking sheets. Top each wafer with 1 scoop of ice cream. Put cookie sheets in freezer. Prepare meringue. Whip egg whites with cream of tartar; gradually add sugar, whipping until stiff. Just before serving, remove ice cream-topped wafers from the freezer. Cover each with meringue. Bake at 400° for 3 minutes or until brown. Serve immediately.

Serves 8

WHISKEY SAUCE

- *1 stick butter*
- *¾ cup sugar*
- *4 tablespoons milk*
- *2 jiggers whiskey*

Cream together the butter and sugar; add milk and whiskey. Heat and serve over baked bread pudding (recipe at left).

SUMMER
DESSERT

• 1 (½ gallon)
carton vanilla ice
cream
• crème de menthe
• 6 chocolate-
covered toffee candy
bars, crushed

In parfait glasses,
layer vanilla ice
cream, crème de
menthe, and
crushed candy bars.
Repeat with
another layer,
finishing with
candy bar.

Makes 6

BAKLAVA

1 (1 pound) package frozen phyllo pastry, thawed
1¼ cups butter, melted
1 cup ground pecans
½ cup ground almonds
2 tablespoons brown sugar
1½ teaspoons ground cinnamon
¼ teaspoon ground nutmeg
½ cup sugar
½ cup water
¼ cup honey
1 tablespoon lemon juice

Grease a 9" x 13" x 2" baking pan. Cut phyllo in half crosswise; cut each half to fit the pan. Layer 15 sheets of phyllo in the greased pan, brushing each sheet with melted butter. (As you work, keep remaining phyllo covered with a damp towel to prevent it from drying out.) Set remaining butter aside. Combine pecans and next 4 ingredients, stirring well. Sprinkle half of nut mixture over phyllo in baking pan. Drizzle with a little melted butter. Top nut mixture with 15 additional sheets of phyllo, brushing each sheet with melted butter. Top phyllo with remaining nut mixture and drizzle with a little melted butter. Top with remaining phyllo, brushing each sheet with melted butter. Using a sharp knife, score top of phyllo in a diamond design. Bake at 350° for 45 minutes or until golden. Let cool completely. Combine sugar, water, and honey in a saucepan. Bring to a boil; boil 10 minutes, stirring occasionally. Stir in lemon juice. Drizzle honey mixture over phyllo. Cut phyllo along scored lines. Let stand at room temperature 8 hours before serving.

Makes 3 dozen

CREAM PUFFS

PUFFS

1 cup water
½ cup butter
1 cup flour, sifted
4 eggs

In a saucepan, bring water and butter to a boil. Stir in flour. Stir constantly until mixture leaves pan and forms a ball, about 1 minute. Remove pan from heat. Cool. Beat in the eggs, one at a time. Drop dough by teaspoonfuls on to a cookie sheet two inches apart. Bake at 350° for 50 minutes or until browned and dry. Cool on racks.

CUSTARD FILLING

½ cup sugar
½ teaspoon salt
6 tablespoons all-purpose flour
2 cups milk
2 eggs, beaten
2 teaspoons vanilla

Mix together sugar, salt, and flour. Slowly add 2 cups milk. Microwave on high for 7 to 8 minutes or until thickened, rotating bowl and whisking custard every 1½ minutes. Slowly add 2 beaten eggs. Microwave 1½ minutes. Cool and blend in 2 teaspoons vanilla. Slice off top of puffs and hollow out, removing any dough filaments from inside. Spoon in custard. Replace top and cover with Chocolate Glaze (recipe below).

CHOCOLATE GLAZE

1 cup confectioners' sugar
2 tablespoons cocoa
1 tablespoon butter
Milk

Mix together confectioners' sugar, cocoa, and butter. Add a few drops of milk; blend.

Makes 3 dozen

Before scalding milk, rinse the pan in cold water to prevent sticking.

Use a plastic ketchup bottle filled with chocolate sauce to decorate dessert plates.

Keep skin from forming on puddings or custards by pressing a piece of wax paper or plastic wrap directly on the surface while it's still warm. An alternative would be to stretch several layers of damp paper towels over the bowl. (The towels let steam escape while keeping the top of the pudding smooth.)

About 7 drops of lemon juice added to a pint of whipping cream makes it beat firm in half the time.

Rainbow Tart

2   (8 ounce) packages cream cheese, softened
½   cup margarine
1¼ cups flour
¼   teaspoon salt
⅓   cup sugar
1   tablespoon lemon juice
1   cup whipping cream, whipped
Assorted fresh fruit, such as strawberries, blueberries, kiwi, and peaches
¼   cup apricot preserves
1   tablespoon water

Mix ½ package cream cheese and margarine until blended. Add flour and salt; mix well. Form dough into a ball and chill. On a lightly floured surface, roll chilled dough into a 14" circle. Place rolled out dough in a 12" torte or pizza pan. Prick bottom and sides of dough with a fork. Bake at 425° for 12 to 15 minutes or until golden brown. Mix remaining cream cheese, sugar, and lemon juice until blended. Fold in whipped cream and spoon into cooled crust. Arrange fruit on cream cheese mixture. Combine preserves and water and brush over fruit. Chill 2 to 3 hours before serving.

Serves 10

Frozen Grand Marnier Soufflé

4   large oranges
6   egg yolks
¾   cup sugar
2⅔ cups heavy cream, whipped
⅓   cup Grand Marnier

Cut oranges in half and carefully scoop out flesh without tearing outer skin to form cups. In a bowl, beat egg yolks and sugar until stiff. Fold in 2 cups cream; add Grand Marnier. Fill orange cups with mixture and freeze at least 2 hours. Before serving, top with remaining whipped cream, dust with cocoa, and garnish with sprigs of mint.

Serves 8

Zingy Lemon Dessert

5 tablespoons cornstarch
1 pinch salt
1 cup sugar
3 eggs, separated
1 cup water, boiling
6 tablespoons lemon juice
1 tablespoon butter, softened
1 cup whipped cream
12 lady fingers, split

Line mold or 9" x 5" loaf pan with split lady fingers. Set aside. In a saucepan, mix together cornstarch, salt, and sugar. In a bowl, beat egg yolks and add to cornstarch mixture. Add water, lemon juice, and butter. Cook over low heat until thick and smooth, stirring constantly. Beat egg whites until stiff. Fold beaten egg whites into the cooked mixture. Cool mixture; fold in whipped cream. Pour into mold lined with split lady fingers. Chill overnight. Serve with whipped cream.

Serves 6

Caramel Apple Fondue

¼ cup butter
1 cup dark brown sugar
½ cup light corn syrup
2 tablespoons water
6 ounces sweetened condensed milk
1 tablespoon vanilla extract
Apple slices

Mix all ingredients together in saucepan. Cook over medium heat until thickened. Pour into a fondue pot. Skewer apple slices with fondue forks and dip into caramel sauce.

Makes 2 cups

This recipe is also delicious as an ice cream topping or spooned over your favorite pound cake.

Fruit Pizza

1 (20 ounce) roll sugar cookie dough
1-2 (8 ounce) packages cream cheese, softened
½ cup sugar, or to taste
1 (8 ounce) can crushed pineapple, drained, with juice reserved
1 (8 ounce) can mandarin orange slices, drained, with juice reserved
Fresh fruit, sliced or whole
¼ to ⅓ cup tapioca beads (optional)

Press cookie dough flat onto round or square pizza pan, making a raised crust around edge. Bake at 350° for 10 to 15 minutes or until lightly browned. Mix together cream cheese and sugar. Spread on crust in desired thickness. Sprinkle crushed pineapple over cream cheese. Arrange orange slices and other fruit over pizza. If desired, make a glaze by mixing the reserved pineapple and orange juices together; add enough water so that it equals 2 cups. Stir in the tapioca beads and let stand for 5 minutes. Transfer to a saucepan and boil for 5 to 8 minutes, stirring frequently. Pour or spread hot glaze over top of fruit. Allow entire pizza to cool at room temperature or in the refrigerator before serving.

Serves 8

Pineapple Belle Hélène

1 ripe pineapple
¼ cup dark rum
3 tablespoons confectioners' sugar
Juice of ½ lemon
6 ounces semi-sweet chocolate
½ cup heavy cream

Halve the pineapple vertically and carefully hollow out each half, removing the flesh in 1" or smaller cubes. Place the cubes in a bowl. Stir in the rum, confectioners' sugar, and lemon juice. Let stand for 4 hours at room temperature. Place the chocolate and cream in a double boiler over low heat. Stir frequently until the chocolate is melted. Cool to lukewarm. To serve, place the pineapple cubes into the hollowed out pineapple halves. Pour chocolate sauce over them or place the chocolate sauce in a serving bowl and allow guests to pour the chocolate over their servings.

Serves 2-4

Bananas Foster

3 tablespoons banana cordial
¼ cup dark rum
4 tablespoons butter
¼ cup firmly packed dark brown sugar
2 bananas, peeled and halved lengthwise
¼ teaspoon ground cinnamon
Vanilla ice cream

Stir the banana cordial and rum together in a small bowl and set aside. Place the butter in a 9" x 9" microwave dish and melt on high for 1½ minutes. Stir the brown sugar into the melted butter. Turn the banana halves in the mixture, coating well. Arrange bananas in the dish, flat side down. Sprinkle with cinnamon. Cover and cook for 1½ minutes in the microwave on high power. Drizzle the rum mixture over the bananas. Cover and cook for 1 minute in the microwave on high power. To serve, place a scoop of ice cream on two dessert plates. Arrange the bananas around ice cream. Spoon the hot sauce over the ice cream and serve immediately.

Serves 2

It's easy to flame a dessert or other dishes without using brandy. Simply sprinkle drops of fresh lemon extract over the dish and flame!

Blueberry Crunch

1 quart blueberries or other fresh fruit, such as peaches or blackberries
1 stick margarine, melted
1 cup sugar
1 cup flour

Rinse berries or slice fruit and place in a greased 9" x 9" baking dish. In a bowl, mix together margarine, sugar, and flour. Sprinkle mixture over the berries. Bake at 325° for 1 hour. Serve with ice cream or other topping.

Serves 4–6

Always select blueberries that are plump, firm, clean, and deep blue in color. Immature blueberries have a reddish color.

Apple Cranberry Casserole

3   cups apples, unpeeled and chopped (about 4 apples)
2   cups fresh or frozen cranberries, whole
¼   cup sugar
1   cup brown sugar, divided
3   tablespoons butter or margarine
2   teaspoons cinnamon or apple pie spice
½   cup butter or margarine
1   cup old-fashioned oatmeal
⅓   cup flour
⅓   cup chopped pecans
1½   teaspoons cinnamon

Combine apples, cranberries, sugar, and ½ cup brown sugar in a bowl. Dot with 3 tablespoons butter; sprinkle with 2 teaspoons cinnamon or apple pie spice. Mix well and pour into a greased 2-quart casserole dish. In another bowl, mix together ½ cup butter, oatmeal, flour, remaining ½ cup brown sugar, pecans, and 1½ teaspoons cinnamon. Sprinkle mixture over apples. Bake at 350° for 45 minutes. May be served with ice cream or whipped cream.

Serves 6-8

Pear Crisp

4   cups fresh pears, sliced
1   cup citrus juice, any flavor
½   cup butter
1   cup brown sugar
½   teaspoon vanilla
⅛   teaspoon salt
½   cup flour
½   cup oatmeal
¼   cup chopped pecans (optional)

Place pears in a buttered 9" baking dish. Coat with juice. Mix remaining ingredients together. Sprinkle mix over the fruit. Bake at 350° for 30 to 45 minutes.

Serves 6

Spiced Pears

2   tablespoons butter, melted
⅓   cup firmly packed light brown sugar
½   teaspoon cinnamon
¼   teaspoon ginger
1   can pear halves, drained
1   pint vanilla ice cream

Mix all ingredients together in a saucepan. Simmer over medium heat for 10 minutes, turning pears once. Spoon ice cream into dessert glasses. Top with hot pears and sauce. Serve immediately before ice cream melts.

Serves 4

Home-Style Peach Cobbler

½   cup butter
1   cup all-purpose flour
1½ cups sugar, divided
½   teaspoon salt
3   teaspoons baking powder
1   cup milk
2   cups sliced peaches

Melt butter in a 2-quart casserole dish. Mix together flour, 1 cup sugar, salt, baking powder, and milk. Pour mixture over butter; do not stir. Sweeten peaches to taste using about ½ cup of sugar. Place peaches on top of mix, do not stir. Bake at 350° for about 45 minutes or until bubbly. Serve warm with ice cream.

Serves 8

You may substitute 1 cup self-rising flour for the all-purpose flour, salt, and baking powder. Other fruits, such as blueberries, blackberries, or fruit combinations may also be used.

PEACH CRUMBLE

1   egg, beaten
1   cup sugar
1   cup chopped pecans or walnuts
1   (6 ounce) package instant vanilla pudding
1   cup sour cream
1   cup milk
1   cup diced fresh peaches

Beat together egg and sugar. Add nuts. Line a cookie sheet with foil and coat it with a good layer of non-stick cooking spray. Pour mixture onto the middle of the sheet. Spread mixture thin; it will not cover the sheet completely. Bake at 350° for about 15 to 20 minutes or until brown. Cool and crumble. Mix together the pudding mix, sour cream, and milk. Fold in peaches. Divide ½ the crumble into 6 parfait glasses. Spoon pudding mixture over the crumble in the glasses. Top each glass with remaining crumble. Chill before serving.

Serves 6

ELEGANT GRILLED PEACHES WITH RASPBERRY PURÉE

½   (10 ounce) package frozen raspberries in light syrup, slightly
      thawed
1½ teaspoons lemon juice
2   medium peaches, peeled, halved and pitted
1½ tablespoons brown sugar
¼   teaspoon ground cinnamon
1½ teaspoons rum flavoring
1½ teaspoons margarine

Combine raspberries and lemon juice in blender or food processor; process until smooth. Strain raspberry purée; discard seeds. Cover and chill. Cut heavy duty foil in an 18" x 18" sheet. Place peach halves, cut side up, on foil. Combine brown sugar and cinnamon. Spoon evenly in center of each peach half. Sprinkle with rum flavoring. Dot with margarine. Fold foil over peaches and loosely seal. Place grill rack over medium-hot coals. Place foil bundle on rack. Cook 15 minutes or until peaches are thoroughly heated. Spoon 2 tablespoons of the raspberry purée over each grilled peach half. (This recipe may be made in the broiler.)

Serves 4

The natural sweetness of fruit makes it a perfect ending to any meal. More than just flavor, you will enjoy the benefit of fruits' fiber, vitamins, and minerals. The low-fat recipe for Grilled Peaches at right can be made even lower by completely eliminating the margarine.

*Barbra Crumpacker,
Registered Dietitian*

Kahlúa Pie

24 large marshmallows
¼ cup milk
¼ cup brewed coffee
14 chocolate chip cookies
2 tablespoons butter
½ pint whipping cream
8 tablespoons kahlúa

In a saucepan over low heat, melt marshmallows with milk and coffee. Set aside to cool completely. While marshmallow mixture cools, make crust. Crush the cookies and melt butter. Mix well and press into the bottom of an 8" round or square pan. Whip the cream until stiff and fold in kahlúa. Then fold in cooled marshmallow mixture. Pour into crust and freeze until firm. Garnish with chocolate curls or chocolate chips.

Serves 6-8

Coconut Pie

½ cup all-purpose flour
½ cup sugar
¼ teaspoon salt
1½ cups milk
3 egg yolks
2 tablespoons butter
1 teaspoon vanilla
1 (3½ ounce) can coconut (reserve ¼ cup for meringue)
1 9" deep-dish pie shell, baked
3 egg whites
1 teaspoon cream of tartar
⅓ cup sugar

Mix flour, sugar, and salt in heavy saucepan; add milk and egg yolks. Cook over medium heat until thick; remove from heat. Add butter, vanilla, and coconut. Pour into baked 9" deep-dish pie shell. In a bowl, beat egg whites with cream of tartar. Gradually add sugar and beat until stiff peaks form. Spread meringue on top of pie. Sprinkle with ¼ cup of coconut. Brown meringue at 350˚.

Serves 6-8

Key Lime Pie

• *2 eggs*
• *¾ cup lime juice*
• *1 (14 ounce) can sweetened condensed milk*
• *1 cup whipping cream, whipped*
• *1 graham cracker pie crust*

Beat eggs until frothy; gradually add sweetened condensed milk, beating until well blended. Gradually add lime juice; mix well. Fold in whipped cream and pour into prepared crust. Freeze at least 1 hour. Top with additional whipped cream before serving.

Serves 8

1   cup sugar
2   tablespoons flour
3   egg yolks, beaten
1   cup milk
4   (1 ounce) blocks unsweetened chocolate
½   stick butter
1   teaspoon vanilla
1   baked 9" pie shell
4   egg whites
¼   teaspoon cream of tartar
3   tablespoons sugar

In a double boiler, mix together sugar and flour. Combine the next 4 ingredients and pour into double boiler. Cook until thick, stirring constantly. Remove from double boiler and add vanilla. Pour mixture into a baked pie shell. Make meringue by beating together egg whites with cream of tartar; gradually add sugar until stiff peaks form. Top pie with meringue. Bake at 325° until meringue is browned.

Serves 6–8

Grandmama's Pumpkin Pie

1   medium pumpkin
1   stick butter
3   small eggs
2   cups sugar
2   teaspoons vanilla
1-3 tablespoons flour
Salt to taste
1-4 tablespoons milk
1   unbaked 9" pie shell

Cook pumpkin until tender; drain. Add butter, eggs, sugar, and vanilla. If thickening is needed, add a little flour. Add just enough salt to bring out the flavor. Add milk to taste, if desired. Bake in uncooked 9" pie shell at 350° until crust is well browned, approximately 30 minutes.

Serves 8

Peanut Butter Pie

• ½ cup crunchy peanut butter
• 1 (3 ounce) package cream cheese
• ½ cup confectioners' sugar
• 1 (8 ounce) non-dairy whipped cream
• 1 chocolate crumb pie shell
• shaved chocolate (optional)

Mix peanut butter and cream cheese together with an electric mixer. Add the confectioners' sugar and fold in the whipped cream. Pour into a prepared chocolate crumb pie shell. Decorate with additional whipped cream and shaved chocolate. Refrigerate before and after serving.

Serves 6–8

Festive Cranberry-Cherry Pie

1 (21 ounce) can cherry pie filling
1 (16 ounce) can whole berry cranberry sauce
½ cup golden or dark seedless raisins
2 tablespoons cornstarch
½ teaspoon ground ginger
1 teaspoon cinnamon
1 (10-11 ounce) package pie crust mix (or Basic Pastry Recipe on page 281)
5-7 tablespoons orange juice
Milk
Sugar

In large bowl, stir cherry pie filling, cranberry sauce, raisins, cornstarch, and ginger. Prepare pie crust mix as label directs for a 2-crust pie, but substitute orange juice for water. Divide pastry into 2 pieces, one slightly larger. On lightly floured surface, with floured rolling pin, roll larger piece of pastry into a 12" round. Gently ease pastry into 9" pie pan; trim edge leaving 1" overhang. Spoon filling into pie crust. Preheat oven to 400°. Roll pastry for top crust into 11" round; cut into 14 strips. Moisten edge of bottom crust with water. To weave lattice crust, place 7 pastry strips across pie; do not seal ends. Fold every other strip back halfway from center. Place center cross strip on pie and replace folded part of strips. Now fold back alternate strips; place second cross strip in place. Repeat to weave cross strips into a lattice. Seal ends. Turn overhang up over ends of strips; pinch to seal. Make high fluted edge. Brush pastry with milk then sprinkle lightly with sugar. Bake pie 50 minutes or until fruit mixture begins to bubble and crust is golden. If edge of crust browns too quickly, cover loosely with foil to prevent over-browning. Cool pie slightly on wire rack to serve warm. Or, cool completely to serve later.

Serves 8-10

Pat-It Crust

- *1½ cups plus 3 tablespoons all-purpose flour*
- *1½ teaspoons sugar*
- *½ teaspoon salt*
- *½ cup vegetable oil*
- *3 tablespoons cold milk*

Place flour, sugar, and salt in pie pan and mix with hands. In measuring cup, combine oil and milk, beat with fork until creamy. Pour all at once over flour mixture. Mix with fork until the flour mixture is completely moistened. Pat the dough with your fingers, first up the sides of the pan, then across the bottom. Flute edges. If to be used as a prebaked crust, preheat oven to 425°. Prick surface with fork and bake 15 minutes, checking often.

Makes 1 pie crust

This is an ideal crust for those who have not mastered rolling out pie pastry.

To rescue food that is browning too fast, place a piece of aluminum foil over top rack. This will deflect the heat and allow cakes, cookies, pies, or soufflés to bake through.

Tipsy Chip Pie

Pie

2   eggs, slightly beaten
1   cup sugar
½   cup all-purpose flour
½   cup butter, melted and cooled
1   cup chopped pecans
1   (6 ounce) package semisweet chocolate morsels
1   teaspoon vanilla extract
1   unbaked 9" pie shell

Combine first 4 ingredients in a medium mixing bowl; beat with an electric mixer just until blended. Stir in pecans, chocolate morsels, and vanilla. Pour filling into pastry shell and bake at 350° for 45 to 50 minutes. Serve pie warm with bourbon-laced whipped cream topping.

Topping

1   cup whipping cream
1   tablespoon bourbon
¼   cup confectioners' sugar, sifted

Beat whipping cream and bourbon until foamy; gradually add sugar, beating until soft peaks form.

Serves 6-8

Blueberry Pie

1   cup sugar
¼   cup cornstarch
1½ cups water
Dash of salt
1   (3 ounce) box black cherry or blackberry gelatin
1   pint blueberries, rinsed and drained
2   8" graham cracker pie shells
Whipped cream (optional)

Strawberries and strawberry gelatin may be substituted for the blueberries and black cherry gelatin.

Substitute frozen fruit for fresh in a pie and use only ½ the sugar called for in the recipe.

Combine sugar and cornstarch in heavy saucepan. Add 1½ cups water and a dash of salt. Cook until mixture is thick. Add the gelatin and stir until the gelatin is dissolved. Let mixture cool. Carefully stir in blueberries. Pour mixture into the 2 pie shells. Refrigerate for about 4 hours. Serve with whipped cream.

Serves 12-16

CREAMY FRUIT PIE

1 (24 ounce) can peaches
1 (3 ounce) package orange gelatin
1 pint vanilla ice cream
1 (1 pound) can peach slices, for garnish
1 baked 9" pie shell

Strain peaches from large can and save 1 cup of liquid. (If necessary, add water to peach liquid to make 1 cup.) Mash peaches and measure 1 cup. Heat peach juice until almost boiling. Add orange gelatin and stir with wooden spoon until dissolved. Remove from heat. Immediately add ice cream by tablespoons to hot liquid, stir until ice cream is melted. Blend in mashed peaches and mix well. Chill in saucepan until mixture is thickened, but not completely set, about 25 minutes. Turn into baked pie shell and top with sliced peaches. Freeze before serving.

Serves 6–8

DELICIOUS PASTRY

1½ cups all-purpose flour, sifted
½ teaspoon salt
¼ cup vegetable shortening
¼ cup butter
4 tablespoons ice cold water

Combine flour and salt; cut in shortening and butter with pastry blender until mixture is crumbly. Sprinkle cold water 1 tablespoon at a time, mix with fork just until pastry holds together and leaves sides of bowl. Wrap in wax paper and chill slightly. Roll out on floured surface, fill and bake according to pie recipe. For prebaked crust, prick surface with fork and bake at 425° for 10 to 15 minutes.

Makes 1 pie crust

BASIC PASTRY (DOUBLE CRUST)

• *2 cups all-purpose flour*
• *1 teaspoon salt*
• *⅔ cup vegetable shortening*
• *5 to 6 table-spoons ice cold water*

Combine flour and salt; cut in shortening with pastry blender until course and crumbly. Add water 1 table-spoon at a time, blend with fork until it holds together and leaves sides of bowl. Chill in wax paper at least 1 hour before using. Roll on floured surface.

Makes 1 double crust

If a pastry shell is to be baked unfilled, prick it thoroughly with a fork to prevent buckling.

Spicy Ginger Snaps

¾ cup vegetable shortening
1 cup sugar
¼ cup molasses
1 egg
2 cups all-purpose flour
2 teaspoons cinnamon
1 teaspoon ground cloves
1½ teaspoons ground ginger
½ teaspoon salt
Granulated sugar

Cream sugar and shortening until light and fluffy. Add molasses and egg; blend well. Combine dry ingredients and add slowly to first mixture, blending well. Cover and chill for at least 1 hour. Roll into 1" balls; then roll into granulated sugar. Place on greased cookie sheets about 2" apart. Bake at 375° for 8 to 10 minutes until golden brown. Let stand for 1 to 2 minutes; remove to wire rack to cool.

Makes 4 dozen

Crunchy Picnic Cookies

1 cup butter, softened
1 cup sugar
1 cup firmly packed brown sugar
1 egg
1 cup oil
1 teaspoon vanilla
3½ cups all-purpose flour
1 teaspoon baking soda
½ teaspoon salt
1 cup regular oats, uncooked
1 cup crushed cornflakes
½ cup flaked coconut
1 cup chopped nuts

Cream butter, sugar, and brown sugar; add egg and beat well. Add oil and vanilla; mix well. Set aside. Combine flour, soda, and salt; add to creamed mixture and mix well. Stir in oats, cornflakes, coconut, and nuts. Shape into 1" balls. Place on ungreased cookie sheet and flatten with fork. Bake at 325° for 12 to 15 minutes.

Makes 6 dozen

CRACKLE TOP COOKIES

2   cups all-purpose flour, sifted
2   teaspoons baking powder
1   teaspoon cinnamon
¾   teaspoon salt
½   cup shortening
1⅔ cups firmly packed brown sugar
2   eggs
1   teaspoon vanilla
2   (1 ounce) squares unsweetened chocolate, melted
⅓   cup milk
⅔   cup chopped nuts
Confectioners' sugar

Sift together flour, baking powder, cinnamon, and salt. Set aside.
Cream shortening and sugar until light and fluffy. Beat in eggs and
vanilla. Add chocolate. Add flour mixture alternately with milk.
Stir in nuts. Chill until firm, about 2 to 3 hours. Shape into 1" balls
and roll in confectioners' sugar. Bake on greased cookie sheets at
350° for 20 minutes.

Makes 5 dozen

If a cookie recipe calls for 2 eggs and there is only 1 egg in the house, use 1 egg plus 1 tablespoon water.

Parchment paper is great to use for lining your cookie sheets. This eliminates the need for greasing the sheets.

Run out of wire cooling racks? Spread wax paper on the kitchen counter and sprinkle with sugar. Cookies will cool on the sugared paper without getting soggy.

For even baking, begin baking cookies on the middle rack of the oven for ½ of the baking time. Rotate cookies to the top rack and finish baking.

Crispy Orange Bites

1   cup butter or margarine, softened
½   cup sugar
½   cup firmly packed brown sugar
1   egg
1   tablespoon grated orange rind
2   tablespoons orange juice
¼   teaspoon vanilla
2½ cups all-purpose flour
¼   teaspoon salt
¼   teaspoon baking soda
½   cup finely chopped pecans

Orange or lemon juice does not produce a distinct flavor in baked goods — but grated rind of either does.

Cream butter, sugar, and brown sugar until light and fluffy. Add egg, orange rind, juice, and vanilla. Beat well. In separate bowl, combine flour, salt, and soda. Gradually add to creamed mixture. Stir in pecans. Shape dough into 2 long rolls, about 1½" in diameter. Wrap each roll in waxed paper and chill 3 hours or until firm. Unwrap rolls, cut into ¼" thick slices. Place cookies 2" apart on greased cookie sheets. Bake at 375° for 8 to 10 minutes or until edges are lightly browned.

Makes 6 dozen

Fudgy Chocolate Chippers

1   cup margarine
1½   cups sugar
2   eggs
1½   teaspoons vanilla
2   cups all-purpose flour
¾   cup cocoa
1   teaspoon baking soda
2   cups chopped pecans
1   (12 ounce) package chocolate chips

To keep drop cookies from spreading, chill the dough first. Cookie dough stored in a tightly covered container can be refrigerated up to one week or frozen up to six months. Allow dough to soften before baking.

Cream margarine and sugar. Add eggs and vanilla. In a medium bowl, combine dry ingredients and add slowly to creamed mixture. Stir in pecans and chips. Dough will be thick and dry. Drop cookies by spoonfuls on greased cookie sheets. Flatten dough with hands. Bake at 375° until dry to touch but still soft, about 10 minutes.

Makes twenty 3½" cookies or 4 dozen 1½" cookies

Old-Time Favorite Oatmeal Cookies

1   cup firmly packed brown sugar
1   cup sugar
1   cup vegetable shortening
2   eggs
2   teaspoons vanilla
1½ cups all-purpose flour
1   teaspoon salt
1   teaspoon baking soda
3   cups oatmeal
½   teaspoon cinnamon (optional)
½   cup chopped nuts (optional)
½   cup raisins (optional)

Cream sugars and shortening. Add eggs and vanilla. Mix in dry ingredients in order given. Batter will be stiff. Drop by heaping tablespoons onto greased cookie sheet. Bake at 350° for 10 to 12 minutes. Cool slightly before removing from pan.

Makes 3 dozen

Always use a shiny cookie sheet. Dark or stained cookie sheets absorb heat and may over-brown cookie bottoms.

Party Time Sugar Cookies

2   cups all-purpose flour
2   teaspoons baking powder
½   teaspoon salt
½   cup margarine
1   cup sugar
1   egg
½   teaspoon vanilla
½   teaspoon lemon extract

Sift together flour, baking powder, and salt. Set aside. Cream margarine and sugar until light and fluffy. Beat in egg, vanilla, and lemon. Slowly add dry ingredients. Chill until firm. Roll out to ⅛" thickness. Cut into shapes with cookie cutters. Decorate with colored sugar or candy sprinkles as desired. Bake on greased cookie sheets at 400° until golden brown, about 8 to 10 minutes. Watch closely, as they will burn easily.

Makes 3 dozen

Don't forget to make a double batch of cookies and freeze half for later use. Drop cookie dough onto cookie sheets and freeze until firm. Once frozen, transfer mounds into zip-top plastic freezer bags and store in freezer. When ready to bake, place frozen mounds on cookie sheets and follow recipe directions.

Lightly grease your measuring cup before measuring honey, syrups, or molasses. This way you will use every drop.

Nutjammer Cookies

1   cup butter, softened
8   ounce package cream cheese, softened
2   cups all-purpose flour, sifted
½   teaspoon baking powder
2   cups finely chopped walnuts
1   (12 ounce) jar apricot or peach jam
2   teaspoons granulated sugar
⅓   cup confectioners' sugar

Place cookies 2-3 inches apart on cookie sheet unless specified otherwise in recipe.

Cream butter and cream cheese. Sift flour and baking powder; add to creamed mixture. Chill dough 2 to 3 hours. Mix nuts, jam, and granulated sugar. Divide dough into 4 equal parts; work with ¼ dough at a time. Refrigerate remaining dough. On a lightly floured cloth-covered board, roll dough very thin, about 1/16". Cut into 2" squares. Place squares on greased baking sheet. Place 1 teaspoon nut mixture in center of each square and top with another square of dough. Press edges together with floured tines of a fork. Bake at 375° for 15 to 20 minutes or until lightly browned. When completely cooled, sprinkle tops with confectioners' sugar.

Makes 3 dozen

Shortening will come out of a measuring cup easily if eggs have been beaten or measured in the cup beforehand.

Tea Party Cakes

½   cup shortening
1   cup sugar
2   eggs
1   teaspoon nutmeg
½   teaspoon vanilla extract
2   cups all-purpose flour
2   teaspoons baking powder
Nutmeg

Blend shortening and sugar. Add eggs, nutmeg, vanilla, flour, and baking powder. Beat until smooth. Form into small balls, using floured hands. Place on greased cookie sheet. Pat with fingers to flatten slightly. Sprinkle lightly with nutmeg. Bake at 350° for 10 minutes.

Makes 4 dozen

Georgia Peanut Cookies

1   cup sugar
1   cup firmly packed brown sugar
1   cup vegetable shortening
1   cup crunchy peanut butter
2   eggs, beaten
2   cups all-purpose flour
1   teaspoon baking soda

Cream sugars, shortening, and peanut butter. Add eggs, flour, and baking soda. Mix well and chill dough slightly. Roll into 1" balls. Using a fork, press a criss-cross pattern on top of each ball. Bake on greased cookie sheets at 375˚ for 8 to 10 minutes. Watch closely, as they will burn easily.

Makes 6 dozen

Minty Chocolate Rounds

1¾ cups flour
½   teaspoon baking powder
½   teaspoon salt
½   cup butter or margarine
¾   cup sugar
¼   cup cocoa
1   egg
2   teaspoons vanilla
¼   cup crushed peppermint hard candy

Combine dry ingredients; set aside. Cream butter and sugar until fluffy. Add cocoa, egg, and vanilla. Beat well. Add dry ingredients. Stir in crushed candy. Shape into two 6" rolls. Wrap in wax paper and chill. Cut into ¼" slices. Bake on greased cookie sheets at 375˚ for 8 to 10 minutes.

Makes 4 dozen

♡ Sugars and fats are necessary ingredients in baked goods as they act as tenderizers while helping to provide the crispness. They can be reduced, though, to make a healthier product. Begin by reducing the sugar by ⅓ to ½, and using brown sugar or honey in place of white sugar. Brown sugar and honey are sweeter than white sugar, so less is needed to achieve the same sweetness. Spices and extracts such as cinnamon, nutmeg, cloves, vanilla, almond, or lemon extract help enhance the flavor of recipes. Dried fruits also add natural sweetness. Reduce the amount of fat in baked goods recipes by ¼ or ⅓. Always use unsaturated fats instead of saturated. To make up for some moisture loss, you may need to add a liquid such as water, fruit juice, or skim milk.

Barbra Crumpacker, Registered Dietitian

To crisp up cookies that have become soft, try reheating them in the oven on low.

Just for Fun Cookies

• 1 (20-ounce) roll refrigerated chocolate chip cookie dough
• 1 (14 ounce) package miniature peanut butter cups

Grease mini muffin tins. Slice cookie dough into 48 pieces. Press dough pieces into pans, bake for 15 minutes at 350°. Unwrap peanut butter cups. Remove pans from oven and immediately press the cups into soft cookies. Cool in freezer. Remove with thin spatula or dull knife. Store in refrigerator.

Makes 4 dozen

Note: 1 (20 ounce) roll of peanut butter refrigerated cookie dough can be substituted for delicious results!

Florida Cookies

1	pound margarine
2	cups sugar
1	cup firmly packed brown sugar
4	eggs
6	cups all-purpose flour
1	cup crispy rice cereal
3	teaspoons cream of tartar
2	teaspoons baking soda
1	teaspoon vanilla
1	cup coconut
1	cup chopped nuts
1	cup chopped dates (optional)
1	cup raisins

Cream margarine and sugars. Add eggs, one at a time; mix well after each. Slowly add flour, cream of tartar, and soda. Add vanilla. Stir in remaining ingredients. Chill slightly to firm. Shape into 5 rolls. Rolls can be wrapped in wax paper and stored in refrigerator or freezer. Cut into ½" slices and bake in 350° oven for 10 minutes.

Makes 8 dozen

Pecan Grove Shortbread Cookies

1	cup unsalted butter
1	cup loosely packed light brown sugar
½	teaspoon vanilla extract
Pinch salt	
2¼	cups cake flour, sifted
½	cup finely chopped pecans

Beat together butter, sugar, vanilla, and salt. Add flour, then nuts. Chill for about 30 minutes. Preheat oven to 325° and position rack in top ⅓ of oven. Lightly grease cookie sheets. Roll dough on lightly floured board until ¼" thick. Cut into desired shapes with cookie cutters. Set 1 to 2 inches apart on cookie sheets. Bake for 20 minutes or just until edges are golden. Cool on racks.

Makes 2 dozen

Jam Diagonals

½ cup butter or margarine, softened
¼ cup granulated sugar
1 teaspoon vanilla
⅛ teaspoon salt
1¼ cups flour
¼ cup seedless raspberry jam
¾ cup confectioners' sugar
4 teaspoons lemon juice

In a large bowl, cream butter, granulated sugar, vanilla, and salt until fluffy. Gradually stir in flour until blended. Divide dough into thirds. On a lightly floured surface, using hands, roll dough into 9" ropes. Place 3" apart on lightly greased cookie sheet. With finger, make ½" depression down center of each rope. (Ropes will flatten into about 1" wide strips.) Fill depressions with jam. Bake in preheated 350° oven for 12 to 15 minutes or until lightly golden. Cool on cookie sheet. Blend confectioners' sugar and lemon juice until smooth; drizzle over baked strips. When icing is set, cut strips diagonally into 1" cookies.

Makes 2½ dozen

Rich 'n Chewy Cake

½ cup butter or margarine
1 (1 pound) box light brown sugar
3 eggs
2 cups self-rising flour
2 cups chopped nuts
1 teaspoon vanilla

Melt butter over low heat; mix in brown sugar and stir until well blended. Add eggs one at a time, mixing well after each. Add flour ½ cup at a time. Add nuts; stir in vanilla. Mix well. Pour into greased 9" x 13" pan. Bake 30 minutes at 325°.

Makes 4 dozen

When homemade cookies are a gift, don't forget a special container! Decorative tins, bags, unusual baskets and jars will be a reminder of your gift long after the treats are gone. Wrap cookies with pretty colored tissue paper or cellophane. Sources for unusual container and wraps – antique stores, craft shops, houseware sections of department stores and flea markets.

Divine Chocolate Mint Squares

2	(1 ounce) squares unsweetened chocolate
½	cup butter or margarine
2	eggs
1	cup sugar
½	cup all-purpose flour
½	cup chopped walnuts or pecans
1½	cups sifted confectioners' sugar
3	tablespoons whipping cream
¾	teaspoon peppermint extract
2	drops green food coloring (optional)
2	(1 ounce) squares sweet baking chocolate
5	tablespoons butter or margarine, divided
1	teaspoon vanilla

Melt unsweetened chocolate and ½ cup butter in top of a double boiler over simmering water; cool. Combine eggs and 1 cup sugar, beating until light and fluffy; stir in flour, walnuts, and cooled chocolate. Spread mixture in a greased 9" square baking pan. Bake at 350° for 25 minutes. Cool in pan on a wire rack. Combine confectioners' sugar, 3 tablespoons butter, whipping cream, and peppermint extract. Stir in food coloring, if desired. Beat until smooth. Spread evenly over baked layer; cover and chill 1 hour or until firm. Melt sweet chocolate and 2 tablespoons butter on top of a double boiler over simmering water; stir in vanilla, and drizzle over peppermint layer. Cover and chill 1 hour or until firm. Cut into 1" squares.

Makes 3 dozen

Ultimate Chocolate Brownies

BROWNIES

¾ cup cocoa
½ teaspoon baking soda
⅔ cup butter or margarine, melted
½ cup boiling water
2 cups sugar
2 eggs
1⅓ cups all-purpose flour
1 teaspoon vanilla
¼ teaspoon salt
1 cup semi-sweet chocolate chips
1 cup chopped nuts

Blend cocoa and baking soda, add ⅓ cup melted butter and add water. Stir until mixture thickens. Stir in sugar, eggs, and remaining ⅓ cup butter. Stir until smooth. Add flour, vanilla, and salt. Blend completely. Stir in nuts and chocolate chips. Bake in a greased 9" x 13" pan at 350° for 35 to 40 minutes. Frost with recipe below.

Makes 4 dozen

FROSTING

6 tablespoons butter or margarine, softened
½ cup cocoa
2⅔ cups confectioners' sugar
⅓ cup milk
1 teaspoon vanilla

Cream 6 tablespoons butter. Add cocoa and confectioners' sugar alternately with milk. Beat to spreading consistency. Add vanilla; spread on cooled brownies.

PARK AVENUE SQUARES

• 1 box butter cake mix
• 1 stick butter or margarine
• 1 egg
• 1 cup chopped nuts
• 1 (8 ounce) package cream cheese
• 2 eggs
• 1 (1 pound) box confectioners' sugar

Mix cake mix, butter, 1 egg, and nuts together and press into a greased 9" x 13" x 2" pan. Mix cream cheese, 2 eggs and confectioners' sugar until smooth; spread on top of crust mixture. Bake at 350° for 30 to 40 minutes.

Makes 4 dozen

To Make
Chocolate Caramel
Bars --
Add 2 (1 ounce) squares unsweetened chocolate to caramel mixture while melting over low heat.

Streusel Caramel Bars

2   cups all-purpose flour
¾   cup firmly packed light brown sugar
1   egg, beaten
¾   cup margarine or butter, divided
¾   cup chopped nuts
24   caramels, unwrapped
1   (14 ounce) can sweetened condensed milk

In large bowl, combine flour, sugar, and egg. Cut in ½ cup margarine until mixture becomes crumbly. Stir in nuts. Reserve 2 cups of mixture, and press remaining dough into a greased 9" x 13" pan. Bake at 350° for 15 minutes. While crust is baking, melt caramels, sweetened condensed milk, and ¼ cup margarine in saucepan, over low heat. Pour over prepared crust. Top with reserved crumb mixture. Bake at 350° for 30 minutes or until bubbly. Cool and cut into squares.

Makes 4 dozen

Before chopping nuts in a processor, lightly flour the knife blade.

Marvelous Orange Nut Bars

3   eggs
1   (6 ounce) can frozen orange juice concentrate
1   cup sugar
2   cups graham cracker crumbs
1   teaspoon baking powder
¼   teaspoon salt
1   cup chopped nuts
1   (8 ounce) package pitted dates, chopped
1   teaspoon vanilla
1¼ cups confectioners' sugar
2½ tablespoons prepared orange juice

Grease and lightly flour a 9" square pan. Beat eggs until light and fluffy. Beat in orange juice concentrate. Stir in next 7 ingredients and mix well. Bake at 350° for 50 minutes. Cool. To make icing, mix confectioners' sugar and orange juice. Frost bars and serve.

Makes 2 dozen

Delicate Lemon Squares

1 cup plus 2 tablespoons all-purpose flour
1 stick cold unsalted butter, cut into bits
¼ cup confectioners' sugar; plus additional for garnish
2 large eggs
¾ cup granulated sugar
3 tablespoons fresh lemon juice
½ teaspoon baking powder

In a medium bowl, blend together 1 cup flour, butter, and ¼ cup confectioners' sugar until the mixture is crumbly. Pat the mixture into an 8" square baking pan. Bake on the middle rack of a preheated 350° oven for 12 to 15 minutes, or until pale golden. In another bowl, with an electric mixer, beat eggs until thick and pale. Beat in granulated sugar and lemon juice and beat mixture for 8 minutes. Sift in the remaining 2 tablespoons flour and the baking powder. Stir well and pour over baked layer. Bake in the middle of preheated 350° oven for 20 minutes or until golden brown. Sift confectioners' sugar over top and let cool in pan on rack. Cut into 2" squares.

Makes 16

After School Peanut Butter Bars

½ cup peanut butter
½ cup margarine
1½ cups sugar
2 eggs
1 teaspoon vanilla
1 cup flour
1½ teaspoons baking powder
½ teaspoon salt

In a skillet, over medium heat, combine peanut butter, margarine, and sugar. When mixture is well blended, remove from heat. When cool, add eggs, vanilla, flour, baking powder, and salt. Bake in a greased 9" x 13" pan at 350° for 25 to 30 minutes.

Makes 4 dozen

Cookie Cheesecake Squares

• 1 (20 ounce) roll refrigerated sugar cookie dough, unbaked
• ¾ cup strawberry preserves
• 1 (8 ounce) package cream cheese
• 1 cup sour cream
• 1 egg
• ½ teaspoon vanilla

Slice cookie dough into ¼" thick slices. Place slices on ungreased 9" x 13" pan. Bake at 375° for 12 to 15 minutes or until golden brown. Spread with preserves. In a large bowl, combine remaining ingredients and beat at medium speed until smooth. Spread over preserves. Bake at 375° for 25 to 30 minutes. Cool; cut into squares.

Makes 4 dozen

Tailgate Party Cupcakes

¾ cup butter
2 (1 ounce) squares semi-sweet chocolate
1 (1 ounce) square unsweetened chocolate
1¾ cups sugar
4 eggs
1 teaspoon vanilla
1 cup all-purpose flour
2 tablespoons cocoa
⅛ teaspoon salt
1 cup chopped toasted pecans

Place butter and chocolate squares in a heavy saucepan and cook over low heat, stirring constantly until melted. Remove from heat, stir in sugar. Add eggs one at a time, stirring well after each. Stir in vanilla. Combine flour, cocoa, and salt; add to chocolate mixture, stirring with wire whisk until smooth. Stir in pecans. Spoon batter into paper-lined muffin pans, filling each ¾ full. Bake at 350° for 35 minutes.

Makes 16

Holiday Chocolate Coconut Bon-Bons

2   (1 pound) boxes confectioners' sugar
1   stick butter, softened
1   (14 ounce) can sweetened condensed milk
1½ cups chopped nuts
14 ounces coconut
1   (6 ounce) package chocolate chips
1   block paraffin

Mix together first five ingredients with hands. Roll into balls. Place on baking sheet lined with wax paper. Freeze until chilled. In a saucepan, heat chocolate chips and paraffin over low heat until dissolved. Dip frozen balls into chocolate mixture. Place on wax paper and let harden.

Makes 4 dozen

Peanut Butter Balls

1   (1 pound) box confectioners' sugar
1   (14 ounce) can sweetened condensed milk
1   cup peanut butter
⅓ cup finely chopped pecans (optional)
1   (1 pound) package candy coating chocolate

Mix together first 4 ingredients. Roll into 4 logs, about 1" diameter. Refrigerate slightly. Melt chocolate. Slice logs about ½" to ¾" thick and roll into balls. Refrigerate until cool. Dip balls into chocolate. Place on wax paper and cool.

Makes 5-7 dozen

DIANE'S HEAVENLY HASH

• 2½ pounds solid milk chocolate
• 1 cup toasted slivered almonds
• 1 (26 ounce) package tiny marshmallows

Melt chocolate in double boiler. Remove from heat; add almonds and mix. Add marsh-mallows and pour onto a cookie sheet lined with foil. To set chocolate, drop cookie sheet several times onto counter top or table from a height of about 1 foot. Let harden in refrigerator. Cut or break into pieces.

Makes 3 dozen

DELICIOUS CARAMELS

1 cup granulated sugar
1 cup dark corn syrup
1 cup butter
1 (14 ounce) can sweetened condensed milk
1 teaspoon vanilla

Mix first 3 ingredients in a medium saucepan. Stir to mix well and continue stirring until mixture comes to a boil. Boil, without stirring, for 5 to 7 minutes. Remove from heat and add condensed milk. Stir to mix well, return to heat, and bring back to slow boil, stirring constantly. Cook for an additional 12 to 15 minutes, stirring constantly. Pour into lightly buttered 8" x 8" pan. Cool overnight at room temperature. Cut into 1" squares and wrap with plastic wrap or wax paper.

Makes 5 dozen

MILLION DOLLAR FUDGE

4½ cups sugar
1 (12 ounce) can evaporated milk
¼ pound butter
2 (4 ounce) bars sweet chocolate, chopped fine
1 (8 ounce) bar semi-sweet chocolate, chopped fine
1 pint marshmallow creme
2 cups chopped nuts

Place first 3 ingredients in large boiler. Heat stirring constantly. Boil for 5 minutes; remove from heat. Add last 4 ingredients and stir to mix well. Pour into a buttered 9" x 13" pan, let stand until firm. Cut into squares.

Makes 8 dozen

APPETIZING APRICOT BALLS

• *1 pound dried apricots*
• *1 pound coconut*
• *1 (14 ounce) can sweetened condensed milk*
• *confectioners' sugar*

Grind apricots. Add coconut and condensed milk. Roll into small balls, then roll in confectioners' sugar. May be frozen.

Makes 7-8 dozen

Fudge

4 squares unsweetened chocolate
6 ounces cream cheese, softened to room temperature
½ teaspoon vanilla extract
⅛ teaspoon salt
1 pound confectioners' sugar, sifted
1 cup chopped pecans or walnuts

Place chocolate in top of double boiler over warm water on medium heat. Stir until melted. Cool and set aside. Mix cream cheese with electric mixer until soft and smooth. Add sugar. Mix until smooth. Add vanilla, salt, and chocolate. Mix in the nuts. Line an 8" square pan with wax paper or foil. Refrigerate until firm. Cut into squares.

Makes 1½ pounds

Place fudge in an airtight container for 24 hours. It will be softer and more velvety.

In candy making, weather is an important factor. On a hot humid day, cook candy 2 degrees higher than in cold, dry weather.

Emily Neel's Candy

½ (14 ounce) can sweetened condensed milk
1 (1 pound) box confectioners' sugar
½ stick butter, melted
1½ cups finely chopped nuts
½ block (4 ounces) bittersweet chocolate
½ block paraffin
Pecan halves

Mix together milk, sugar, and melted butter gradually. Blend well. Add chopped nuts and mix well. Roll into balls and shape. Chill in refrigerator. Melt chocolate and paraffin together on stove. Use toothpicks to dip balls into chocolate. Place 1 pecan half on each piece immediately.

Makes 2 dozen

Chocolate should be stored for no more than one year. Keep it tightly wrapped in a cool dry place (between 60° - 75°F.) If storage temperature goes above 75° some of the cocoa butter may separate and rise to the surface. This causes the whitish cast or "bloom." Chocolate with a bloom is still edible. In hot weather, chocolate can be stored in the refrigerator. But be aware that chocolate can absorb odors of other foods.

Party Praline Strips

1   (1 pound) box graham crackers
½   cup butter
½   cup margarine
1   cup light brown sugar
1   cup chopped pecans
1   teaspoon vanilla extract

Line a 9" x 15" baking sheet with aluminum foil. Cover completely with as many graham crackers as needed. In a saucepan, bring butter, margarine, and sugar to a boil; boil for 2 minutes. Stir in pecans and vanilla. Spread mixture evenly over crackers. Bake at 350° for 10 to 15 minutes. Cut while warm.

Makes 4 dozen

Candy Coated Pecans

4   cups pecan halves
2   egg whites
1   cup sugar
Pinch salt
½   cup butter

Place pecans on a baking sheet and bake at 300° for 15 minutes or until lightly browned. Melt butter in saucepan. In a bowl, beat egg whites to a peak. Fold in sugar and salt. Remove pecans from cookie sheet. Pour melted butter onto cookie sheet. Mix the pecans in with the sugar mixture. Pour onto cookie sheet and distribute evenly. Place in oven at 275° for 10 minutes. Stir pecans on sheet, then bake 10 more minutes or until mixture begins to brown.

Makes 4 cups

Cindy's Best Caramel Corn

5   quarts popped popcorn (remove unpopped kernels)
2   sticks margarine
2   cups brown sugar
½   cup light corn syrup
1   teaspoon baking soda
1   teaspoon vanilla
1   teaspoon salt

Melt margarine, sugar, and syrup in a saucepan. Boil for 5 minutes.
Add salt, soda, and vanilla. Put popcorn in large baking pan(s).
Pour syrup over popcorn and stir. Bake for 40 minutes at 250°,
stirring every 10 minutes.

Makes 5 quarts

Peanut Butter Crunch

1   stick butter
1   (6 ounce) package chocolate chips
1   (18 ounce) jar peanut butter
1   (12.3 ounce) box crispy corn and rice cereal
1   (1 quart) jar dry roasted peanuts
2   cups raisins
1   (1 pound) box confectioners' sugar

In a microwave or on the stove, melt together the first 3 ingredients. In a large container, mix together the cereal, nuts, and raisins.
Pour melted mixture over cereal mix. Stir until coated. Sprinkle
confectioners' sugar over mixture; toss until coated. Store in airtight
container away from heat.

Makes 3 quarts

COOKBOOK COMMITTEE 1992-93

CHAIRMEN

Caren McKenzie Jones   Marta Jones Turner

PHOTO STYLIST
Natalie Braswell

FOOD STYLISTS

Diana Cone   Cindy Lawson

PHOTO TEAMS

Penny Woodward, *Team Leader*	Sara Martha Vann, *Team Leader*	Julia Taylor, *Team Leader*
Stylists:	*Stylists:*	*Stylists:*
Gwyn Mallet	Karen Maxwell	Dayna Hardy
Sherri Barnes	Diane Glaccum	Suzanne Fullington
Gina Shumake	Jennifer Culbreth	Rebecca Sanford
Karen Burklow	Peggy Barhite	Donna Kelly
Kathy Smith	Kathy MacQuirter	Nell McPherson
Mary Wolek	Sherriee Kinsey	Maria Garland
Martha Hanna	Sandra Hall	Diedre Hamil
Food Preparation:	*Food Preparation:*	*Food Preparation:*
Sharon B. Johnson	Ashley Ivey-Jackson	Dale Gurley
Beverly Gee	Susan Harvard	Lee Bryant
Louise Duke	Machelle Watt	Devy Moore
Georgia Richardson	Claire Singer	Denise Watt
Sherri Burks	Becky Miller	Kim Bragg
Debbie Folsom	Shannon Balfour	Jane Allen

PRELIMINARY RECIPE EDITING
Sharon C. Johnson, Editor
Linda Elliott and Eve Rumble

RESEARCH COMMITTE
Boo Ivey, Chairman

Beverly Cox	Robin Gay	Sandra Daniel
Cynthia Gibbs	Sabrina Williams	Jamie Jones

MARKETING CHAIRMEN

Cindy Lawson   Pam Rosenbury

Latrelle Cone	Marge Shaw	Mary Wolek
Allison Davis	Sheila Scott	Claudia Grooms

September 1990 – May 1993
PRESIDENTS

Kay Yarbrough	Diana Cone	Mary Wolek
1990–1991	1991–1992	1992–1993

Allen, Jane
Balfour, Linda
Balfour, Shannon
Barhite, Peggy
Barnes, Sherri
Beeson, Debbie
Bragg, Kim
Brandenburg, Leigh
Braswell, Natalie
Bryant, Lee
Burklow, Karen
Burks, Sherri
Cernogorsky, Sharon
Chavaux, Melanie
Collins, Jan
Cone, Diana
Cone, Latrelle
Cox, Beverly
Culbreth, Jennifer
Daniel, Sandra
Davis, Allison
Dollar, Penny
Duke, Louise
Dunham, Indy
Eckles, Kay
Elliott, Linda
Fenlon, Denise
Fiveash, Debra
Folsom, Debbie
Fullington, Suzanne
Garland, Maria
Gay, Robin
Gee, Beverly
Gibbs, Cynthia
Glaccum, Diane

Grooms, Claudia
Gurley, Dale
Hall, Sandra J.
Hall, Susan E.
Hall, Susan J.
Hamil, Diedre
Hanna, Martha
Hanna, Stephanie
Hardy, Dayna
Hardy, Joanne
Harvard, Susan
Hjort, Emily
Hutchison, Lynn
Ivey, Boo
Ivey-Jackson, Ashley
Johnson, Karen
Johnson, Sharon B.
Johnson, Sharon C.
Jones, Angela
Jones, Caren
Jones, Jamie
Kelly, Donna
Kinsey, Sherriee
Lang, Barbara
Lawson, Cindy
Lattay, Julie
Lewis, Anne
Lewis, Jane
Liles, Janet
Lilly, Nelray
Loomis, Kathy
MacQuirter, Kathy
Mallett, Gwyn
Mathes, Connie
Maxwell, Karen

McCollum, Margaret
McPherson, Nell
Miller, Becky
Miller, Merrie
Mixon, Denise
Moore, Devy
Mott, Tammi
Richardson, Georgia
Riddle, Cheryl
Rosenbury, Pam
Rumble, Eve
Sanford, Rebecca
Scott, Sheila
Shaw, Marge
Shumake, Gina
Singer, Claire
Singletary, Julia
Smith, Kathy
Spence, Julie
Stephenson, Cynthia
Taylor, Julia
Taylor, Sunny
Thomas, Carol
Thomas, Elsie
Turner, Marta Jones
Vann, Sara Martha
Watt, Denise
Watt, Machelle
Whitehead, Judy
Williams, Sabrina
Wolek, Mary
Woodward, Penny
Wright, Pam
Yarbrough, Kay

ℛECIPE CONTRIBUTORS

The publication of GOOD FOOD, GOOD COMPANY *would not have been possible without the generous contributions of hundreds of fabulous recipes. Our heartfelt gratitude goes to all those listed here and to those whose names may have been inadvertently omitted.*

Allen, Jane

Allen, Kathy

Allen, Rebecca

Arce, Leesa M.

Autry, Janice

Bailey, Dee

Bain, Sally

Balfour, Linda

Balfour, Shannon

Barhite, Peggy

Barhite, Sherry

Barnes, Merle

Barnes, Sherri

Beeson, Debbie

Beverly, Mary Jo

Bibb, Mildred

Bracey, BettyLou

Bragg, Chip

Bragg, Kim

Braswell, Natalie

Burks, Sherri

Cable, Kathy

Calloway, Sherri

Celeschi, Beth

Cheney, Nancy

Chubb, Lee

Clark, Lona

Clay, Pam

Clay, Pat

Cone, Diana

Cone, Latrelle

Cox, Beverly H.

Culbreth, Jennifer

Daniel, Sandra

Davis, Roz

Day, Linda

Dixon, Sis

Duke, Louise

Echols, Kay

Elliot, Linda

Enfinger, Sandra

Eubanks, Frances

Evans, Peggy

Faircloth, Janice

Feinberg, Julie

Fender, Pat Davis

Ferguson, Georgia

Filbert, Martha

Fink, Robin

Fiveash, Deborah

Gaston, Janet

Gay, Robin

Gee, Beverly

Gibbs, Cynthia

Grant, Ginger

Greenland, Ursa C.

Grooms, David

Gurley, Dale

Gurley, Paul

Hall, Susan E.

Hall, Susan J.

Hancock, Andrea

Hanna, Martha

Hardy, Dayna

Hargrave, Clara

Harkins, Patricia G.

Harvard, Susan

Henderson, Leigh

Higginbotham, Joann

Hjort, Emily

Holland, Jimmie

Horne, Nancy

Hughes, Mary Ann Murphy

Hurst, Margaret S.

Ivey-Jackson, Ashley

Ivey, Boo

Jackson, Beverly

Johnson, Sharon B.

Johnson, Sharon C.

Johnson, Susan Clark

Jones, Caren

Jones, Jamie

Jones, Velma

Kelly, Donna

King, Anne

King, Clarice

Kres, Margaret

Krier, Mary

Lauder, Annelle

Lawson, Bill

Lawson, Cindy

Lawson, Diane D.

Lewis, Anne Lester

Lewis, Jane

Lilly, Nelray

MacQuirter, Kathy

Mallett, Gwyn

Mathes, Connie

Maxwell, Karen

Maxwell, Ruth Ann

May, Martha

McCollum, Lorna

McCollum, Margaret

McKenzie, Blanford

McMillan, Florence

McPherson, Nell

Milberg, Fran

Miller, Becky

Miller, Charlotte

Milton, Evie

Mobley, Mary Lou

Mooney, Cathy

Moore, Anne Lester

Moore, Devy

Myers, Bob

Myerscough, Cleo

Neel, Josie

Neel, Phoebe

Olson, Sis

Palmer, Brenda

Palmer, Leslie

Powell, Pat

Quinif, Alice

Red Rocker Inn,
    Black Mountain, N.C.

Richardson, Georgia

Riddle, Cheryl

Rockett, Bonnie

Rosenbury, Pam

Rumble, Eve

Sanford, Rebecca

Sauerbrey, Nancy

Schlemmer, Gloria G.

Searcy, Emily

Sewell, Carey

Singer, Claire

Singer, Rip

Singletary, Jimmy

Singletary, Nan

Smith, Kathy

Spence, Julie

Summitt, Melissa

Tanner, Peggy

Taylor, Betty

Taylor, Julia

Taylor, Sunny

Thomas, Carol

Thomas, Elsie

Thomasville Cultural
    Center, Inc.

Turner, Margaret

Turner, Marta Jones

Vann, Ann A.

Vann, Kay

Vann, Mildred

Vann, Sara Martha

Waters, Martha

Watt, Denise

Watt, Jane

Watt, Julie

Watt, Machelle

Watt, Mercer

Wilson, Gladys

Wolek, Mary

Wolff, Tammie

Wood, Daphne

Wortman, Randi

Yarbrough, Kay

Index

A

Alice's Rice Salad, 86
Alligator Eyes Dip, 51
All Seasons Seafood Marinade, 54
Always-A-Hit Spinach Dip, 50
Angel Hair Pasta with Tomato-Basil Sauce, 99
Anitra Alle Olive, 222
APPETIZERS
 Alligator Eyes Dip, 51
 All Seasons Seafood Marinade, 54
 Always-A-Hit Spinach Dip, 50
 Bacon Wrapped Surprise, 58
 Barbecue Baby Spareribs, 63
 Blue Cheese Biscuits, 39
 Brie Wrapped in Pastry, 63
 Carter's Mushroom Caps, 42
 Charleston Cheese, 46
 Chili Cheese, 45
 Cool Vegetable Tray with Fresh Dill Dip, 44
 Crab Mold, 60
 Crabmeat Crisps, 64
 Cucumber Lites, 38
 Curried Cheese Toasts, 40
 Down-Home Boiled Peanuts, 42
 Fabulous Franks, 56
 Fernandina Shrimp Dip, 51
 Florida Lobster Butter Log, 46
 Freckled Cheese Sticks, 57
 Happy Hour Ham Biscuits, 54
 Hearts of Palm Spread, 60
 Hot Onion Canapé, 47
 Jo's Cheese Ball, 47
 Kiwi and Prosciutto, 44
 Lona's Hot Mushroom Turnovers, 61
 Magnificent Mini-Reubens, 59
 Margaret's Pimiento Spread with
  Bagel Chips, 62
 Marinated Mushrooms, 43
 Mexi-Dip, 49
 Never Fail Cocktail Meatballs, 37
 Newlywed Crab Dip, 51
 Nutty Brie Appetizer, 64
 Open-Faced Ham Sandwiches, 38
 Our Cheese Straws, 41
 Parmesan Pastry Twists, 40
 Pawley's Island Pickled Shrimp, 52
 Pineapple Cheese Ball, 48
 Pizza Popcorn, 58
 Potatoes Nouveau, 45
 Quick and Easy Quesadillas, 64
 Savory Tenderloin with Horseradish Sauce, 55
 Shrimp in Fresh Dill Marinade, 53
 Shrimp in Suds, 51
 Shrimp Mousse, 46
 Shrimp Stuffed Cherry Tomatoes, 52
 Smoked Cheese, 216
 Smoked Oysters, 228
 Southern Popcorn, 42
 Spicy Greek Toast, 41
 Spinach Beef Dip, 50
 Steve's Shrimp Spread, 53
 Stuffed Artichoke Hearts, 56
 Summer Fruit Tray, 45
 Super Sandwich Filling, 39
 Sweet Vidalia Spread, 62
 Swiss Onion Spread, 47
 Tomato Salsa, 49
 Tortilla Roll-Ups, 57
 Tuna Cream Ball, 48
 Venison Chili, 219
 Versatile Cocktail Puffs, 60
 Whirligigs, 57
Appetizing Apricot Balls, 296
Apple Cranberry Casserole, 274
APPLES
 Apple Cranberry Casserole, 274
 Applesauce Cake, 244
 Caramel Apple Fondue, 271
 Fresh Apple Cake, 247
 Pat's Applesauce Muffins, 110
 Sausage and Apple Casserole, 182
Applesauce Cake, 244
APRICOTS
 Appetizing Apricot Balls, 296
 Apricot Linguine, 99
Apricot Linguinie, 99
Artichoke and Spinach Casserole, 129
ARTICHOKES
 Artichoke and Spinach Casserole, 129
 Shrimp and Artichoke Casserole, 205
 Stuffed Artichoke Hearts, 56
ASPARAGUS
 Asparagus and Pea Casserole, 130
 Congealed Asparagus Salad, 84
 Marinated Asparagus, 129
Asparagus and Pea Casserole, 130
Aunt Ginger's Chocolate Pie, 278
Avocado Crab Salad, 92

B

Bacon Wrapped Surprise, 58
Baked Brazilian, 267
Baked Duck Beverly, 221
Baked Lima Beans, 132
Baklava, 268
Banana Oatmeal Muffins, 110
Banana Split Dessert, 266
BANANAS
 Banana Oatmeal Muffins, 110
 Banana Split Dessert, 266
 Bananas Foster, 273
Bananas Foster, 273
Banker's Red Beans and Rice, 183

BARBECUE
    Barbecue Sauce, 63
    Barbecued Chicken, 238
    Barbecued Spareribs, 63
    South Carolina Chopped Barbecue, 191
Barbecue Sauce, 63
Barbecued Chicken, 238
Barbecued Baby Spareribs, 63
Basic Pastry, 281
Basil Sauce, 201
Bean Bundles, 130
BEANS
    Baked Lima Beans, 132
    Banker's Red Beans and Rice, 183
    Bean Bundles, 130
    Bourbon Beans, 131
    Delicious Baked Beans, 131
    Herbed Green Beans, 130
    Marinated Green Bean Salad, 88
    Paul's Baked Beans, 237
    Smoked Turkey, Bean, and Barley Soup, 78
    Tangy Green Bean Salad, 89
    Tortilla Black Bean Casserole, 160
    White Bean Soup, 75
Béarnaise Mayonnaise, 109
BEEF
    Billy's Brunswick Stew, 74
    Boeuf Bourguignon, 189
    Fabulous Franks, 56
    Filet Mignon with Red Wine
      Sauce, 190
    Grilled Steak with Rum Butter, 233
    Magnificent Mini-Reubens, 59
    Marinated Sirloin Kabobs, 233
    Martini Stew, 185
  Ground
    Easy Spaghetti Meat Sauce, 108
    How To Add Zip To Plain 'Ole
      Hamburgers, 234
    League Lasagna, 104
    Mama's Famous Meat Loaf, 186
    Manicotti with Beef, 185
    Never Fail Cocktail Meatballs, 37
    Texas Hash, 186
  Tenderloin
    Beef Medallions in Sherry Mushroom
      Sauce, 188
    Beef Tenderloin with Mustard
      Sauce, 188
    Grilled Beef Tenderloin, 232
    Savory Tenderloin with Horseradish
      Sauce, 55
Beef Medallions in Sherry Mushroom Sauce, 188
Beef Tenderloin with Mustard Sauce, 188
BEETS
    Mildred's Beets, 132

BEVERAGES
    Christmas Punch, 70
    Ciderific, 69
    Cider-Spritzer, 69
    Coffee Punch, 65
    Cozy Cocoa Mix, 68
    Fruited Tea Punch, 67
    Fuzzie Peach, 65
    Georgia Peach Punch, 66
    Pink Baby Shower Punch, 68
    Poppa Tom's Eggnog, 68
    Very Bloody Mary, 66
    Warm Winter Coffee, 67
    Wassail Supreme, 69
Billy's Brunswick Stew, 74
Bing Cherry Salad, 80
BISCUITS
    Flaky Biscuits, 125
    Happy Hour Ham Biscuits, 54
    Pandora's Biscuits, 124
Black-eyed Peas and Sausage, 184
BLUEBERRIES
    Blueberry Crunch, 273
    Blueberry Ginger Cupcakes with
      Lemon Frosting, 252
    Blueberry Pie, 280
    Blueberry Teacake, 253
Blueberry Crunch, 273
Blueberry Ginger Cupcakes with Lemon Frosting, 252
Blueberry Pie, 280
Blueberry Teacake, 253
Blue Cheese Biscuits, 39
Blue Cheese Chicken, 166
Blue Cheese Dressing, 93
Blue Crab Broccoli Casserole, 194
Boeuf Bourguignon, 189
Bourbon and Praline Ham, 191
Bourbon Beans, 131
Braised Chicken with Garlic and Spinach, 162
Bran Muffins, 111
BREADS
    Croutons, 76
    Curried Cheese Toasts, 40
    Garlic Italian Bread, 102
    Homemade Salad Croutons, 90
    Spicy Greek Toast, 41
  Coffeecakes
    Caramel Coffeecake, 112
    Cranberry Coffeecake, 112
    Jack's Favorite Coffeecake, 114
    Pandora's Coffeecake, 125
  Cornbreads
    Hushpuppies, 121
    Lacy Cornbread, 121
    Mexican Cornbread, 122
    Sour Cream Cornbread, 122

Quick Breads
Banana Oatmeal Muffins, 110
Blue Cheese Biscuits, 39
Bran Muffins, 111
Butter Dips, 120
Cranberry Bread, 116
Dill Muffins, 118
Favorite Pancakes, 113
Mama's Gingerbread, 116
Pandora's Box All-Purpose Mix, 124
Pandora's Biscuits, 124
Pandora's Muffins, 125
Pandora's Pancakes, 124
Parmesan Bread Sticks, 121
Pat's Applesauce Muffins, 110
Poppy Seed Bread, 117
Quick Mayonnaise Rolls, 120
Sesame Parmesan Rolls, 120
Southern Spoon Bread, 123
Strawberry Bread, 117
Zucchini Muffins, 111

Yeast Breads
Dixie Rolls, 118
Granny's Rolls, 119
High Rise Rolls, 119
Holiday Coffee Wreath, 113
Overnight Cinnamon Rolls, 115
Sourdough Bread, 126
One Hundred Percent Whole Wheat
Bread, 123
Bread Pudding with Whiskey Sauce, 267
Breaded Veal with Lemon and Mushrooms, 180
Brie Wrapped in Pastry, 63

BROCCOLI
Broccoli Balls, 133
Broccoli Ring with Parmesan Cheese
Sauce, 134
Broccoli Surprise, 133
Cream of Broccoli Soup, 75
Molded Broccoli Salad, 83
Broccoli Balls, 133
Broccoli Mushroom Salad, 89
Broccoli Ring with Parmesan Cheese Sauce, 134
Broccoli Surprise, 133
Broiled Scallops, 214
Brown Sugar Chocolate Cake, 242
Butter Dips, 120
Butternut Squash Casserole, 151

C

CABBAGE
Marinated Cole Slaw, 88
Oriental Cabbage, 135
Sweet and Sour Cabbage Soup, 73
Cajun Chicken, 161
CAKES
Applesauce Cake, 244

Blueberry Ginger Cupcakes with
Lemon Frosting, 252
Blueberry Teacake, 253
Brown Sugar Chocolate Cake, 242
Caramel Cake, 245
Chocolate Chip Cake, 242
Chocolate Ice Box Cake, 243
Chocolate Meringue Torte, 255
Cocoa Chocolate Pound Cake, 243
Coconut Sour Cream Cake, 241
Creamy Lemon Cake, 251
Dicey's Chocolate Cake, 241
Fresh Apple Cake, 247
Grandmother Watt's Orange Cake, 250
Mocha Almond Torte, 254
Oh So Good Oatmeal Cake, 249
Orange Blossoms, 250
Red Velvet Cake, 246
Strawberry Patch Cake, 248
Tailgate Party Cupcakes, 294
CANDIES
Appetizing Apricot Balls, 296
Candy Coated Pecans, 298
Cindy's Best Caramel Corn, 299
Delicious Caramels, 296
Diane's Heavenly Hash, 295
Emily Neel's Candy, 297
Holiday Chocolate Coconut Bon-Bons, 295
Million Dollar Fudge, 296
Party Praline Strips, 298
Pecan Meringues, 298
Peanut Butter Balls, 295
Peanut Butter Crunch, 299
Phudge, 297
Candy Coated Pecans, 298
Caramel Apple Fondue, 271
Caramel Cake and Frosting, 245
Caramel Coffeecake, 112
Caribbean Chicken, 167
Carrot Soufflé, 135
CARROTS
Carrots à la Crème, 136
Carrot Soufflé, 135
Cheesy Carrot Casserole, 136
Steamed Carrots, 136
Carrots à la Crème, 136
Carter's Mushroom Caps, 42
Cartwheel Pasta Salad, 100
CASSEROLES
Apple Cranberry Casserole, 274
Artichoke and Spinach Casserole, 129
Asparagus and Pea Casserole, 130
Blue Crab Broccoli Casserole, 194
Broccoli Surprise, 133
Butternut Squash Casserole, 151
Carrot Soufflé, 135
Cheesy Carrot Casserole, 136

Cheesy-Chive Potatoes, 144
Cheesy Eggplant Casserole, 139
Cheesy Tomato and Onion Casserole, 151
Cultural Center Chicken Casserole, 171
Green Tomato Casserole, 153
Hot Fruit Casserole, 151
Individual Mushroom Casseroles, 141
Irish Potato Casserole, 144
Macaroni Supreme, 105
Mexican Corn Pudding, 137
Mixed Vegetable Casserole, 154
Mushrooms au Gratin, 140
Onions Baked with Cheese, 142
Praline Sweet Potato Casserole and
   Orange Sauce, 146
Sausage and Apple Casserole, 182
Savory Baked Eggplant, 138
Savory Baked Onions, 143
Shrimp and Artichoke Casserole, 205
Shrimp and Cheese Casserole, 204
Shrimp Casserole, 204
Southern-Style Deviled Spinach, 149
Spinach Cheese Bake, 148
Squash Parmesan, 150
Sweet Corn Pudding, 138
Swiss Cheesy Potatoes, 145
Tortilla Black Bean Casserole, 160
Charcoaled Marinated Duck Breasts, 224
Charleston Cheese, 46
Cheese Gratiné, 76

CHEESE
Brie Wrapped in Pastry, 63
Charleston Cheese, 46
Cheese Gratiné, 76
Cheesy Carrot Casserole, 136
Cheesy-Chive Potatoes, 144
Cheesy Eggplant Casserole, 139
Cheesy Tomato and Onion Casserole, 151
Chili Cheese, 45
Cream of Cheese Soup, 77
Freckled Cheese Sticks, 57
Jo's Cheese Ball, 47
Margaret's Pimiento Spread with
   Bagel Chips, 62
Nutty Brie Appetizer, 64
Our Cheese Straws, 41
Pimiento Cheese, 79
Pineapple Cheese Ball, 48
Smoked Cheese, 216
Swiss Cheesy Potatoes, 145
Tuna Cream Ball, 48

CHEESECAKES
Chocolate Cheesecake, 256
Chocolate Turtle Cheesecake, 259
Cookie Cheesecake Squares, 293
Frozen Peppermint Cheesecake, 260
Miniature Cherry Cheesecakes, 259

Triple Layer Chocolate Cheesecake, 258
White Chocolate Cheesecake, 257
Cheesy Carrot Casserole, 136
Cheesy-Chive Potatoes, 144
Cheesy Eggplant Casserole, 139
Cheesy Tomato and Onion Casserole, 151

CHERRIES
Bing Cherry Salad, 80
Festive Cranberry-Cherry Pie, 279
Miniature Cherry Cheesecake, 259

CHICKEN
Barbecued Chicken, 238
Billy's Brunswick Stew, 74
Blue Cheese Chicken, 166
Braised Chicken with Garlic and Spinach, 162
Cajun Chicken, 161
Caribbean Chicken, 167
Chicken and Sausage Jambalaya, 174
Chicken Breasts in Triple Mustard Sauce, 161
Chicken Chutney Stir-Fry, 165
Chicken Enchiladas, 163
Chicken Florentine with Mornay Sauce, 172
Chicken Pasta Salad, 100
Chicken with Sun-Dried Tomatoes, 169
Chicken with Tarragon Sauce, 166
Christmas Chicken, 165
Cultural Center Chicken Casserole, 171
Dijon Chicken Breasts, 167
Exotic Chicken Salad, 90
Fancy Fettuccine, 102
Garlic and Tomato Chicken, 168
Ginger Chicken, 164
Greek Lemon Chicken, 170
Grilled Lemon Chicken, 238
Honey Mustard Chicken with Wine, 173
Japanese Chicken Salad, 91
Jazzy Chicken Livers, 179
Mediterranean Chicken, 173
Molded Chicken Salad, 90
Orange-Glazed Cornish Hens, 177
Oriental Vegetables and Chicken, 171
Parmesan Chicken, 175
Penne Pasta and Grilled Chicken, 108
Pinky's Chicken, 170
Southern Fried Chicken, 169
Spicy Southwestern Oven-Fried Chicken, 176
Stuffed Cornish Hens, 178
Chicken and Sausage Jambalaya, 174
Chicken Breasts in Triple Mustard Sauce, 161
Chicken Chutney Stir-Fry, 165
Chicken Enchiladas, 163
Chicken Florentine with Mornay Sauce, 172
Chicken Pasta Salad, 100
Chicken with Sun-Dried Tomatoes, 169
Chicken with Tarragon Sauce, 166
Chili Bean Tacos, 186
Chili Cheese, 45

Chili St. George, 187
CHOCOLATE
    Aunt Ginger's Chocolate Pie, 278
    Chocolate Cheesecake, 256
    Chocolate Chip Cake, 242
    Chocolate Ice Box Cake, 243
    Chocolate Leaves, 264
    Chocolate Meringue Torte, 255
    Chocolate Sauce, 260
    Chocolate Turtle Cheesecake, 259
    Cocoa Chocolate Pound Cake, 243
    Decadent Chocolate Soufflé, 261
    Diane's Heavenly Hash, 295
    Dicey's Chocolate Cake, 241
    Divine Chocolate Mint Squares, 290
    Fudgy Chocolate Chippers, 284
    Holiday Chocolate Coconut Bon-Bons, 295
    Luscious Chocolate Mousse, 264
    Million Dollar Fudge, 296
    Minty Chocolate Rounds, 287
    Normandy Chocolate Mousse, 263
    Phudge, 297
    Triple Layer Chocolate Cheesecake, 258
    Ultimate Chocolate Brownies, 291
    White Chocolate Cheesecake, 257
Chocolate Cheesecake, 256
Chocolate Chip Cake, 242
Chocolate Glaze, 258
Chocolate Ice Box Cake, 243
Chocolate Leaves, 264
Chocolate Meringue Torte, 255
Chocolate Sauce, 260
Chocolate Turtle Cheesecake, 259
Christmas Chicken, 165
Christmas Punch, 70
Ciderific, 69
Cider-Spritzer, 69
Cindy's Best Caramel Corn, 299
CLAMS
    Spaghetti and Minced Clams, 108
Cocoa Chocolate Pound Cake, 243
COCONUT
    Coconut Pie, 277
    Coconut Sour Cream Cake, 241
Coconut Pie, 277
Coconut Sour Cream Cake, 241
Coffee Punch, 65
Congealed Asparagus Salad, 84
Congealed Spiced Peach Salad, 81
Cookie Cheesecake Squares, 293
COOKIES
    Crackle Top Cookies, 283
    Crispy Orange Bites, 284
    Crunchy Picnic Cookies, 282
    Florida Cookies, 288
    Fudgy Chocolate Chippers, 284
    Georgia Peanut Cookies, 287

    Jam Diagonals, 289
    Just For Fun Cookies, 288
    Minty Chocolate Rounds, 287
    Nutjammer Cookies, 286
    Old-Time Favorite Oatmeal
      Cookies, 285
    Party Time Sugar Cookies, 285
    Pecan Grove Shortbread Cookies, 288
    Pecan Meringues, 298
    Spicy Ginger Snaps, 282
    Tea Party Cakes, 286
  Bar Cookies
      After School Peanut Butter Bars, 293
      Cookie Cheesecake Squares, 293
      Delicate Lemon Squares, 293
      Divine Chocolate Mint Squares, 290
      Marvelous Orange Nut Bars, 292
      Park Avenue Squares, 291
      Party Praline Strips, 298
      Rich 'n Chewy Cake, 289
      Streusel Caramel Bars, 292
      Tailgate Party Cupcakes, 294
      Ultimate Chocolate Brownies, 291
Cookies 'n Lime Fluff, 266
Cool Vegetable Tray with Fresh Dill Dip, 44
CORN
    Sweet Corn Pudding, 138
Cozy Cocoa Mix, 68
CRABMEAT
    Avocado Crab Salad, 92
    Blue Crab Broccoli Casserole, 194
    Crabmeat Crisps, 64
    Crab Mold, 60
    Newlywed Crab Dip, 51
    Veal with Shrimp and Crabmeat, 181
Crabmeat Crisps, 64
Crab Mold, 60
Crackle Top Cookies, 283
CRANBERRIES
    Apple Cranberry Casserole, 274
    Cranberry Bread, 116
    Cranberry Coffeecake, 112
    Cranberry Salad Ring, 81
    Festive Cranberry-Cherry Pie, 279
    Layered Cranberry Salad, 80
Cranberry Bread, 116
Cranberry Coffeecake, 112
Cranberry Salad Ring, 81
Cream Gravy, 227
Cream of Broccoli Soup, 75
Cream of Cheese Soup, 77
Cream Puffs, 269
Creamy Fruit Pie, 281
Creamy Lemon Cake, 251
Creamy Peas with Bacon and Mushrooms, 143
Creamy Vegetable Medley, 154
Crispy Orange Bites, 284

Criss Cross Salad, 91
Croutons, 76
Crunchy Picnic Cookies, 282
Cucumber Lites, 38
Cultural Center Chicken Casserole, 171
Curly Pasta with Breadcrumbs, 101
Curried Cheese Toast, 40
Curried Pumpkin Soup, 74

D

Decadent Chocolate Soufflé, 261
Delicate Lemon Squares, 293
Delicious Baked Beans, 131
Delicious Caramels, 296
Delicious Pastry, 281
DESSERTS (Also see Cakes, Candies,
Cheesecakes, Cookies, Pies)
    Appetizing Apricot Balls, 296
    Apple Cranberry Casserole, 274
    Baked Brazilian, 267
    Baklava, 268
    Bananas Foster, 273
    Banana Split Dessert, 266
    Blueberry Crunch, 273
    Bread Pudding with Whiskey Sauce, 267
    Caramel Apple Fondue, 271
    Cookies 'N Lime Fluff, 266
    Cream Puffs, 269
    Decadent Chocolate Soufflé, 261
    Elegant Grilled Peaches with
      Raspberry Purée, 276
    Forgery, 263
    Frozen Grand Marnier Soufflé, 270
    Fruit Pizza, 272
    Ginger Mousse Trifle, 263
    Home-Style Peach Cobbler, 275
    Luscious Chocolate Mousse, 264
    Normandy Chocolate Mousse, 263
    Peach Crumble, 276
    Pear Crisp, 274
    Pineapple Belle Hélène, 272
    Praline Soufflé with Raspberry Sauce, 262
    Rainbow Tart, 270
    Raspberry Cream, 265
    Robin's Caramel Flan, 260
    Spiced Pears, 275
    Summer Dessert, 268
    Vanilla Cream with Raspberries, 265
    Zingy Lemon Dessert, 271
Deviled Eggplant, 140
Deviled Eggs, 140
Diane's Heavenly Hash, 295
Dicey's Chocolate Cake, 241
Dijon Chicken Breasts, 167
Dill Muffins, 118
Dinner Party Salad, 104
DIPS (Also see Salad Dressing, Spreads)

Alligator Eyes Dip, 51
Always-A-Hit Spinach Dip, 50
Fernandina Shrimp Dip, 51
Green Goddess Salad Dressing and Dip, 94
Herb Dip, 44
Honey Dressing for Fresh Fruit, 96
Mexi-Dip, 49
Newlywed Crab Dip, 51
Spinach Beef Dip, 50
Tomato Salsa, 49
Divine Chocolate Mint Squares, 290
Dixie Rolls, 118
DOVE
    Dove Stew, 225
    Grilled Dove, 224
    Merrily Plantation Deep Dish Dove Pie, 226
Dove Stew, 225
Down-Home Boiled Peanuts, 42
DRESSINGS (See Salad Dressings)
DUCK
    Anitra Alle Olive, 222
    Baked Duck Beverly, 221
    Charcoaled Marinated Duck Breasts, 224
    Roast Duck, 223

E

Easy Garlic Pork Roast, 191
Easy Spaghetti Meat Sauce, 108
EGGPLANT
    Cheesy Eggplant Casserole, 139
    Deviled Eggplant, 140
    Savory Baked Eggplant, 138
    Southern Fried Eggplant, 139
EGGS
    Deviled Eggs, 140
    Melissa's Spinach Salad Quiche, 159
Elegant Grilled Peaches with Raspberry Purée, 276
Emily Neel's Candy, 297
ENTRÉES
    Anitra Alle Olive, 222
    Baked Duck Beverly, 221
    Banker's Red Beans and Rice, 183
    Barbecued Chicken, 238
    Beef Medallions in Sherry Mushroom
      Sauce, 188
    Beef Tenderloin with Mustard Sauce, 188
    Billy's Brunswick Stew, 74
    Black-eyed Peas and Sausage, 184
    Blue Crab Broccoli Casserole, 194
    Blue Cheese Chicken, 166
    Boeuf Bourguignon, 189
    Bourbon and Praline Ham, 191
    Braised Chicken with Garlic and Spinach, 162
    Breaded Veal with Lemon and
      Mushrooms, 180
    Broiled Scallops, 214
    Broiled Tuna, 209

Cajun Barbecued Shrimp, 200
Cajun Chicken, 161
Cajun Spiced Oysters, 215
Caribbean Chicken, 167
Charcoaled Marinated Duck Breasts, 224
Chicken and Sausage Jambalaya, 174
Chicken Breasts in Triple Mustard Sauce, 161
Chicken Chutney Stir-Fry, 165
Chicken Enchiladas, 163
Chicken Florentine with Mornay Sauce, 172
Chicken Pasta Salad, 100
Chicken with Sun-Dried Tomatoes, 169
Chicken with Tarragon Sauce, 166
Chili Bean Tacos, 186
Chili St. George, 187
Chinese Crabmeat with Celery Cabbage, 196
Christmas Chicken, 165
Crab Fritters, 195
Crab Imperial, 195
Crabmeat in Pastry Shells, 194
Cultural Center Chicken Casserole, 171
Dijon Chicken Breasts, 167
Dove Stew, 225
Duck and Wild Rice Casserole, 223
Easy Garlic Pork Roast, 191
Easy Spaghetti Meat Sauce, 108
Escargot with Scallops, 214
Exotic Chicken Salad, 90
Fancy Fettuccine, 102
Fettuccine Alfredo, 101
Filet Mignon with Red Wine Sauce, 190
Fish and Vegetable Dinner, 196
Fish Fillets Italiano 198
Fried Shrimp, 206
Garlic and Tomato Chicken, 168
Ginger Chicken, 164
Great Grouper, 231
Greek Lemon Chicken, 170
Greek Shrimp and Pasta Salad, 103
Grilled Beef Tenderloin, 232
Grilled Boston Butt, 236
Grilled Dove, 224
Grilled Fish and Vegetables, 230
Grilled Leg of Lamb, 237
Grilled Lemon Chicken, 238
Grilled Pork Tenderloin, 235
Grilled Salmon Steaks with Caper Dill
   Sauce, 229
Grilled Scallops, 231
Grilled Sesame Trout, 229
Grilled Steak with Rum Butter, 233
Ham Salad in Cantaloupe Rings, 87
Honey Mustard Chicken with Wine, 173
Hot Seafood Salad, 208
How To Add Zip To Plain 'Ole
   Hamburgers, 234
Hunter's Pie, 219

Japanese Chicken Salad, 91
Jazzy Chicken Livers, 176
Key West Shrimp, 232
Lamb Chops Made Simple, 192
League Lasagna, 104
Lemon Steamed Fish, 197
Light Mexican-Style Fish, 197
Mama's Famous Meat Loaf, 186
Manicotti with Beef, 185
Marinated Sirloin Kabobs, 233
Martini Stew, 185
Mediterranean Chicken, 173
Melissa's Spinach Salad Quiche, 159
Merrily Plantation Deep Dish Dove Pie, 226
Molded Chicken Salad, 90
Orange-Glazed Cornish Hens, 177
Oriental Shrimp, 207
Oriental Vegetables and Chicken, 171
Oyster Stew, 198
Oysters Lizbeth, 199
Parmesan Chicken, 175
Pasta Primavera, 107
Patsy's Pasta Salad, 106
Penne Pasta and Grilled Chicken, 108
Pineapple Garlic Pork Chops, 235
Pinky's Chicken, 170
Poached Fish, 210
Pork Medallions in Creamy Peppercorn
   Sauce, 193
Rack of Lamb with Mustard Sauce, 193
Roast Duck, 223
Roasted Pork, 192
Royal Seafood Casserole, 209
Salmon and Noodles Romanoff, 213
Salmon Croquettes, 211
Salmon Florentine, 210
Salmon Loaf, 211
Salmon Ring, 212
Sausage and Apple Casserole, 182
Sausage Pizzas, 182
Sautéed Shrimp, 215
Savory Tenderloin with Horseradish Sauce, 55
Seafood Casserole, 208
Seafood Frying Batter, 206
Seafood Primavera with Basil Sauce, 201
Shrimp and Artichoke Casserole, 205
Shrimp and Cheese Casserole, 204
Shrimp and Green Noodles, 202
Shrimp and Sausage Gumbo, 204
Shrimp and Scallop Sauté, 214
Shrimp and Spinach Pasta, 203
Shrimp Butter Cream Sauce, 206
Shrimp Carolyn, 203
Shrimp Casserole, 204
Shrimp Curry, 202
Shrimp in Suds, 51
Shrimp Salad, 200

Shrimp St. George, 200
Shrimp with Lemon-Garlic Sauce, 205
Smoked Oysters, 228
Smoked Salmon, 228
Smoked Turkey, 216
South Carolina Chopped Barbecue, 191
Southern Fried Chicken, 169
Southern Fried Quail with Cream Gravy, 227
Spaghetti and Minced Clams, 108
Spicy Chops, 192
Spicy Southwestern Oven-Fried Chicken, 176
Spinach Lasagna, 105
Springwood Plantation Grilled
  Amberjack, 230
Steamed Florida Lobster, 197
Stuffed Cornish Hens, 178
Stuffed Flounder, 199
Stuffed Quail, 227
Swordfish, Pasta and Pecan Salad, 109
Tallokas Quail, 226
Texas Hash, 186
Tortilla Black Bean Casserole, 160
Veal Chops à la Palmer, 236
Veal Chops Provençal, 180
Veal with Shrimp and Crabmeat, 181
Venison in Red Wine, 220
Venison Chili, 219
Venison Sausage Gumbo, 218
Wild Turkey with Oyster Pecan Dressing, 217
Woodfield Springs Plantation Venison
  Stew, 220
Zesty Scalloped Oysters, 210
Exotic Chicken Salad, 90

F

Fabulous Franks, 56
Famous Potato Salad, 87
Fancy Fettuccine, 102
Favorite Pancakes, 113
Festive Cranberry-Cherry Pie, 279
Fernandina Shrimp Dip, 51
Fettuccine Alfredo, 101
Filet Mignon With Red Wine Sauce, 190
FISH
  Grilled Fish and Vegetables, 230
  Grilled Salmon Steaks with Caper Dill
    Sauce, 229
  Grilled Sesame Trout, 229
  Great Grouper, 231
  Poached Fish, 210
  Smoked Salmon, 228
  Springwood Plantation Grilled
    Amberjack, 230
  Swordfish, Pasta and Pecan Salad, 109
Flaky Biscuits, 125
Florida Cookies, 288
Florida Lobster Butter Log, 46

Forgery, 263
FOWL (See Chicken, Dove, Duck, Game, Quail)
Freckled Cheese Sticks, 57
Fresh Apple Cake, 247
Fresh Collard Greens, 137
Fresh Ginger Salad Dressing, 93
Fried Green Tomatoes, 153
Fried Rice, 207
FROSTINGS & ICINGS
  Brown Sugar Chocolate Cake Frosting, 242
  Caramel Frosting, 245
  Chocolate Glaze, 258
  Chocolate Sauce, 260
  Lemon Frosting, 252
  Seven Minute Icing, 241
Frozen Fruit Salad, 82
Frozen Grand Marnier Soufflé, 270
Frozen Peppermint Cheesecake, 260
FRUIT (Also see Apples, Apricots, Bananas,
Blueberries, Cherries, Coconut, Cranberries, Kiwi,
Lemons, Limes, Oranges, Peaches, Pears,
Pineapples, Pumpkin, Raspberries, Strawberries)
  Frozen Fruit Salad, 82
  Fruit Pizza, 272
  Hot Fruit Casserole, 151
  Summer Fruit Tray, 45
Fruit Pizza, 272
Fruited Tea Punch, 67
Fudgy Chocolate Chippers, 284
Fuzzie Peach, 65

G

GAME
  Baked Duck Beverly, 221
  Charcoaled Marinated Duck Breasts, 224
  Dove Stew, 225
  Grilled Dove, 224
  Hunter's Pie, 219
  Merrily Plantation Deep Dish Dove Pie, 226
  Roast Duck, 223
  Southern Fried Quail with Cream Gravy, 227
  Stuffed Quail, 227
  Tallokas Quail, 226
  Venison Chili, 219
  Venison in Red Wine, 220
  Venison Jerky, 219
  Venison Sausage Gumbo, 218
  Woodfield Springs Plantation Venison
    Stew, 220
Garden Vegetable Rice Salad, 85
Garlic and Tomato Chicken, 168
Garlic Cheese Grits, 230
Garlic Italian Bread, 102
Georgia Peach Punch, 66
Georgia Peanut Cookies, 287
Ginger Chicken, 164
Ginger Mousse Trifle, 263

Golden Dressing, 94
Golden Glow Salad, 83
Grandmama's Pumpkin Pie, 278
Grandmother Watt's Orange Cake, 250
Granny's Rolls, 119
Great Grouper, 231
Greek Lemon Chicken, 170
Greek Potato Salad, 86
Greek Salad, 78
Greek Shrimp and Pasta Salad, 103
Green Goddess Salad Dressing and Dip, 94
Green Pasta Salad, 102
Green Tomato Casserole, 153
Grilled Beef Tenderloin, 232
Grilled Boston Butt, 236
Grilled Dove, 224
Grilled Fish and Vegetables, 230
Grilled Leg of Lamb, 237
Grilled Lemon Chicken, 238
Grilled Pork Tenderloin, 235
Grilled Salmon Steaks with Caper Dill Sauce, 229
Grilled Scallops, 231
Grilled Sesame Trout, 229
Grilled Steak with Rum Butter, 233
Grilled Vegetables, 236
GRILLING
    Barbecued Chicken, 238
    Barbecued Baby Spareribs, 63
    Charcoaled Marinated Duck Breasts, 224
    Elegant Grilled Peaches with
        Raspberry Purée, 276
    Great Grouper, 231
    Grilled Beef Tenderloin, 232
    Grilled Boston Butt, 236
    Grilled Dove, 224
    Grilled Fish and Vegetables, 230
    Grilled Leg of Lamb, 237
    Grilled Lemon Chicken, 238
    Grilled Pork Tenderloin, 235
    Grilled Salmon Steak with Caper Dill
        Sauce, 229
    Grilled Scallops, 231
    Grilled Sesame Trout, 229
    Grilled Steak with Rum Butter, 233
    Grilled Vegetables, 236
    How To Add Zip To Plain 'Ole
        Hamburgers, 234
    Key West Shrimp, 232
    Marinated Sirloin Kabobs, 233
    Penne Pasta and Grilled Chicken, 108
    Pineapple Garlic Pork Chops, 235
    Smoked Cheese, 216
    Smoked Oysters, 228
    Smoked Salmon, 228
    Smoked Turkey, 216
    Springwood Plantation Grilled
        Amberjack, 230

Tallokas Quail, 226
Veal Chops à la Palmer, 236
Guacamole Potatoes, 145

H
Ham Salad in Cantaloupe Rings, 87
Happy Hour Ham Biscuits, 54
Hearts of Palm Spread, 60
Heavenly Hash Browns, 147
Herb Dip, 44
Herbed Green Beans, 130
High Rise Rolls, 119
Holiday Chocolate Coconut Bon-Bons, 295
Holiday Coffee Wreath, 113
Home-Style Peach Cobbler, 275
Homemade Salad Croutons, 90
Honey Dressing for Fresh Fruit, 96
Honey Mustard Chicken with Wine, 173
Hot Fruit Casserole, 151
Hot Onion Canapé, 47
How To Add Zip To Plain 'Ole Hamburgers, 234
Hunter's Pie, 219
Hushpuppies, 121

I
ICE CREAM
    Baked Brazilian, 267
    Forgery, 263
    Creamy Fruit Pie, 281
    Summer Dessert, 268
ICINGS & GLAZES (See Frostings)
Individual Mushroom Casseroles, 141
Irish Potato Casserole, 144

J
Jack's Favorite Coffeecake, 114
Jam Diagonals, 289
Japanese Chicken Salad, 91
Jazzy Chicken Livers, 179
Jo's Cheese Ball, 47
Julienne Vegetables, 155
Julie's Fresh Italian Dressing, 94
Just For Fun Cookies, 288

K
Kahlúa Pie, 277
Key Lime Pie, 277
Key West Shrimp, 232
KIWI
    Kiwi and Proscuitto, 44
    Rainbow Tart, 270
Kiwi and Prosciutto, 44

L
Lacy Cornbread, 121

LAMB

    Grilled Leg of Lamb, 237

    Lamb Chops Made Simple, 192

    Rack of Lamb with Mustard Sauce, 193

    Spicy Chops, 192

Lamb Chops Made Simple, 192

Layered Cranberry Salad, 80

League Lasagna, 104

Lemon Frosting, 252

LEMONS

    Delicate Lemon Squares, 293

    Creamy Lemon Cake, 251

    Grilled Lemon Chicken, 238

    Lemon Frosting, 252

    Zingy Lemon Dessert, 271

LIMES

    Cookies 'n Lime Fluff, 266

    Key Lime Pie, 277

Linda's Squash Soufflé, 150

LOBSTER

    Florida Lobster Butter Log, 64

    Steamed Florida Lobster, 197

Lona's Hot Mushroom Turnovers, 61

Luscious Chocolate Mousse, 264

M

Macaroni Supreme, 105

Magnificent Mini-Reubens, 59

Mama's Famous Meat Loaf, 186

Mama's Gingerbread, 116

Mandarin Orange Salad, 92

Manicotti with Beef, 185

Margaret's Pimiento Spread with Bagel Chips, 62

MARINADE

    All Seasons Seafood Marinade, 54

    Grilled Beef Tenderloin, 232

    Shrimp in Fresh Dill Marinade, 53

Marinara Sauce, 103

Marinated Asparagus, 129

Marinated Cole Slaw, 88

Marinated Green Bean Salad, 88

Marinated Mushrooms, 43

Marinated Onion and Tomato Slices, 141

Marinated Sirloin Kabobs, 233

Marinated Vegetables, 53

Marinated Zucchini, 43

Martini Stew, 185

Marvelous Orange Nut Bars, 292

MEATS

    Beef

        Beef Medallions in Sherry Mushroom Sauce, 188

        Beef Tenderloin with Mustard Sauce, 188

        Billy's Brunswick Stew, 74

        Boeuf Bourguignon, 189

        Fabulous Franks, 56

        Filet Mignon with Red Wine Sauce, 190

        Grilled Beef Tenderloin, 232

        Grilled Steak with Rum Butter, 233

        Marinated Sirloin Kabobs, 233

        Martini Stew, 185

        Savory Tenderloin with Horseradish Sauce, 55

    Corned Beef

        Magnificent Mini-Reubens, 59

    Ground Beef

        Chili Bean Tacos, 186

        Chili St. George, 187

        Easy Spaghetti Meat Sauce, 108

        How To Add Zip To Plain 'Ole Hamburgers, 234

        League Lasagna, 104

        Mama's Famous Meat Loaf, 186

        Manicotti with Beef, 185

        Never Fail Cocktail Meatballs, 37

        Quick and Easy Quesadillas, 64

        Texas Hash, 186

    Ham

        Bourbon and Praline Ham, 191

        Ham Salad in Cantaloupe Rings, 87

        Happy Hour Ham Biscuits, 54

        Kiwi and Prosciutto, 44

        Open-Faced Ham Sandwiches, 38

    Lamb

        Grilled Leg of Lamb, 237

        Lamb Chops Made Simple, 192

        Rack of Lamb with Mustard Sauce, 193

        Spicy Chops, 192

    Pork

        Barbecued Spareribs, 63

        Easy Garlic Pork Roast, 191

        Grilled Boston Butt, 236

        Grilled Pork Tenderloin, 235

        Pineapple Garlic Pork Chops, 235

        Pork Medallions in Creamy Peppercorn Sauce, 193

        Roasted Pork, 192

        South Carolina Chopped Barbecue, 191

    Pork Sausage

        Banker's Red Beans and Rice, 183

        Billy's Brunswick Stew, 74

        Black-eyed Peas and Sausage, 184

        Chicken and Sausage Jambalaya, 174

        Sausage and Apple Casserole, 182

        Sausage Pizzas, 182

        Shrimp and Sausage Gumbo, 204

    Veal

        Breaded Veal with Lemon and Mushrooms, 180

        Veal Chops à la Palmer, 236

        Veal Chops Provençal, 180

        Veal with Shrimp and Crabmeat, 181

Venison
Hunter's Pie, 219
Venison in Red Wine, 220
Venison Beef Jerky, 219
Venison Sausage Gumbo, 218
Woodfield Springs Plantation
Venison Stew, 220
Mediterranean Chicken, 173
Melissa's Spinach Salad Quiche, 159
Merrily Plantation Deep Dish Dove Pie, 226
Mexican Cornbread, 122
Mexican Corn Pudding, 137
Mexi-Dip, 49
Mildred's Beets, 132
Million Dollar Fudge, 296
Miniature Cherry Cheesecakes, 259
Minty Chocolate Rounds, 287
Mixed Vegetable Casserole, 154
Mocha Almond Torte, 254
Molded Broccoli Salad, 83
Molded Chicken Salad, 90
Molded Tomato Salad, 85
MOUSSES
Ginger Mousse Trifle, 263
Luscious Chocolate Mousse, 264
Normandy Chocolate Mousse, 263
Shrimp Mousse, 46
MUFFINS
Banana Oatmeal Muffins, 110
Bran Muffins, 111
Dill Muffins, 118
Pandora's Muffins, 125
Pat's Applesauce Muffins, 110
Zucchini Muffins, 111
MUSHROOMS
Carter's Mushroom Caps, 42
Individual Mushroom Casseroles, 141
Lona's Hot Mushroom Turnovers, 61
Marinated Mushrooms, 43
Mushrooms au Gratin, 140
Mushrooms au Gratin, 140

N

Never Fail Cocktail Meatballs, 37
Newlywed Crab Dip, 51
Normandy Chocolate Mousse, 263
Nutjammer Cookies, 286
NUTS
Candy Coated Pecans, 298
Down-Home Boiled Peanuts, 42
Pecan Meringues, 298
Swordfish, Pasta and Pecan Salad, 109
Nutty Brie Appetizer, 64

O

OATMEAL
Oh So Good Oatmeal Cake, 249

Old-Time Favorite Oatmeal Cookies, 285
Ocean Pond Tomatoes, 152
Oh So Good Oatmeal Cake, 249
OKRA
Southern Popcorn, 42
Old-Time Favorite Oatmeal Cookies, 285
Onion Soufflé, 142
Onion Soup Les Halles, 76
ONIONS
Cheesy Tomato and Onion Casserole, 151
Hot Onion Canapé, 47
Marinated Onion and Tomato Slices, 141
Onions Baked with Cheese, 142
Onion Soufflé, 142
Onion Soup Les Halles, 76
Savory Baked Onions, 143
Sweet Vidalia Spread, 62
Swiss Onion Spread, 47
Vidalia Onion Pie, 141
Onions Baked with Cheese, 142
Open-Faced Ham Sandwiches, 38
Orange Blossoms, 250
Orange-Glazed Cornish Hens, 177
ORANGES
Grandmother Watt's Orange Cake, 250
Mandarin Orange Salad, 92
Marvelous Orange Nut Bars, 292
Orange Blossoms, 250
Orange-Glazed Cornish Hens, 177
Praline Sweet Potatoes and Orange Sauce, 146
Oriental Cabbage, 135
Oriental Shrimp, 207
Oriental Vegetables and Chicken, 171
Orzo with Onions and Parsley, 103
Our Cheese Straws, 41
Overnight Cinnamon Rolls, 115
OYSTERS
Smoked Oysters, 228

P

Party Meatball Sauce, 37
Pandora's Box All-Purpose Mix, 124
Pandora's Biscuits, 124
Pandora's Coffeecake, 125
Pandora's Muffins, 125
Pandora's Pancakes, 124
Park Avenue Squares, 291
Parmesan Bread Sticks, 121
Parmesan Chicken, 175
Parmesan Pastry Twists, 40
Parmesan Zucchini and Tomatoes, 156
Parsley New Potatoes, 229
Party Praline Strips, 298
Party Time Sugar Cookies, 285
PASTA
Angel Hair Pasta with Tomato-Basil Sauce, 99
Apricot Linguine, 99

Cartwheel Pasta Salad, 100
Chicken Pasta Salad, 100
Curly Pasta with Bread Crumbs, 101
Fancy Fettuccine, 102
Fettuccine Alfredo, 101
Greek Shrimp and Pasta Salad, 103
Green Pasta Salad, 102
League Lasagna, 104
Macaroni Supreme, 105
Manicotti with Beef, 185
Orzo with Onions and Parsley, 103
Pasta Primavera, 107
Pasta Salad, 107
Patsy's Pasta Salad, 106
Penne Pasta and Grilled Chicken, 108
Seafood Primavera with Basil Sauce, 201
Sea Shell Salad, 106
Shrimp and Spinach Pasta, 203
Spaghetti and Minced Clams, 108
Spinach Lasagna, 105
Swordfish, Pasta & Pecan Salad, 109
Pasta Primavera, 107
Pasta Salad, 107
Pat-It Crust, 279
Pat's Applesauce Muffins, 110
Patsy's Pasta Salad, 106
Paul's Baked Beans, 237
Pawley's Island Pickled Shrimp, 52
Peach Crumble, 276
PEACHES
Congealed Spiced Peach Salad, 81
Creamy Fruit Pie, 281
Elegant Grilled Peaches with Raspberry
Purée, 276
Fuzzie Peach, 65
Georgia Peach Punch, 66
Home-Style Peach Cobbler, 275
Peach Crumble, 276
Peaches and Mincemeat, 133
Peaches and Mincemeat, 133
Peanut Butter Balls, 295
Peanut Butter Bars, 293
Peanut Butter Pie, 278
Pear Crisp, 274
PEARS
Pear Crisp, 274
Spiced Pears, 275
PEAS
Asparagus and Pea Casserole, 130
Creamy Peas with Bacon and
Mushrooms, 143
Pecan Grove Shortbread Cookies, 288
Pecan Meringues, 298
Penne Pasta and Grilled Chicken, 108
Perfect Wild Rice, 149
Phudge, 297

PIES & PASTRY
Aunt Ginger's Chocolate Pie, 278
Basic Pastry, 281
Blueberry Pie, 280
Coconut Pie, 277
Creamy Fruit Pie, 281
Delicious Pastry, 281
Festive Cranberry-Cherry Pie, 279
Grandmama's Pumpkin Pie, 278
Kahlùa Pie, 277
Key Lime Pie, 277
Pat-It Crust, 279
Peanut Butter Pie, 278
Tipsy Chip Pie, 280
Tomato Pie, 152
Vidalia Onion Pie, 141
Zucchini Crescent Pie, 155
Pimiento Cheese, 79
Pineapple Belle Hélène, 272
Pineapple Cheese Ball, 48
Pineapple Garlic Pork Chops, 235
PINEAPPLES
Golden Glow Salad, 83
Pineapple Belle Hélène, 272
Pineapple Cheese Ball, 48
Pineapple Garlic Pork Chops, 235
Pink Baby Shower Punch, 68
Pinky's Chicken, 170
Pizza Popcorn, 58
Poached Fish, 210
Poppa Tom's Eggnog, 68
Poppy Seed Bread, 117
Poppy Seed Dressing, 95
PORK
Banker's Red Beans and Rice, 183
Barbecued Baby Spareribs, 63
Billy's Brunswick Stew, 74
Black-eyed Peas and Sausage, 184
Bourbon and Praline Ham, 191
Chicken and Sausage Jambalaya, 174
Easy Garlic Pork Roast, 191
Grilled Pork Tenderloin, 235
Ham Salad in Cantaloupe Rings, 87
Happy Hour Ham Biscuits, 54
Kiwi and Prosciutto, 44
Open-Faced Ham Sandwiches, 38
Pineapple Garlic Pork Chops, 235
Pork Medallions in Creamy Peppercorn
Sauce, 193
Roasted Pork, 192
Sausage and Apple Casserole, 182
Sausage Pizzas, 182
Shrimp and Sausage Gumbo, 204
South Carolina Chopped Barbecue, 191
Pork Medallions in Creamy Peppercorn Sauce, 193
Potato Soup, 77

POTATOES

Famous Potato Salad, 87
Guacamole Potatoes, 145
Irish Potato Casserole, 144
Parsley New Potatoes, 229
Potatoes Nouveau, 45
Potato Soup, 77
Swiss Cheesy Potatoes, 145
Potatoes Nouveau, 45

POULTRY (See Chicken, Game, Turkey)
Praline Soufflé with Raspberry Sauce, 262
Praline Sweet Potato & Orange Sauce, 146

PUMPKIN

Curried Pumpkin Soup, 74
Grandmama's Pumpkin Pie, 278

Q

QUAIL

Southern Fried Quail with Cream Gravy, 227
Stuffed Quail, 227
Tollokas Quail, 226

QUICHE

Melissa's Spinach Salad Quiche, 159
Quick and Easy Quesadillas, 64
Quick Basic Mayonnaise, 84
Quick Mayonnaise Rolls, 120

R

Rack of Lamb with Mustard Sauce, 193
Rainbow Tart, 270

RASPBERRIES

Elegant Grilled Peaches with
Raspberry Purée, 276
Praline Soufflé with Raspberry Sauce, 265
Raspberry Cardinal Sauce, 262
Raspberry Cream, 265
Vanilla Cream with Raspberries, 265
Raspberry Cardinal Sauce, 262
Raspberry Cream, 265
Red Velvet Cake, 246

RICE

Alice's Rice Salad, 86
Banker's Red Beans and Rice, 183
Perfect Wild Rice, 149
Seasoned Rice, 147
Wild Rice Soup, 73
Rich 'n Chewy Cake, 289
Roast Duck, 223
Roasted Pork, 192
Robin's Caramel Flan, 260

S

SALAD DRESSINGS (Also see Dips, Spreads)
Blue Cheese Dressing, 93
Fresh Ginger Salad Dressing, 93
Golden Dressing, 94
Green Goddess Salad Dressing and Dip, 94

Honey Dressing For Fresh Fruit, 96
Julie's Fresh Italian Dressing, 94
Poppy Seed Dressing, 95
Quick Basic Mayonnaise, 84
Spinach Salad Dressing, 95
Strawberry Dressing, 96

SALADS

Congealed Salads
Bing Cherry Salad, 80
Congealed Asparagus Salad, 84
Congealed Spiced Peach Salad, 81
Crab Mold, 60
Cranberry Salad Ring, 81
Golden Glow Salad, 83
Layered Cranberry Salad, 80
Molded Broccoli Salad, 83
Molded Chicken Salad, 90
Molded Tomato Salad, 85
Tangy Spinach Salad, 82
Tomato Aspic, 84

Fruit Salads
Bing Cherry Salad, 80
Congealed Spiced Peach Salad, 81
Cranberry Salad Ring, 81
Frozen Fruit Salad, 82
Golden Glow Salad, 83
Layered Cranberry Salad, 80
Mandarin Orange Salad, 92

Meat, Poultry, Seafood Salads
Avocado Crab Salad, 92
Chicken Pasta Salad, 100
Exotic Chicken Salad, 90
Greek Shrimp and Pasta Salad, 103
Ham Salad in Cantaloupe Rings, 87
Japanese Chicken Salad, 91
Molded Chicken Salad, 90
Swordfish, Pasta and Pecan Salad, 109

Pasta, Rice Salads
Alice's Rice Salad, 86
Cartwheel Pasta Salad, 100
Garden Vegetable Rice Salad, 85
Pasta Salad, 107
Patsy's Pasta Salad, 106
Sea Shell Salad, 106

Vegetable Salads
Broccoli Mushroom Salad, 89
Congealed Asparagus Salad, 84
Criss Cross Salad, 91
Dinner Party Salad, 104
Famous Potato Salad, 87
Greek Potato Salad, 86
Greek Salad, 78
Mandarin Orange Salad, 92
Marinated Cole Slaw, 88
Marinated Green Bean Salad, 88
Molded Broccoli Salad, 83
Molded Tomato Salad, 85

Tangy Green Bean Salad, 89
Tangy Spinach Salad, 82

SALMON
Grilled Salmon Steak with Caper Dill
   Sauce, 229
Salmon and Noodles Romanoff, 213
Salmon Croquettes, 211
Salmon Florentine, 210
Salmon Loaf, 211
Salmon Ring, 212
Smoked Salmon, 228

SANDWICHES
Cucumber Lites, 38
Magnificent Mini-Reubens, 59
Open-Faced Ham Sandwiches, 38
Savannah Open-Faced Tomato Sandwich, 75
Super Sandwich Filling, 39
Sausage and Apple Casserole, 182
Sausage Pizzas, 182

SAUCES
Barbecue Sauce, 63
Basil Sauce, 201
Béarnaise Mayonnaise, 109
Chocolate Sauce, 260
Cream Gravy, 227
Easy Spaghetti Meat Sauce, 108
Marinara Sauce, 103
Party Meatball Sauce, 37
Raspberry Cardinal Sauce, 262
Shrimp Butter Cream Sauce, 206
Whiskey Sauce, 267
Sautéed Fresh Spinach, 148
Sautéed Shrimp, 215
Savannah Open-Faced Tomato Sandwich, 75
Savory Baked Eggplant, 138
Savory Baked Onions, 143
Savory Tenderloin with Horseradish Sauce, 55

SCALLOPS
Broiled Scallops, 214
Grilled Scallops, 231
Shrimp and Scallop Sauté, 214

SEAFOOD (See Crab, Fish, Lobster, Scallops,
Shrimp, Oysters)
Sea Shell Salad, 106
Seafood Frying Batter, 206
Seafood Primavera with Basil Sauce, 201
Seasoned Rice, 147
Sesame Parmesan Rolls, 120
Seven Minute Icing, 241

SHRIMP
All Season's Seafood Marinade, 54
Fernandina Shrimp Dip, 51
Greek Shrimp and Pasta Salad, 103
Key West Shrimp, 232
Oriental Shrimp, 207
Pawley's Island Pickled Shrimp, 52
Sautéed Shrimp, 215

Seafood Primavera with Basil Sauce, 201
Shrimp and Artichoke Casserole, 205
Shrimp and Cheese Casserole, 205
Shrimp and Sausage Gumbo, 204
Shrimp and Scallop Sauté, 214
Shrimp and Spinach Pasta, 203
Shrimp Butter Cream Sauce, 206
Shrimp Carolyn, 203
Shrimp Casserole, 204
Shrimp in Suds, 51
Shrimp with Lemon-Garlic Sauce, 205
Shrimp Mousse, 46
Shrimp St. George, 200
Shrimp Salad, 200
Shrimp Stuffed Cherry Tomatoes, 52
Veal with Shrimp and Crab Meat, 181
Shrimp and Artichoke Casserole, 205
Shrimp and Cheese Casserole, 205
Shrimp and Sausage Gumbo, 204
Shrimp and Scallop Sauté, 214
Shrimp and Spinach Pasta, 203
Shrimp Butter Cream Sauce, 206
Shrimp Carolyn, 203
Shrimp Casserole, 204
Shrimp in Suds, 51
Shrimp Mousse, 46
Shrimp St. George, 200
Shrimp Salad, 200
Shrimp Stuffed Cherry Tomatoes, 52
Shrimp with Lemon-Garlic Sauce, 205

SIDE DISHES
Artichoke and Spinach Casserole, 129
Asparagus and Pea Casserole, 130
Baked Lima Beans, 132
Bean Bundles, 130
Bourbon Beans, 131
Broccoli Balls, 133
Broccoli Ring with Parmesan Cheese
   Sauce, 134
Broccoli Surprise, 133
Butternut Squash Casserole, 151
Carrots à la Crème, 136
Carrot Soufflé, 135
Cheesy Carrot Casserole, 136
Cheesy-Chive Potatoes, 144
Cheesy Eggplant Casserole, 139
Cheesy Tomato and Onion Casserole, 151
Creamy Peas with Bacon and Mushrooms, 143
Creamy Vegetable Medley, 154
Curly Pasta with Bread Crumbs, 101
Delicious Baked Beans, 131
Deviled Eggplant, 140
Deviled Eggs, 140
Fettuccine Alfredo, 101
Fresh Collard Greens, 137
Fried Green Tomatoes, 153
Fried Rice, 207

Garlic-Cheese Grits, 230
Green Tomato Casserole, 153
Grilled Vegetables, 236
Guacamole Potatoes, 145
Heavenly Hash Browns, 147
Herbed Green Beans, 130
Hot Fruit Casserole, 151
Individual Mushroom Casseroles, 141
Irish Potato Casserole, 144
Julienne Vegetables, 155
Linda's Squash Soufflé, 150
Marinated Asparagus, 129
Marinated Onion and Tomato Slices, 141
Marinated Vegetables, 153
Marinated Zucchini, 43
Mexican Corn Pudding, 137
Mildred's Beets, 132
Mixed Vegetable Casserole, 154
Mushroom au Gratin, 140
Ocean Pond Tomatoes, 152
Onions Baked with Cheese, 142
Onion Soufflé, 142
Oriental Cabbage, 135
Parmesan Zucchini and Tomatoes, 156
Parsley New Potatoes, 229
Paul's Baked Beans, 237
Peaches and Mincemeat, 133
Perfect Wild Rice, 149
Pimiento Cheese, 79
Praline Sweet Potato Casserole & Orange
    Sauce, 146
Sautéed Fresh Spinach, 148
Savory Baked Eggplant, 138
Savory Baked Onions, 143
Seasoned Rice, 147
Southern Fried Eggplant, 139
Southern-Style Deviled Spinach, 149
Spinach Cheese Bake, 148
Spinach-Stuffed Tomatoes, 232
Squash Parmesan, 150
Steamed Carrots, 136
Sweet Corn Pudding, 138
Swiss Cheesy Potatoes, 145
Tomato Pie, 152
Vidalia Onion Pie, 141
Yam Peanut Puffs, 154
Zucchini Crescent Pie, 155
Zucchini Sauté, 156
Smoked Cheese, 216
Smoked Oysters, 228
Smoked Salmon, 228
Smoked Turkey, 216
Smoked Turkey, Bean, and Barley Soup, 78
SOUFFLÉS
Carrot Soufflé, 135
Decadent Chocolate Soufflé, 261
Frozen Grand Marnier Soufflé, 270

Linda's Squash Soufflé, 150
Onion Soufflé, 142
Praline Soufflé with Raspberry Sauce, 262
SOUPS & STEWS
Billy's Brunswick Stew, 74
Cream of Broccoli Soup, 75
Cream of Cheese Soup, 77
Curried Pumpkin Soup, 74
Dove Stew, 225
Martini Stew, 185
Onion Soup Les Halles, 76
Potato Soup, 77
Shrimp and Sausage Gumbo, 204
Smoked Turkey Bean and Barley Soup, 78
Sweet and Sour Cabbage Soup, 73
Tomato Zucchini Soup, 79
Venison Sausage Gumbo, 218
White Bean Soup, 75
Wild Rice Soup, 73
Woodfield Springs Plantation Venison
    Stew, 220
Zucchini Soup, 78
Sour Cream Cornbread, 122
Sourdough Bread, 126
South Carolina Chopped Barbecue, 191
Southern Fried Chicken, 169
Southern Fried Eggplant, 139
Southern Fried Quail with Cream Gravy, 227
Southern Popcorn, 42
Southern Spoon Bread, 123
Southern-Style Deviled Spinach, 149
Spaghetti and Minced Clams, 108
Spiced Pears, 275
Spicy Chops, 192
Spicy Ginger Snaps, 282
Spicy Greek Toast, 41
Spicy Southwestern Oven-Fried Chicken, 176
SPINACH
Always-A-Hit Spinach Dip, 50
Sautéed Fresh Spinach, 148
Southern-Style Deviled Spinach, 149
Spinach Beef Dip, 50
Spinach Cheese Bake, 148
Spinach Lasagna, 105
Spinach Salad Dressing, 95
Spinach Stuffed Tomatoes, 232
Tangy Spinach Salad, 82
Spinach Beef Dip, 50
Spinach Cheese Bake, 148
Spinach Lasagna, 105
Spinach Salad Dressing, 95
Spinach-Stuffed Tomatoes, 232
SPREADS (Also see Dips)
Charleston Cheese, 46
Chili Cheese, 45
Hearts of Palm Spread, 60
Hot Onion Canapé, 47

Steve's Shrimp Spread, 53
Sweet Vidalia Spread, 62
Swiss Onion Spread, 47
Springwood Plantation Grilled Amberjack, 230
SQUASH
Butternut Squash Casserole, 151
Linda's Squash Soufflé, 150
Squash Parmesan, 150
Squash Parmesan, 150
Steamed Carrots, 136
Steamed Florida Lobster, 197
Steve's Shrimp Spread, 53
STRAWBERRIES
Strawberry Bread, 117
Strawberry Dressing, 96
Strawberry Patch Cake, 248
Strawberry Bread, 117
Strawberry Dressing, 96
Strawberry Patch Cake, 248
Streusel Caramel Bars, 292
Stuffed Artichoke Hearts, 56
Stuffed Cornish Hens, 178
Stuffed Quail, 227
Summer Dessert, 268
Summer Fruit Tray, 45
Super Sandwich Filling, 39
Sweet and Sour Cabbage Soup, 73
Sweet Corn Pudding, 138
SWEET POTATOES
Praline Sweet Potato Casserole and
Orange Sauce, 146
Yam Peanut Puffs, 154
Sweet Vidalia Spread, 62
Swiss Cheesy Potatoes, 145
Swiss Onion Spread, 47
Swordfish, Pasta, and Pecan Salad, 109

T
Tailgate Party Cupcakes, 294
Tallokas Quail, 226
Tangy Green Bean Salad, 89
Tangy Spinach Salad, 82
Texas Hash, 186
Tipsy Chip Pie, 280
Tomato Aspic, 84
Tomato Pie, 152
Tomato Salsa, 49
Tomato Zucchini Soup, 79
TOMATOES
Cheesy Tomato and Onion Casserole, 151
Fried Green Tomatoes, 153
Green Tomato Casserole, 153
Marinara Sauce, 103
Marinated Onion and Tomato Slices, 141
Molded Tomato Salad, 85
Ocean Pond Tomatoes, 152
Parmesan Zucchini and Tomatoes, 156

Shrimp Stuffed Cherry Tomatoes, 52
Spinach-Stuffed Tomatoes, 232
Tomato Aspic, 84
Tomato Pie, 152
Tomato Salsa, 49
Tomato Zucchini Soup, 79
Tortilla Black Bean Casserole, 160
Tortilla Roll-Ups, 57
Triple Layer Chocolate Cheesecake, 258
TROUT
Grilled Sesame Trout, 229
Tuna Cream Ball, 48
TURKEY
Smoked Turkey, 216
Smoked Turkey, Bean, and Barley Soup, 78
Wild Turkey with Oyster Pecan Dressing, 217

U
Ultimate Chocolate Brownies, 291

V
Vanilla Cream with Raspberries, 265
VEAL
Breaded Veal with Lemon and Mushrooms, 180
Veal Chops à la Palmer, 236
Veal Chops Provençal, 180
Veal with Shrimp and Crab Meat, 181
Veal Chops à la Palmer, 236
Veal Chops Provençal, 180
Veal with Shrimp and Crabmeat, 181
VEGETABLES (Also see Artichokes, Asparagus,
Beans, Beets, Broccoli, Cabbage, Carrots, Corn,
Eggplant, Mushrooms, Okra, Onions, Peas, Potatoes,
Spinach, Squash, Sweet Potatoes, Tomatoes, Zucchini)
Cool Vegetable Tray with Fresh Dill Dip, 44
Creamy Vegetable Medley, 154
Grilled Vegetables, 236
Julienne Vegetables, 155
Marinated Vegetables, 153
Mexican Corn Pudding, 137
Mixed Vegetable Casserole, 154
Vegetables on the Grill, 236
VENISON
Hunter's Pie, 219
Venison Chili, 219
Venison Beef Jerky, 219
Venison in Red Wine, 220
Venison Sausage Gumbo, 218
Woodfield Springs Plantation Venison Stew, 220
Venison Chili, 219
Venison Beef Jerky, 219
Venison in Red Wine, 220
Venison Sausage Gumbo, 218
Versatile Cocktail Puffs, 60
Very Bloody Mary, 66
Vidalia Onion Pie, 141

W

Warm Winter Coffee, 67
Wassail Supreme, 69
Whirligigs, 57
Whiskey Sauce, 267
White Bean Soup, 75
White Chocolate Cheesecake, 257
One Hundred Percent Whole Wheat Bread, 123
Wild Rice Soup, 73
Wild Turkey with Oyster Pecan Dressing, 217
Woodfield Springs Plantation Venison Stew, 220

Y

Yam Peanut Puffs, 154

Z

Zingy Lemon Dessert, 271
ZUCCHINI
   Marinated Zucchini, 43
   Parmesan Zucchini and Tomatoes, 156
   Tomato Zucchini Soup, 79
   Zucchini Crescent Pie, 155
   Zucchini Muffins, 111
   Zucchini Sauté, 156
   Zucchini Soup, 78
Zucchini Crescent Pie, 155
Zucchini Muffins, 111
Zucchini Sauté, 156
Zucchini Soup, 78

NOTES

Event Planner

Date/Time: _____ Number of Guests: _____

Location: _____ Theme/Style: _____

Good Food

Menu	Page Number/Comments
Appetizers _____	_____
Soup/Salad _____	_____
Bread/Pasta _____	_____
Side Dishes _____	_____
Entrée _____	_____
Dessert _____	_____
Beverages _____	_____

Good Company

Guests

_____	_____	_____
_____	_____	_____
_____	_____	_____
_____	_____	_____
_____	_____	_____
_____	_____	_____

Things to Consider

	Notes
Invitations _____	_____
Linens _____	_____
Flowers/Decorations _____	_____
Tableware _____	_____
Stemware _____	_____
Serving Dishes _____	_____
Special Needs _____	_____

NOTES

Event Planner

Date/Time: _____   Number of Guests: _____
Location: _____   Theme/Style: _____

Good Food

Menu	Page Number/Comments
Appetizers _____	_____
Soup/Salad _____	_____
Bread/Pasta _____	_____
Side Dishes _____	_____
Entrée _____	_____
Dessert _____	_____
Beverages _____	_____

Good Company

Guests

_____   _____   _____
_____   _____   _____
_____   _____   _____
_____   _____   _____
_____   _____   _____
_____   _____   _____

Things to Consider

Notes

Invitations _____	_____
Linens _____	_____
Flowers/Decorations _____	_____
Tableware _____	_____
Stemware _____	_____
Serving Dishes _____	_____
Special Needs _____	_____

NOTES

Make checks payable to:
GOOD FOOD, GOOD COMPANY
Thomasville Junior Service League
P.O. Box 279, Thomasville, GA 31799

	QTY	TOTAL	
GOOD FOOD, GOOD COMPANY @ $18.95		$	**SHIP TO:** Name_____ Street Address_____ City/State/Zip_____
GA residents add 5% sales tax ($.95 ea.)			Phone (day)_____ (night) _____ Payment by ☐ check ☐ money order
Shipping/Handling $3. 95 each			Charge to ☐ Mastercard ☐ Visa Expiration date___ Account Number_____
TOTAL		$	Name as it appears on card _____ Signature_____

- -

GOOD FOOD GOOD COMPANY

Make checks payable to:
GOOD FOOD, GOOD COMPANY
Thomasville Junior Service League
P.O. Box 279, Thomasville, GA 31799

	QTY	TOTAL	
GOOD FOOD, GOOD COMPANY @ $18.95		$	**SHIP TO:** Name_____ Street Address_____ City/State/Zip_____
GA residents add 5% sales tax ($.95 ea.)			Phone (day)_____ (night) _____ Payment by ☐ check ☐ money order
Shipping/Handling $3. 95 each			Charge to ☐Mastercard ☐Visa Expiration date___ Account Number_____
TOTAL		$	Name as it appears on card _____ Signature_____

- -

GOOD FOOD GOOD COMPANY

Make checks payable to:
GOOD FOOD, GOOD COMPANY
Thomasville Junior Service League
P.O. Box 279, Thomasville, GA 31799

	QTY	TOTAL	
GOOD FOOD, GOOD COMPANY @ $18.95		$	**SHIP TO:** Name_____ Street Address_____ City/State/Zip_____
GA residents add 5% sales tax ($.95 ea.)			Phone (day)_____ (night) _____ Payment by ☐check ☐money order
Shipping/Handling $3. 95 each			Charge to ☐Mastercard ☐Visa Expiration date___ Account Number_____
TOTAL		$	Name as it appears on card _____ Signature_____

Junior Service League of Thomasville appreciates your purchase of this copy of our cookbook. All money raised from the sale of GOOD FOOD, GOOD COMPANY will be used for children's programs in Thomasville and Thomas County.

Please see the reverse side of this page to order additional copies of GOOD FOOD, GOOD COMPANY.